FOREVER FREE

FOREVER FREE

THE STORY OF EMANCIPATION AND RECONSTRUCTION

ERIC FONER

Illustrations edited and with commentary by
Joshua Brown

FOREVER FREE PROJECT
Peter O. Almond & Stephen Brier
Senior Producers
Christine Doudna, *Editor*

ALFRED A. KNOPF • NEW YORK • 2005

THIS IS A BORZOI BOOK
PUBLISHED BY ALFRED A. KNOPF

Knopf, Borzoi Books, and the colophon are registered
trademarks of Random House, Inc.

Library of Congress Cataloging-in-Publication Data
Foner, Eric.
Forever free : the story of emancipation and Reconstruction / Eric Foner;
illustrations edited and with commentary by Joshua Brown.—1st ed.
p.   cm.
"Forever Free project : Peter O. Almond, Stephen Brier, senior producers;
Christine Doudna, editor."
Includes bibliographical references and index.
ISBN 0-375-40259-4 (alk. paper)
1. Reconstruction (U.S. history, 1865–1877)   2. Slaves—Emancipation—United States.
3. United States—History—Civil War, 1861–1865—African Americans.
4. United States—Race relations—History—19th century.
5. United States—Politics and government—1865–1900.
I. Brown, Joshua, 1949–   II. Forever Free, Inc.   III. Title.

E668.F655 2005
973.8—dc22   2005040706

Manufactured in the United States of America
First Edition

To the late
W. W. Law of Savannah, Georgia, historian, citizen, activist,
whose life and work embody the first and second Reconstructions;
and to
Herbert Gutman, scholar, mentor, enthusiast;
and to
Sergei Bodrov, Jr.;
and to
Cornelia Bailey and the Bailey family of Sapelo Island, Georgia,
who live the tradition of Emancipation and Reconstruction

The most magnificent drama in the last thousand years of human history is the transportation of ten million human beings out of the dark beauty of their mother continent into the new-found Eldorado of the West. They descended into Hell; and in the third century they arose from the dead, in the finest effort to achieve democracy for the working millions which this world had ever seen.

. . .

The unending tragedy of Reconstruction is the utter inability of the American mind to grasp its real significance, its national and world-wide implications. . . . This problem involved the very foundations of American democracy, both political and economic.

—W. E. B. Du Bois, *Black Reconstruction in America,* 1935

CONTENTS

FOREWORD

The struggle for equality in America, like that of the ancient Israelites, is of biblical proportions. The story of four million slaves and their transformation from bondage to citizenship is one of the great and inspiring events in world history. We were compelled by this history because it revealed a little recognized commitment to and embrace of freedom by the nation's African American population before, during, and in the immediate aftermath of slavery's demise. And yet this critical moment in our nation's history has failed to establish itself in the national memory, at least with any accuracy or full depth of understanding. Here was a critical and revolutionary moment of change that was essentially unknown to most Americans, a period that involved not only the destruction of slavery, but also a dozen-year period, known as Reconstruction, of profound political, legal, economic, and racial transformation that followed the end of the Civil War.

The understanding of the Civil War and of the war's root causes reveals the contested meaning of the era of emancipation and Reconstruction. What had the war accomplished? Who had benefited and who had suffered? What had freedpeople sought and what had they and their allies achieved in the aftermath of freedom? David Blight argues, in his influential book *Race and Reunion: The Civil War in American Memory* (2001), that the desire in the half-dozen decades following the Civil War to obscure the real causes of the war—the emancipation of four million slaves—led to the "denigration of black dignity and the attempted erasure of emancipation from the national narrative of what the war had been about." W. E. B. Du Bois drew similar conclusions sixty-six years earlier in *Black Reconstruction:* "Little effort has been made to preserve the records of Negro effort and speeches, action, work and wages, homes and families. Nearly all of this has gone down beneath a mass of ridicule and caricature, deliberate omission and misstatement."

As a result, one of the great triumphs for equal rights in American history was obliterated, overwhelmed by a fascination with the valor of combat. That undue fascination tended to reduce the war to a noble tragedy, pitting "brother against brother." Whether in novels, popular histories, feature films, or television series such as *The Civil War,* the tragedy and glory of armed combat overrode the central fact that, by its end, the war was about the future of the institution of slavery and the people whom it enslaved. Because such attitudes continue to dominate the historical consciousness of most Americans—and because the "facts" of Reconstruction remain largely unknown—we felt both humbled and challenged by the opportunity to tell this story anew.

The great irony about the titanic struggles that took place during emancipation and Reconstruction is the nature of the role that the freedpeople played. Rather than passive recipients of freedom bestowed upon them by the Union army and the federal government, millions of African Americans actively sought their own freedom during the war by running away from slavery, by sabotaging Confederate efforts on the plantations, and by fighting valiantly as Union soldiers. The freedpeople also asserted their new-won freedoms in the war's immediate aftermath. A rich array of documents from the period reveals that African Americans embraced the simple rights of citizenship and its responsibilities: they wanted to vote, sit on juries, marry, worship as they chose, ride public conveyances, and own land. They wanted, in short, the chance to participate in the American dream.

The violent suppression of that dream haunts us to this day. The "what-ifs" of the story are legion: What if the brief flowering of equality in the war's immediate aftermath had been allowed to flourish rather than being brutally suppressed? What if the federal government had upheld the Constitution and guaranteed the rights of all its citizens? The story is at once poignant and urgent. The complex legacy of Reconstruction is lived every day in America. Until Americans understand that history, we are, as the saying goes, condemned to repeat it.

The book, and the project from which it emerged, grows out of a long-standing collaboration among historians, writers, and filmmakers. We began work in the late 1980s on film projects about "ordinary" people and their impact on American history intended for a broad popular audience. We set out to produce a pilot episode for a television series that would focus on the years immediately following the revolutionary transformations ushered in by the North's victory in the Civil War. In Savannah, Georgia, where we were filming the pilot, we met Wallace Westley

Law (W. W. Law). "Mr. Law," as we came to know him, was the living embodiment of the civil rights history of his beloved city and the carrier of
its civil rights tradition extending all the way back to the first days of emancipation. Mr. Law spoke eloquently about the "Colloquy," a little-known
encounter in January 1865 between two of the highest-ranking figures in
the U.S. government—Secretary of War Edwin Stanton and Union army
general William Tecumseh Sherman—and representatives of Savannah's African American community. Mr. Law communicated a reverence
for the Colloquy to everyone who had the privilege of meeting him,
including those of us working on the *Forever Free* television project. It is
the clarity and sheer scope of the vision that "ordinary" black Americans,
recently liberated from slavery, revealed in their exchange with Stanton
and Sherman that gave us the central idea for the television series and
this book.

Our colleague and the author of the central narrative in this volume,
Eric Foner, has spent two decades on the history of this critical era, most
expansively in his critically acclaimed book *Reconstruction: America's Unfinished Revolution, 1863–1877* (1988). In this book, Foner synthesizes the
recent scholarship on slavery, emancipation, and Reconstruction into an
accessible narrative. In doing so, he makes a powerful case that history is as
much about the present as it is about the past. To this end, Foner carries the
story forward from slavery to our current era, exploring the many ways in
which ideas about race and rights have shaped and continue to shape our
experience as citizens.

Joshua Brown's essays, interspersed with Foner's chapters, illuminate
several themes of the *Forever Free* project. They are called *visual essays* in
this book because Brown analyzes the impact of race on the rapidly
expanding visual culture that suffused American society throughout the
nineteenth and twentieth centuries. In that sense, Brown's essays literally
and figuratively illustrate a central theme about American popular culture: it is and always has been a battleground on which cultural attitudes
are contested and through which popular attitudes are influenced and
shaped.

The shape and structure of this book deserve some explanation. The
Foner chapters and Brown essays interact in ways perhaps more akin to
jazz than to a standard historical narrative supplemented by traditional
"illustrations." Each stands on its own; but each also enhances the overall
argument of the book, playing off the others in considering common
themes and the larger meaning of American history.

When we brought our editor at Knopf a proposal for a book with visual essays embedded within the narrative, he did not flinch. *Forever Free* the book got to the finish line before our planned television series. It remains a story that we believe needs to reach the widest possible audience.

Peter O. Almond
Stephen Brier
December 2004

SEEING RACE AND RIGHTS:
A NOTE ABOUT THE VISUAL ESSAYS

The six visual essays that appear in this book chart the ways American visual culture embraced, ignored, and distorted issues of race and equality from the 1840s to the 1920s. In the last thirty years, scholars have recovered the suppressed history of emancipation and Reconstruction. That rediscovered past is in part based on a vast visual record of the people, places, events, experiences, and ideas that shaped the era. It is a record that was the result of an antebellum pictorial revolution that itself helped spur the Civil War and transform American society. With the invention and rapid adoption of photography, innovations in printing, the rise of a national illustrated press, and the ever-expanding system of roads, canals, and railroad lines, pictures became a standard part of the news that Americans previously had obtained solely through the closely packed print in their daily or weekly papers. Methods of pictorial reproduction were labor intensive and not always reliable—photographic reproduction would not be perfected until the end of the nineteenth century—but by the middle of the nineteenth century the American public could see reasonably accurate depictions of the people, locations, and issues that were inevitably moving sectional tension toward all-out war.

To our twenty-first-century sensibilities, the stiff photographic poses, regimented wood-engraved lines, crude caricatures, and other nineteenth-century visual conventions seem quaint and disconnected from the tumultuous events of war and peace. But, thanks to the recent work of history and art history scholars, we can begin to discern the ways in which the conflicts, anxieties, and profound changes of the Reconstruction era were directly and indirectly enacted in its popular visual media and fine art. To contemporary Americans, the prints they bought on the street, the news engravings and cartoons they viewed in weekly and monthly magazines, the paintings and photographs displayed in studios, and the statues erected in town squares often conveyed critically important information and ideas—and in provocative ways that we need to recover in order to fully comprehend what nineteenth-century Americans did and why.

Nowhere was the immediacy and urgency of viewing more apparent than in the ways that slavery, the Civil War, emancipation, and Reconstruction were depicted in an expanding range of visual media. Ways of seeing and understanding what one saw rapidly changed under the pressure of unprecedented events and social upheaval. The ubiquitous portraits, cartoons, and monuments became battlegrounds on which newly claimed rights of visual representation were fought. African Americans were the focal point of most of these struggles, and the fate of their visualization in popular media of the day would measure how far the nation had moved from old modes of pictorial representation. In short, pictures mattered, and part of the mission of this book is to show some of the ways those nineteenth-century images changed popular perceptions, and were in turn changed by the opportunities and limits presented and imposed.

I make no claim that these visual essays provide a comprehensive overview. But with the aid of a generation of groundbreaking studies, I have tried to convey how the visual was one of the realms over which Americans contended in a time of social and political upheaval. The first essay, "True Likenesses," explores the ways public portraiture in the antebellum years became a significant weapon for the antislavery movement as it struggled against traditional and anti-abolitionist uses of African American caricatures. "Re-visions of War" moves to the Civil War to examine how the actions of tens of thousands of slaves combined with the changing fortunes of the Northern war effort to transform the pictorial depiction of African Americans. The third essay, "Altered Relations," takes us into the first years of Reconstruction and the possibilities for a new visual dispensation based on equality of "representation." "On the Offensive" chronicles the betrayal of that promise as the nation's commitment to Reconstruction—and reconstructing the nature of graphic representation—flagged. The Gilded Age is the focus of "Countersigns," the fifth essay, which considers the concerted effort to construct a postwar visual culture based on racial inequality—and the pockets of pictorial resistance that the creators and purveyors of the Redemptionist vision of the Southern white cause continued to encounter. The final essay, "Jim Crow," marks the nadir of U.S. race relations and the ways the nation's visual culture, comprising both old and new forms of media, helped legitimate legalized discrimination and vigilante terror. I also gesture at the end of the final essay to efforts by contemporary black artists to appropriate and reinterpret the images that helped oppress African Americans in that era.

Together, these essays demonstrate that history is not a triumphant forward march, that the visual realm was perpetually contested terrain, and that it provided Americans, black and white, with meanings and methods of expression that text could not provide. Finally, it is my hope that these essays reveal that neither the images of the past nor the people who created and viewed them should be subjected to the condescension of the present, where we, the enlightened, assume that stereotypes were never challenged or that real alternatives, even with the most limited of means and opportunities, were not being constantly sought.

Joshua Brown, December 2004

PROLOGUE

No one can argue, at the dawn of the twenty-first century, that America's long struggle with racial inequality has ended or that the contradictions created by the existence of slavery in a country that considers itself an embodiment of freedom have been fully resolved. This book examines the era of emancipation and Reconstruction, a crucial moment when conflicts over racial justice, political democracy, and the meaning of American freedom reached their greatest intensity. That era witnessed a profound experiment in reshaping the country's social and political institutions. One hundred forty years later, it remains vitally important to understand that experiment, and what one historian has called its "splendid failure," because the unresolved legacy of Reconstruction remains a part of our lives. In movements for social justice that have built on the legal and political accomplishments of Reconstruction, and in the racial tensions that still plague American society, the momentous events of Reconstruction reverberate in modern-day America.

The effort to recover the historical memory of Reconstruction has been part of the larger movement for racial equality. This book hopes to reclaim, and reintroduce to the nation's memory, Reconstruction's remarkable cast of characters and their enduring accomplishments. It also depicts the often violent opposition that helped to overthrow the Reconstruction experiment and contributed to the misrepresentation of its legacy. The struggles of Reconstruction remain an important part of our present and future. As James Baldwin has written, "History does not merely refer to the past . . . history is literally present in all we do." In that sense, Reconstruction remains an inspiration for those who hope to build a freer and more equal America.

Reconstruction was a crucial chapter in the long struggle for racial justice. When the Civil War brought freedom to four million slaves, the United States underwent a profound social revolution. The vast economic and political power of the South's white elite hung in the balance, as did the lives and dreams of the former slaves. Indeed, the nature of the new social order created in the South profoundly affected the entire nation. For a brief moment, the country experimented with genuine interracial democracy. Then Reconstruction was overturned by a violent racist reaction. This book tells the story of that turbulent era, its successes and failures, and its long-term consequences up until this very day.

Reconstruction witnessed the creation of religious, educational, and political institutions by the newly freed slaves, and their entrance onto the stage of American politics as voters and officeholders. It was a period when Congress engaged in a bitter struggle with President Andrew Johnson over the definition of American citizenship, culminating in the first impeachment of a president. The United States had its first confrontation with widespread terrorism, in the form of the Ku Klux Klan. But the era also produced enduring achievements, among them the ratification of the Thirteenth, Fourteenth, and Fifteenth amendments to the Constitution.

For nearly a century, Reconstruction was tragically misunderstood by both historians and the broader popular culture. Today, it is shrouded as much in ignorance as in myth. For many decades, academic monographs, popular books, and films portrayed Reconstruction as the lowest point in the entire American saga. According to this view, the vindictive Radical wing of the Republican Party, motivated by hatred of the South, overturned the lenient plans for national reunion designed by Abraham Lincoln and his successor, Andrew Johnson, and imposed black suffrage on the defeated Confederacy. There followed a sordid period of corruption and misrule, the argument went, presided over by unscrupulous political opportunists from the North (derisively termed "carpetbaggers"), southern whites who had abandoned their racial and regional loyalties to cooperate with the Radical Republicans (the "scalawags"), and the former slaves, who were allegedly unprepared for the freedom that had been thrust upon them and unfit to participate in government. Eventually, organizations such as the Ku Klux Klan, deemed patriotic by proponents of this interpretation, overthrew this "misgovernment" and restored "home rule" (a euphemism for white supremacy) to the South.

All history, the saying goes, is contemporary history, in the sense that historical interpretation both reflects and shapes the world in which the historian lives. No period in America's past better illustrates this idea than Reconstruction. The portrait of the era that so long held sway originated in the contemporary propaganda of southern Democrats opposed to black suffrage and officeholding after the Civil War. It gained national legitimacy when it became part of the overall process of reconciliation between

North and South that gathered force in the 1880s and 1890s. In popular literature and in memoirs by participants, at veterans' reunions, and in public statuary, the Civil War came to be remembered as a tragic family quarrel among white Americans in which blacks had played no significant part, and Reconstruction as a regrettable time of "Negro rule." This was, to say the least, a highly distorted view.

Battle flags captured by Northern troops during the Civil War are returned to aged Confederate veterans in a 1927 ceremony of reconciliation, in front of the Capitol, supervised by President Calvin Coolidge.

The rush to forget or reinterpret the actual course of events during Reconstruction answered the immediate needs of white America, but the cost was high. Forgotten were the promises of equality and citizenship made to the former slaves by the federal government. Forgotten, too, was the heroism of former slaves who embraced emancipation, participated actively in politics, and struggled to consolidate their families and improve their communities. Also forgotten was slavery's role in precipitating the Civil War, and the service of 200,000 African Americans in the Union army and navy. Of the hundreds of Civil War monuments erected in these years, only a handful contained any reminder of the black men who fought for the

Union. The abandonment during and after Reconstruction of the nation's commitment to equal rights for the former slaves was the basis on which former white antagonists could reunite. The road to what the great black abolitionist Frederick Douglass derisively referred to as "peace among the whites" was paved with the shards of African Americans' broken dreams of genuine equality and full citizenship.

Later known as the Dunning school of Reconstruction historiography, this outlook received its scholarly expression in the early-twentieth-century work at Columbia University by historian William A. Dunning and political scientist John W. Burgess (leading figures in their respective disciplines), and their students. Their account of the era rested, as one member of the Dunning school put it, on the assumption of "negro incapacity." Finding it impossible to believe that blacks could ever be independent actors on the stage of history, with their own aspirations and motivations, Dunning et al. portrayed African Americans either as "children," ignorant dupes manipulated by unscrupulous whites, or as savages, their primal passions unleashed by the end of slavery. Burgess, a founder of American political science, taught that "a black skin means membership in a race of men which has never of itself succeeded in subjecting passion to reason, and has never, therefore, created any civilization of any kind."

For decades, the Dunning school shaped scholarly writing on Reconstruction. Its interpretation reached a non-academic reading public in a great best seller of the late 1920s, *The Tragic Era,* by the journalist Claude G. Bowers. In lurid prose, Bowers described how southern whites "literally were put to the torture" by "emissaries of hate" from the North who inflamed "the negroes' egotism" and inspired "lustful assaults" by blacks upon white womanhood.

But the most influential portrayal of Reconstruction appeared in D. W. Griffith's classic film *The Birth of a Nation,* released in 1915. Based on the 1905 novel *The Clansman,* by Thomas Dixon, Jr., the film glorifies the Ku Klux Klan as the savior of white civilization from blacks bent on appropriating white property and despoiling white women, and presents white supremacy as the underpinning of post-Reconstruction national unity. It had a screening at the White House during the administration of Woodrow Wilson. A Democrat, and the first elected president since before the Civil War who had been born in the South, Wilson shared the racial views of that region's white population. When he took office, he dismissed most of the black employees of the federal government and imposed rigid segregation in federal offices in Washington, D.C. The film quoted the president, a noted scholar of American government, several times. One quote described Reconstruction as "a veritable overthrow of civilization in the South,"

A poster for the 1922 reissue of The Birth of a Nation

which "put the white South under the heel of the black South," and another Wilson statement glorified the Ku Klux Klan.

By this time, nearly all white Americans embraced the Dunning version of history. Even white critics of the film's racist caricatures of blacks, such as the prominent reformer Jane Addams, a founder of the National Association for the Advancement of Colored People, accepted the accuracy of Griffith's account of Reconstruction. Blacks held a different opinion. The NAACP protested the film's showing and persuaded a few municipalities to ban it. Nonetheless, *The Birth of a Nation* played to large audiences throughout the country, and remained popular for decades. It was even viewed at a special screening by members of the Supreme Court (whose chief justice, Edward White, had once been a member of the Klan). Because of its sweeping battle scenes and complex plot development, *The Birth of a Nation* is considered a turning point in the development of American cinema, and one of the most influential films ever made. But it was blamed for touching off race riots and lynchings, and helped to instill a racist and wholly inaccurate view of blacks, and of Reconstruction, in the minds of generations of Americans.

The Birth of a Nation established the pattern for how Hollywood long dealt with slavery, the Civil War, and Reconstruction. The most popular of all American films, *Gone With the Wind* (1939), is filled with stock characters reflecting Hollywood's view of the era's history—loyal slaves, unruly black soldiers, untrustworthy scalawags and carpetbaggers, noble Klansmen. Most viewers watch *Gone With the Wind* to follow Scarlett O'Hara's romantic adventures, not to receive a history lesson. But they imbibe a grossly distorted view of history all the same.

A less renowned film, *Tennessee Johnson*, produced in 1942 and starring Van Heflin as President Andrew Johnson, continued the Hollywood tradition of distortion evident in *The Birth of a Nation* and *Gone With the Wind*. During World War II, for the first time since Reconstruction, the status of

Mammy (Hattie McDaniel) tends to Scarlett O'Hara (Vivien Leigh) in
Gone With the Wind.

African Americans became a subject of major concern to the federal government. With blacks vigorously protesting discrimination in the army and
defense industries and their exclusion from the right to vote in the South,
and the persistence of segregation opening the United States to charges of
hypocrisy as it crusaded abroad for what President Roosevelt called the
Four Freedoms, the administration took steps to ease racial tensions at
home. Along with banning discrimination in defense employment and
emphasizing that ethnic and racial tolerance were what made the United
States different from Nazi Germany, it sought to improve Hollywood's
portrayal of blacks. Despite these efforts, *Tennessee Johnson* showed how
little of substance had changed. The film portrays African Americans as little more than happy slaves, wrongly implicates Radical Republican Thaddeus Stevens in the assassination of Lincoln, and portrays Johnson as a
maligned defender of national reunion and constitutional government.
Alarmed that the film might stir up racial antagonism, the Office of War
Information asked Walter White of the NAACP to review the script. But
the studio made only a few of his recommended changes, and in the end the
OWI endorsed the film as a demonstration of how change in the United
States comes through the ballot box rather than violence (an ironic mes-

sage at a time when millions of blacks were denied the right to vote). After viewing the film, the black sociologist E. Franklin Frazier mused, "Perhaps white America needs this form of hypocrisy to survive."

This image of Reconstruction did not go entirely unchallenged. On the margins of American society, black communities in the late nineteenth and early twentieth centuries continued to celebrate emancipation, the service of black troops, and the Reconstruction principles of equal political and civil rights. During Woodrow Wilson's presidency, John R. Lynch, an African American who had represented Mississippi in Congress during the 1870s, published a series of devastating critiques of the racial biases of prominent historians and offered his own, far more favorable, account of Reconstruction's history. "I do not hesitate to assert," he wrote, "that the Southern Reconstruction governments were the best governments those States ever had."

Indeed, in black communities throughout the country, an alternative memory of Reconstruction survived well into the twentieth century. When the Works Progress Administration collected interviews with former slaves during the 1930s, they found lingering resentment over the failure of land reform and the betrayal of the promise of equality during Reconstruction, but it was tempered by pride in the era's achievements. Black men and women, then in their eighties, could still recall the names of Reconstruction officeholders. Younger family members spoke of being taught by their parents "about the old times, mostly about the Reconstruction, and the Ku Klux." "I know folks think the books tell the truth, but they shore don't," one former slave told the WPA.

It was W. E. B. Du Bois who offered the first full-fledged scholarly critique of the prevailing view of Reconstruction, and whose career best epitomizes the intertwined struggle for racial equality and an accurate understanding of Reconstruction. Poet, scholar, activist, father of pan-Africanism, and founder of the NAACP, Du Bois lived from Reconstruction to the civil rights revolution, which is sometimes called the Second Reconstruction. Born in Great Barrington, Massachusetts, in 1868, in the midst of Reconstruction, Du Bois died in Ghana in August 1963, on the eve of the March on Washington. The unifying theme of his long career was his effort to reconcile the contradiction between what he called "American freedom for whites and the continuing subjection of Negroes."

Among Du Bois's greatest works was his monumental history *Black Reconstruction in America*, published in 1935. Although largely ignored by historians when it first appeared, *Black Reconstruction* has come to be recognized as a brilliant forerunner of modern interpretations of the entire

W. E. B. Du Bois in 1938

Civil War era. Writing at a time when racial inequality was deeply embedded in American life, Du Bois insisted that Reconstruction must be understood as an episode in the struggle for genuine democracy—political and economic—in the United States. He pointed to the contest over access to land and control of the labor of the emancipated slaves as the crucial issues of Reconstruction, and explored the broad ramifications of Reconstruction's failure for the future course of American development.

Du Bois added a long subtitle to his book—"An essay toward a history of the part which black folk played in the attempt to reconstruct democracy in America"—for he believed that the existence of slavery challenged the democratic premises on which the country claimed to have been founded, and he saw Reconstruction as raising the fundamental question, still relevant as he wrote, of who should rule in the United States and other countries. "What were to be the limits of democratic control in the United States?" he asked. "If all labor, black as well as white, became free, were given schools and the right to vote, what control could or should be set to the power and action of these laborers. . . ."

Claude Bowers had called Reconstruction a tragic era. For Du Bois, the tragedy was not that Reconstruction was attempted, but that it failed. Yet Du Bois called it a "splendid failure," since the era demonstrated the capacity of African Americans for the full enjoyment of citizens' rights. And, in the families, schools, and churches created or consolidated after the Civil War, and in constitutional amendments that established the principle of legal and political equality regardless of race, Reconstruction laid the foundation for future struggle. In the final chapter of *Black Reconstruction*, entitled "The Propaganda of History," Du Bois offers a devastating indictment of a historical profession that sacrificed scholarly objectivity on the altar of racism. Any account of Reconstruction based solely on the testimony of whites alone, and grounded in the assumption of black inferiority, he argued correctly, must be hopelessly flawed.

Du Bois understood that more was at stake than competing interpretations of history. There is no better illustration than Reconstruction of how historical interpretation helps to shape contemporary politics. The prevailing account of Reconstruction during the first half of the twentieth century formed an ideological pillar for the system of white supremacy. It provided justification for the white South's unalterable opposition to change in race relations, and for decades of northern indifference to the nullification of the Fourteenth and Fifteenth amendments. Time and again, white southerners invoked the alleged horrors of Reconstruction to justify racial segregation and the disenfranchisement of the region's black voters. The struggle for racial justice and political democracy, Du Bois believed, could not advance without a corrected understanding of Reconstruction. But in 1935, when his book appeared, these goals seemed as remote as ever.

Today, of course, we live in a different America, thanks in large part to the civil rights revolution of the 1960s. And with changes in the nation's politics and racial attitudes has come a wholesale rewriting of the history of the Civil War era, and especially of Reconstruction. Two generations of scholars have overturned virtually every assumption of the traditional viewpoint, abandoning the racism at the base of that interpretation and presenting Reconstruction as an attempt to put into effect the principle of equal citizenship for all Americans. In this scholarship, the reputations of Andrew Johnson, the Radicals, carpetbaggers, scalawags, and Klansmen have all been revised. But the most sweeping transformation has been the new emphasis on the centrality of the black experience for understanding the era. Rather than passive victims of the actions of others, a "problem" confronting white society, or an obstacle to reunion, blacks were active agents in overthrowing slavery, winning the Civil War, and shaping Reconstruction. The former slaves were thwarted in their quest for land ownership. But their demands for civil and political rights and their efforts to create schools, churches, and other institutions of freedom proved crucial for establishing the social and political agenda of Reconstruction. While previous scholars (with a few exceptions, including Du Bois) wrote of Reconstruction exclusively from white sources, more recent ones have delved into congressional documents, plantation records, army reports, black newspapers, the papers of Republican officials, and numerous other sources to recover the voices of the emancipated slaves. Here they have found evidence of the utopian hopes and shattered dreams, the local institution-building and national political involvement that animated black activism during Reconstruction.

That same inquiry has led scholars to look to the slave experience for the antecedents of Reconstruction, and to reevaluate slave culture in light of the actions of African Americans during and after the Civil War.

The modern view of the Civil War and Reconstruction has been reflected in museum exhibitions and in films such as *Freedom Road* (1979), based on the novel by Howard Fast, and *Glory* (1989), which celebrated the accomplishments of the Fifty-fourth Massachusetts, a black Civil War regiment. Cutting-edge scholarship, however, takes a long time to percolate into the broader culture. Long abandoned in the academic world, the traditional view of Reconstruction still survives in popular memory and in everyday life. In 1987, state officials in Tennessee ordered the portrait of William G. Brownlow, the state's Reconstruction governor, removed from the Capitol library because he "was not worthy of emulation" by the state's schoolchildren. Brownlow's offense was to have presided over the disenfranchisement of some Tennessee Confederates after the Civil War. Yet portraits of slaveholding governors, and those who denied the right to vote to black Tennesseans, remained in place—evidently these qualities did not make them unsuitable subjects of emulation.

In 1995, during the civil war in Bosnia, a respected reporter for the *New York Times* commented that the warring sides there should learn a lesson from the United States and avoid the "ruthless" punishment of the defeated side by the victors. Even works of meticulous scholarship on other periods of American history slip into the familiar, outdated pattern when referring to Reconstruction. For example, Robert L. Caro's excellent recent volume on Lyndon Johnson, *Master of the Senate* (2002), repeats long-discarded myths and misconceptions when referring to President Andrew Johnson and his battle with the Republican Congress during Reconstruction.

The greatest obstacle to a broad appreciation of the real history of Reconstruction and its centrality to the American experience, however, is not misinformation as much as sheer ignorance. Of the hundreds of National Park Service sites that introduce visitors to one or another event or theme in American history, only one is devoted to Reconstruction, the Andrew Johnson Homestead, and its portrayal of the former president is more in keeping with Dunning and Bowers than with modern scholarship. (The NPS is today considering establishing a site at Beaufort, South Carolina, devoted to the history of Reconstruction.) In 1990, the Department of Education surveyed sixteen thousand graduating high school seniors, asking them to identify various terms or issues in American history. Reconstruction received the lowest score on the entire test—only one student in five could correctly identify it. E. D. Hirsch's 1988 best seller, *The Dictio-*

nary of Cultural Literacy, did not include Reconstruction on its list of one thousand things a person needs to know to be considered educated.

Occasionally, around Election Day, one hears television commentators referring to the first black person, or the first southern Republican, since Reconstruction to be elected to some office. During the Clinton administration, the impeachment of the president (although for matters less weighty than the issues that pitted Congress against Andrew Johnson) and a disputed presidential election in which Florida played a pivotal role, as in 1876, led to renewed references to Reconstruction. But few commentators on these events seemed to have much of an understanding of their precursors. Indeed, print and television journalists seemed unable to resist linking President Clinton and the first President Johnson—both, allegedly, good men persecuted by vindictive Republicans in Congress.

Ignorance of Reconstruction is unfortunate because, whether we realize it or not, it remains very much a part of our lives, nearly a century and a half after the Civil War ended. Every year, Congress and the Supreme Court debate issues arising from Reconstruction laws and constitutional amendments. The rights of American citizens, the proper roles of the state and federal governments, the possibility of interracial political coalitions, affirmative action, reparations for slavery, the proper ways for the government to protect citizens against terrorist violence, the relationship between political and economic democracy—these and other issues of our own time cannot be properly understood today without knowledge of how they were debated during the Reconstruction era. Versions of the past continue to shape how people think about the present. Those still influenced by the traditional view of Reconstruction often find themselves thinking of the expansion of the rights of African Americans as a punishment to whites rather than as an expansion of democracy; of the Ku Klux Klan as a well-meaning if perhaps overzealous guardian of order and civilization rather than as a homegrown exemplar of violent terrorism; of those who seek to use the power of government to effect social change as meddlesome outsiders rather than as idealistic reformers.

This book seeks to bring the fruits of recent scholarship on Reconstruction to a broad popular audience and in so doing to reinforce the point that knowledge of that turbulent era is indispensable to thinking about American society today. Lingering stereotypes and misconceptions need to be abandoned. I draw upon the writings of numerous recent scholars, as well as my own research on the era. Ever since my Columbia University colleague Richard B. Morris asked me to write the volume on Reconstruction in the New American Nation series in 1975, Reconstruction has been central to my own career as a historian. Since then, I have published several books on the period, have served as curator of an exhibition, "America's Reconstruction," which traveled to several museums during the 1990s and is now available in digital form on the Internet, and have served as an advisor to a public television series on the period. I hope that this book will help to communicate an understanding of the era of emancipation and Reconstruction, and to illustrate why it remains urgently relevant for our own time.

The book begins with slavery, not only because, following Du Bois, modern historians view slavery as the fundamental cause of the Civil War, but because the institutions former slaves created during Reconstruction and the values and aspirations they articulated in the aftermath of emancipation had their roots in the slave experience. The book then turns to the Civil War, highlighting how the actions of African Americans helped to propel white America down the road to emancipation, and how efforts to create a new social order in the South began during the war itself. The bulk of the book examines the years from 1865 to 1877, tracing Reconstruction's rise and fall, its accomplishments and failures. An epilogue continues on through the recent past, the era of the civil rights movement and its aftermath, to look briefly at the nation's second major effort to come to terms with the problem of racial inequality and interracial democracy, and the ongoing efforts today. Six visual essays by Joshua Brown that accompany the text illuminate and add texture to the narrative and illustrate the changing iconography of slavery, the Civil War, and Reconstruction.

We live, of course, in a different world from the America of the Reconstruction era and, indeed, of the civil rights movement. History never really repeats itself. Far more than in the past, the United States today is a multiracial society, not one divided between black and white. Enormous changes have taken place in race relations in the past half century. Nonetheless, in our racial institutions and attitudes, and the social dislocations around us, the unresolved legacy of emancipation is still a part of our lives. The continuing economic plight of many descendants of slavery has less to do with access to farms—the forty acres and a mule demanded during Reconstruction—than to the disruptive impact of globalization and deindustrialization. Yet, in many ways, the United States, both in public memory and public policy, has yet to come to terms with the impact of slavery on its history, and the long-term consequences of the overthrow of Reconstruction. It still matters very much how we remember the era of the Civil War and Reconstruction.

Eric Foner, December 2004

FOREVER FREE

CHAPTER ONE

THE PECULIAR INSTITUTION

ON THE EVENING of January 12, 1865, twenty leaders of the local black community gathered in Savannah, Georgia, for a discussion with General William T. Sherman and Edwin M. Stanton, the Union's secretary of war. The encounter took place at a pivotal moment in American history. Less than three weeks earlier, Sherman, at the head of a sixty-thousand-man Union army, had captured the city, completing his March to the Sea, which cut a swath of destruction through one of the most productive regions of the slave South. On the horizon loomed the final collapse of the Confederacy, the irrevocable destruction of slavery, and the turbulent postwar era known as Reconstruction. Americans, black and white, would now have to come to terms with the war's legacy, and decide whether they would build an interracial democracy on the ashes of the Old South.

One of the most remarkable interchanges of those momentous years, the "Colloquy" between Sherman, Stanton, and the black leaders offered a rare lens through which the experience of slavery and the aspirations that would help to shape Reconstruction came into sharp focus. The meeting, which took place in the house where Sherman had established his headquarters in Savannah, was the brainchild of Secretary Stanton, who, the general later recalled, "seemed desirous of coming into contact with the negroes to confer with them." It was Sherman who invited "the most intelligent of the negroes" of the city to the gathering. The immediate purpose was to assist Union authorities in devising a plan to deal with the tens of thousands of slaves who had abandoned Georgia and South Carolina plantations and followed his army to the city. But in its deeper significance, the discussion, conducted in a dignified, almost solemn manner, revealed how the experience of bondage had shaped African Americans' ideas and hopes at the moment of emancipation.

The group that met with Sherman and Stanton, mostly Baptist and

GEN^L SHERMAN'S H^D OR^S . RESIDENCE OF GREEN, ES^Q , SAVANNAH .

General Sherman's Savannah headquarters, the residence of cotton merchant Charles Green

Methodist ministers, included several men who had already achieved prominence among Savannah's African American population and who would shortly assume positions of leadership in Reconstruction. Ulysses L. Houston, who had worked as a house servant and butcher while in slavery, had since 1861 been pastor of the city's Third African Baptist Church. He would go on to take part in the statewide black convention of 1866, where representatives of the freedpeople demanded the right to vote and equality before the law, and to serve in the state legislature. James Porter, an Episcopal vestryman, before the war operated a clandestine and illegal school for black children, who "kept their secret with their studies; at home." He would soon help to organize the Georgia Equal Rights Association, and, like Houston, become one of the era's black lawmakers. James D. Lynch would rise to prominence in Mississippi's Reconstruction, serving as secretary of state and winning a reputation, in the words of a white contemporary, as "a great orator, fluid and graceful," who "stirred the emotions" of his black listeners "as no other man could do." Most of the other Colloquy participants would play major roles in the consolidation of independent black churches, one of the signal developments of the postwar years.

If the Colloquy looked forward to the era of Reconstruction, it also shed light backward onto slavery. Taking place, as it were, at the dawn of freedom, it underscored both the diversity of the black experience under slavery and the common culture—the institutions, values, and aspirations—that African Americans had managed to construct before the Civil War in the face of the extraordinary repression and dislocations visited by slavery.

The group that met with Sherman was hardly typical of all blacks. Only 5 percent of the nation's black population was free in 1860, but five of the twenty men who met with Sherman were freeborn, and of the remainder, no fewer than six had obtained their liberty before the war, either by self-purchase or through the will of a deceased owner. Although the law forbade teaching slaves to read and write, several at the Colloquy were literate. Houston had been taught to read by white sailors while working in the city's Marine Hospital. Lynch, the only participant in the Colloquy to live in the North before the war, had been educated at Kimball Union Academy, in New Hampshire, taught school in Jamaica, New York, and preached for the African Methodist Episcopal Church in Indiana prior to 1860. These were men of talent, ambition, and standing, fully prepared for the challenges of freedom.

The conversation with Sherman and Stanton revealed that the black leaders possessed clear conceptions of slavery and freedom. The group chose at its spokesman Garrison Frazier, a Baptist minister who had purchased the liberty of his wife and himself in 1856. Asked what he understood by slavery, Frazier responded that it meant one person's "receiving by irresistible power the work of another man, and not by his consent." Freedom he defined as "placing us where we could reap the fruit of our own labor, and take care of ourselves"; the best way to accomplish this was "to have land, and turn it and till it by our own labor." Frazier also affirmed (despite pro-slavery dogma to the contrary) that blacks, free and slave, possessed "sufficient intelligence" to maintain themselves in freedom and to enjoy the equal protection of the laws. Here were the goals—the right to the fruits of one's labor, access to land, equal rights as citizens—that would animate black politics during and after Reconstruction.

Despite Frazier's optimism about blacks' capacity to take full advantage of emancipation, slavery cast a long shadow over the discussion. Asked whether blacks preferred to live in communities of their own or "scattered among the whites," he replied: "I would prefer to live by ourselves, for there is a prejudice against us in the South that will take years to get over." (On this point alone, disagreement followed, for Lynch insisted it would be best for the races to live together; all the others, however, agreed with Frazier.) At the same time, Frazier affirmed the loyalty of African Americans, free and slave, to the federal government. "If the prayers that have gone up for the Union army could be read out," he added, "you would not get through them these two weeks." As for Sherman himself, Frazier remarked that blacks viewed him as a man "specially set apart by God" to "accomplish this work" of emancipation.

BY THE TIME of the Savannah Colloquy, slavery was an old institution in America. Two and a half centuries had passed since the first African Americans set foot in Britain's mainland colonies. Before the American Revolution, slavery existed in all the colonies, and in Spanish Florida and French Louisiana, areas subsequently absorbed into the United States. Slavery is as old as human civilization itself. It was central to the societies of ancient Greece and Rome. After dying out in northern Europe after the collapse of the Roman empire, it persisted in the Mediterranean world, where a slave trade in Slavic peoples survived into the fifteenth century. (The English word *slavery* derives from *Slav.*) Slavery in Africa long predated the coming of Europeans and the opening of the mammoth transatlantic slave trade in the sixteenth century.

The slave system that arose in the western hemisphere differed in significant ways from others that preceded it. Traditionally, Africans enslaved on their own continent tended to be criminals, debtors, and captives in war. They worked within the households of their owners and had well-defined rights, such as possessing property and marrying free persons. It was not uncommon for slaves in Africa to acquire their freedom. Slavery was one of several forms of labor, not the basis of the overall economy as it would become in large parts of the New World. In the western hemisphere, by contrast, slavery centered on the plantation system, in which large concentrations of slave laborers under the control of a single owner produced goods—sugar, tobacco, rice, and cotton—for the world market. The fact that slaves greatly outnumbered whites in plantation regions magnified the prospects for resistance and made it necessary to police the system rigidly. Labor on slave plantations was far more demanding than in household slavery, and the death rate among slaves much higher. And New World slavery was a racial system. Unlike in the ancient world or Africa, slaves who managed to become free remained distinct because of their color, a mark of bondage and a visible sign of being considered unworthy of incorporation as equals into free society.

Slavery proved indispensable to the settlement and development of the New World. Of the approximately 12.5 million persons who crossed the Atlantic to live in the western hemisphere between 1500 and 1820, perhaps 10 million were African slaves. The Atlantic slave trade, which flourished from 1500 into the nineteenth century, was a regularized business in which European merchants, African traders, and American planters engaged in a complex and profitable bargaining over human lives. Most Africans were shipped in inhuman conditions. "The height, sometimes, between decks," wrote one slave trader, "was only 18 inches, so that the unfortunate human beings could not turn around, or even on their sides . . . and here they are usually chained to the decks by their necks and legs." Olaudah Equiano, the eleven-year-old son of a West African village chief, kidnapped by slave traders in the 1750s, later wrote a widely read account of his experiences, in which he described "the shrieks of the women and the groans of the dying" on the ship that carried him to slavery in Barbados. Disease spread rapidly on slave ships; sometimes the ill were thrown overboard to prevent epidemics. The colonies that became the United States attracted a higher percentage of free immigrants than other parts of the New World. Even here, however, of some 800,000 arrivals between 1607 and 1770, more than 300,000 were slaves.

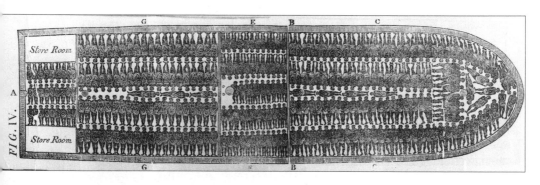

A diagram from an 1808 report on the African slave trade shows the interior of a "slaver."

The first mass consumer goods in international trade were produced by slaves—sugar, rice, coffee, and tobacco. The rising demand for these products fueled the rapid growth of the Atlantic slave trade. The profits from slavery stimulated the rise of British ports such as Liverpool and Bristol, and the growth of banking, shipbuilding, and insurance, and helped to finance the early industrial revolution. The centrality of slavery to the economy of the British empire encouraged an ever-closer identification of freedom with whites and slavery with blacks. This is not to say that all whites enjoyed equality. Many gradations of freedom coexisted in colonial America. The majority of English settlers who crossed the Atlantic in the seventeenth and eighteenth centuries came as indentured servants who agreed to labor for a period of years in exchange for passage. Even after their term of labor ended, many remained poor, landless, and unable to meet the property qualifications for voting.

Slavery and ideas about innate racial difference developed slowly in seventeenth-century America. Some early black arrivals were apparently treated as servants rather than slaves, and gained their freedom after a fixed term of labor. Not until the 1660s did the laws of Virginia and Maryland explicitly refer to slavery. As tobacco planting spread and the demand for labor increased, however, the condition of black and white servants diverged sharply. "Race"—the idea that humanity is divided into well-defined groups associated with skin color—is a modern concept that had not fully developed in the seventeenth century. Nor had "racism"—an ideology based on the belief that some races are inherently superior to others and entitled to rule over them. But as slavery became more and more central to the colonial economy, views of race hardened. In 1762, the Quaker abolitionist John Woolman commented on the strength of "the idea of slavery being connected with the black color, and liberty with the white."

By the mid-eighteenth century, slaves accounted for nearly half of Virginia's population. Virginia had changed from a "society with slaves," in which slavery was one system of labor among others, to a "slave society," where the institution stood at the center of the economic process. Slavery formed the basis of the economy, and the foundation of a powerful local ruling class, in the entire region from Maryland south to Georgia.

Slavery also existed in the middle and northern colonies, although there, slaves generally worked on small farms or in their owners' homes or shops rather than on large plantations. Nonetheless, in 1746, New York City's 2,440 slaves comprised one-fifth of its total population. Among cities on the North American continent, only Charleston and New Orleans counted more slaves than New York. As immigration from Europe increased, the proportion of slaves in the workforce outside the southern colonies declined. But areas where slavery was only a minor institution still profited from slave labor. Merchants in New York, Massachusetts, and Rhode Island participated actively in the slave trade, shipping slaves from Africa to the Caribbean or the South. Much of the grain, fish, and livestock exported from Pennsylvania and other northern colonies was destined for the slave plantations of the West Indies.

The colonial era witnessed the simultaneous expansion of freedom and slavery in Britain's Atlantic empire. These were the years when the idea of the "freeborn Englishman" became powerfully entrenched in the outlook of both colonists and Britons. Yet the eighteenth century was also the great era of the Atlantic slave trade, a commerce increasingly dominated by

British merchants and ships. During that century more than half the Africans shipped to the New World as slaves were carried on British vessels.

The American Revolution threw the future of slavery into doubt. When Thomas Jefferson in 1776 proclaimed mankind's inalienable right to liberty, and he and other leaders of the new nation spoke of the United States as an asylum of freedom for the oppressed peoples of the world, one American in five was a black slave (including more than one hundred owned by Jefferson himself). The same colonial newspapers that carried arguments against British policies and accounts of resistance to British tyranny also printed advertisements for the sale of slaves. The Revolution did, however, make slavery for the first time a matter of widespread public debate. It inspired charges of hypocrisy, not only from British opponents of independence but also within America. How strong, wondered Abigail Adams, could the "passion for liberty" be among those "accustomed to deprive their fellow citizens of theirs"? But the Revolution also inspired hopes that the institution of slavery could be eliminated from American life.

The language of liberty echoed in slave communities, North and South. The first concrete steps toward emancipation in the North were "freedom petitions"—arguments for emancipation presented to New England's courts by slaves who claimed the rhetoric of liberty for themselves. In 1776, Lemuel Haynes, a black minister who served in the Massachusetts militia during the War of Independence, penned an antislavery essay. If liberty were truly "an innate principle" for all mankind," Haynes wrote, "even an African [had] as equally good a right to his liberty in common with Englishmen." The British offered freedom to slaves who joined the royal cause, and nearly one hundred thousand deserted their owners; twenty thousand of them accompanied the British out of the country at the end of the war—to Europe, Canada, Africa, and, in some cases, reenslavement in the West Indies. Perhaps five thousand escaped bondage by enlisting in the Revolutionary army or local American militias.

Motivated by devotion to revolutionary ideals, a considerable number of southern slaveholders, especially in Virginia and Maryland, voluntarily emancipated their slaves during the 1780s and 1790s. The most famous to do so was George Washington, who died in 1799. His will provided for the emancipation of his nearly three hundred slaves upon the death of his wife, Martha, and for the education of the black children so that they could support themselves in freedom. Perhaps fearing that the executors of his will would seek to subvert this provision, Washington couched it in forceful language. He ordered his family to "see that *this* clause, respecting slaves, and every part thereof be religiously fulfilled . . . without evasion, neglect or delay." He added, "I do hereby expressly forbid the sale . . . of any slave I may die possessed of, under any pretence whatsoever." (Uncomfortable living among men and women who looked forward to gaining their freedom upon her death, Martha Washington liberated the family slaves the following year.) George Washington was the only founding father to liberate his slaves in this manner. Thomas Jefferson's will, by contrast, provided for the freedom of only five slaves, all of them relatives of Sally Hemings, a slave woman with whom he appears to have fathered one or more children.

By the beginning of the nineteenth century, all the northern states had provided for gradual emancipation. State laws generally provided that children henceforth born to slaves would become free after working for their owner until adulthood, to compensate him for the loss of property rights. Thus, the end of slavery in the North was a drawn-out process. In 1810, there were fifty thousand free blacks in the North, but twenty-seven thousand slaves remained. A handful of elderly slaves still lived in New Jersey in 1861, when the Civil War began.

Nonetheless, the first large communities of free African Americans now came into existence. By 1860, the number of free blacks would increase to nearly half a million. A majority lived in the slave states, where they had been born and had family connections. In cities such as Charleston and New Orleans, the free black community included numerous persons of education, wealth, and professional accomplishment—individuals well positioned to take the lead in black politics in the early years of Reconstruction. Some free blacks owned slaves; a few were even plantation owners. Most free blacks, however, worked as poor urban or rural laborers and enjoyed few rights other than not being considered a form of property. Willis Hodges, a freeborn Virginian active in the antislavery movement before the Civil War and in Reconstruction politics afterward, described free blacks and slaves as "one man of sorrow." But despite numerous hardships, the very existence of free blacks offered a standing refutation of slaveholders' argument that African Americans could survive only in bondage.

Despite abolition in the North, slavery not only survived the Revolution but also in some ways emerged from it strengthened. No steps toward abolition took place in the South, where slavery was central to the economy and where the large size of the black population fueled the widespread conviction that two races, if free, could not live together on a basis of peace and equality. Slavery, moreover, was deeply embedded in the new federal Constitution (although it was not named in that document; slaves were called "other persons," as a concession to the sensibilities of delegates who feared the word *slavery* would "contaminate the glorious fabric of American liberty"). The Constitution allowed the slave trade from Africa to continue for twenty more years and required states to return to their owners fugitives from bondage. It provided that three-fifths of the slave population be counted in allocating electoral votes and congressmen among the states. (The ratio was a compromise between the southern desire that all the slaves be counted and the northern insistence that none be.) Taken together, these measures ensured an increase in the slave population because of renewed imports from Africa and gave the slave South far greater power in national life than its free population warranted. Slavery, moreover, helped to shape the identity, the sense of self, of all Americans. The first Naturalization Act, of 1790, which created a uniform system of immigration, restricted the process of becoming a citizen from abroad to "free white persons." Thus, from the outset, a racial definition of American citizenship was built into national law.

Slavery not only survived the American Revolution, but also soon entered a period of unprecedented expansion. As in the colonial era, the economic interests of the North, and of England, remained intertwined with slavery. The industrial revolution in England, soon replicated in the antebellum North, created an insatiable desire for cotton, the raw material of the early textile industry. Cotton had been grown for thousands of years in many parts of the globe. The conquistador Cortés was impressed by the high quality of woven cotton clothing worn by the Aztecs. But in the nineteenth century, cotton assumed an unprecedented role in the world economy. Cotton production grew from fewer than three thousand bales in 1790 to nearly five million bales on the eve of the Civil War. By then, cotton was by far the most important export of the United States.

As the nation expanded westward, so too did slavery, giving rise to the Cotton Kingdom of Alabama, Mississippi, Louisiana, and Texas, which soon became the new center of gravity of American slavery. Because of its high rate of natural increase (about equal to that of whites), the slave population grew apace, even after the importation of enslaved Africans was barred in 1808. On the eve of the Civil War, there were nearly four million slaves, and the South had become the largest, most powerful slave society the modern world had known. By 1860, the economic value of property in slaves amounted to more than the sum of all the money invested in railroads, banks, and factories in the United States.

The slave system varied markedly in different parts of the South. In 1860, 40 percent of the slaves still lived in the upper South, where small- and medium-size farms, rather than large plantations, predominated. Throughout the South, slaves engaged in virtually every kind of economic activity—they worked on farms and plantations, in factories and homes, as skilled artisans and field hands. Agricultural slaves, young and old, male and female, generally were required to labor from sunup to "first dark," often under the close supervision of an overseer or driver. Slaves grew a variety of crops, including rice, sugar, and tobacco, but the "white gold," cotton, was central to the southern and national economies. Labor in the cotton fields was arduous and incessant, especially when an overseer directed the work. "The requisite qualifications for an overseer," wrote Solomon Northup, a free black who spent twelve years in slavery after being kidnapped from the North, "are utter heartlessness, brutality, and cruelty. It is his business to produce large crops, no matter [what the] cost."

Slaves also worked in southern cities, where skilled laborers often enjoyed far better conditions than on plantations. Frederick Douglass, who escaped from slavery as a young man and went on to become the era's greatest abolitionist writer and orator, later recalled being sent to work in Baltimore from rural Maryland: "Instead of the cold, damp floor of my master's kitchen, I found myself on carpets; for the corn bay in winter, I now had a good straw bed, well furnished with covers. For the coarse corn-meal in the morning I now had good bread, and mush [a loaf made from cornmeal] occasionally; for my poor tow-linen shirt, reaching to my knees, I had good clean clothes. I was really well-off." Skilled urban slaves such as Douglass were sometimes allowed to "hire their own time"—that is, to live on their own and make their own labor arrangements, surrendering their earnings to their owner. Ulysses Houston, one of the group at the Collo-quy, worked in this manner as a butcher in prewar Savannah. Such slaves had a wide range of choices in living arrangements: they could rent rooms in a boardinghouse, live with family members, or stay in the homes of free blacks. They spent their nonworking time as they wished. Their experience produced a sense of independence and broad experience that helps to explain why so many urban slave artisans emerged as political leaders after the Civil War.

Three out of four white southern families did not own slaves. Since planters monopolized the best land, most small white farmers lived outside the plantation belt, in hilly areas unsuitable for cotton production. They worked the land using family labor rather than slaves or hired workers. Many southern farmers lived comfortable lives of economic self-sufficiency remote from the market revolution. They raised livestock and grew food for their families, and purchased relatively few goods at local stores. Those residing on marginal land in isolated hill areas and in the Appalachian mountains were often desperately poor and, since nearly all the southern states lacked systems of free public education, more often illiterate than their northern counterparts. Rarely in the antebellum period did the non-slaveholding majority pose a political threat to the planter domination of southern politics. But, especially in the mountain areas, many poor whites remained loyal to the Union during the Civil War. During Reconstruction, some would become scalawags—southern-born white Republicans willing to support civil and political rights for the former slaves.

It is essential to bear in mind the overwhelming economic and political power of slavery in order to appreciate the radicalism of emancipation and Reconstruction. Planters dominated antebellum southern society and politics, and exerted enormous influence in national affairs as well. The wealthiest Americans before the Civil War were planters in the South Carolina low country (where rice was the principal crop) and the Mississippi Valley cotton region around Natchez. Frederick Stanton, a cotton broker turned planter in the Natchez area, owned 444 slaves and more than 15,000 acres of land in Mississippi and Louisiana. The South's "peculiar institution" enriched many northerners as well. Northern ships carried cotton to New York and Europe, northern bankers and merchants financed the cotton crop, northern companies insured it, and northern factories turned cotton into textiles. The "free states" had abolished slavery, but they remained intimately linked to the peculiar institution.

As the nineteenth century progressed, the economic importance of slavery increased steadily, even as the institution came under increasing criticism from reformers in the North and from the slaves themselves. White southerners found themselves more and more dependent on an institution under assault from within and without. In response, the southern states drew tighter and tighter the bonds of slavery, closing off nearly every avenue to freedom and increasing the severity of the laws under which slaves lived and labored.

Before the law, slaves were property with virtually no legal rights. Completely subject to the will of their masters and, more generally, of the white community, they could be bought and sold, leased, fought over in court, and passed on to one's descendants. Blacks and whites were tried in separate courts. No black, free or slave, could own arms, strike a white man, or employ a white servant. Any white person could apprehend any black to demand a certificate of freedom or a pass from the black person's owner giving permission for him to be away from his place of residence. In cases where one parent was free and one slave, the status of a child was determined by that of the mother. This provision, first enacted into law in seventeenth-century Virginia, opened the door to the sexual exploitation of slave women by their owners by ensuring that any offspring would have no legal claim on their fathers, who would own them as property. Slaves' family ties had no legal standing, slaves could not leave the plantation or hold meetings without the permission of their owners, and no aspect of their lives, no matter how intimate, was beyond the reach of their owners' interference.

The entire system of southern justice, from the state militia and courts to slave patrols in each locality, was committed to enforcing the masters' control over their human property. In one celebrated case, a Missouri court considered the "crime" of Celia, a slave who had killed her master while resisting a sexual assault. State law deemed "any woman" in such circumstances to be acting in self-defense. But Celia, the court ruled, was not, legally speaking, a "woman." She was a slave, whose master had complete power over her person. The court sentenced her to death. However, since Celia was pregnant, her execution was postponed until the child was born, so as not to deprive Celia's owner's heirs of their property rights.

Slavery, wrote Thomas Jefferson, was "a perpetual exercise of the most boisterous passions, the most unremitting despotism." Masters had almost complete discretion in inflicting punishment, and rare was the slave who went through his or her life without experiencing a whipping. Even the most gentlemanly and prominent owners inflicted brutal, often sadistic punishments. Wesley Norris, a slave of Confederate general Robert E. Lee, later recalled how after he and his family had attempted to run away, Lee ordered a local constable "to strip us to the waist and give us fifty lashes each." Lee, Norris added, "stood by, and frequently enjoined the constable to 'lay it on well,' " then ordered him "to thoroughly wash our backs" with saltwater to increase the pain. At the cotton plantations in Tennessee and Mississippi owned by President James K. Polk, conditions were so brutal that only half the slave children lived to the age of fifteen.

In the face of this grim reality, slaves never surrendered their desire for freedom or their efforts to carve out a degree of autonomy in their day-to-day lives. Despite overwhelming odds, slaves succeeded in creating loose standards of expected work patterns for themselves that included "free time," space in which to forge a semi-independent culture, centered on the family and church. This enabled them to pass from generation to generation a set of ideas and values fundamentally at odds with those of their owners, ideas and values articulated at the Savannah Colloquy and in countless other venues as the war drew to a close. The slave community was the seedbed for the ways African Americans responded to the coming of emancipation and shouldered the responsibilities of freedom during Reconstruction.

The forging of a distinctive African American culture was a long, complex process. The nearly three hundred thousand Africans brought to the mainland colonies during the eighteenth century were not a single people. They came from different cultures, spoke different languages, and practiced many religions. Slavery threw together individuals who would never otherwise have encountered one another and who had never considered their color or their residence on the same continent a source of identity or unity. The process of creating a cohesive African American culture and community took many years, and proceeded at different rates in different regions.

For most of the eighteenth century, the majority of American slaves were African by birth. For many years, they spoke African languages. Advertisements seeking information about runaways often described them by African origin ("young Gambia Negro," "new Banbara Negro fellow") and spoke of their bearing on their bodies "country marks"—visible signs of ethnic identity in Africa. Elements of African culture were evident throughout the southern colonies in eighteenth-century America—in the names of slaves, in their religions (including, in some areas, Islam), in their African food, music, rituals, and dance. Charles Hansford, a white Virginia

An anonymous late-eighteenth-century painting depicts a wedding ceremony in the slave quarters, where, by African custom, the bride and groom jump over a stick.

blacksmith, noted in a 1753 poem that he had frequently heard slaves speak of their desire to "reenjoy" life in Africa:

> *I oft with pleasure have observ'd how they*
> *Their sultry country's worth strive to display*
> *In broken language, how they praise their case*
> *And happiness when in their native place . . .*
> *How would they dangers court and pains endure*
> *If to their country they could get secure!*

By the nineteenth century, slaves no longer identified themselves as Ibo, Ashanti, Yoruba, and so on, but as African Americans. The War of Independence disrupted the slave trade to North America. The trade resumed briefly in the early nineteenth century, but Congress prohibited the further importation of slaves in 1808. Henceforth, the slave population grew almost entirely by natural increase. In music, art, folklore, language, and religion, the slaves' cultural expressions emerged as a synthesis of African traditions, European elements, and conditions in America. The values expressed during Reconstruction were rooted in the culture that slaves developed in bondage.

At the center of the slave community stood the family, even though the law did not recognize slave marriages and many were disrupted by sales. Because of the exigencies of life under slavery, many kinds of family structures coexisted in slave communities. Most adults lived in two-parent households, with ties that often lasted a lifetime. But the slave community had a significantly higher number of female-headed households than among whites, and families in which grandparents, other relatives, or even non-kin assumed responsibility for raising children who had been separated from their parents. To solidify a sense of family continuity, slaves frequently named children after cousins, uncles, grandparents, and other relatives. They developed "fictive" kin relations that supplemented blood ties. Frederick Douglass recalled that on the plantation where he grew up, skilled slaves "were called 'uncles' by all the younger slaves, not because they really sustained that relationship to any, but as a mark of plantation etiquette, a mark of respect due from the younger to the older slaves." Nor did the slave family simply mirror kinship patterns among whites. Slaves, for example, did not marry their first cousins, a practice common among white southerners.

The slave family existed with the constant threat of disruption. The peopling of the Cotton Kingdom involved an immense forced migration. Between 1800 and 1860, at least one million slaves were transported from older southern states to the plantations of the Deep South. Fear of sale pervaded slave life. "Mother, is Massa gwine to sell us tomorrow?" ran a line in a popular slave song. Slave traders gave little attention to preserving family ties. A public notice, "SALE OF SLAVES AND STOCK," announced the 1852 auction of property belonging to a recently deceased Georgia planter. It listed thirty-six individuals, ranging from an infant to a sixty-nine-year-old woman, and ended with the proviso: "SLAVES WILL BE SOLD SEPARATE, OR IN LOTS, AS BEST SUITS THE PURCHASER."

Most of the slaves sold in the interstate trade were young men and women below the age of thirty. "It is better to buy none in families," wrote one slave trader, "but to select only

Sale of Slaves and Stock.

The Negroes and Stock listed below, are a Prime Lot, and belong to the ESTATE OF THE LATE LUTHER McGOWAN, and will be sold on Monday, Sept. 22nd, 1852, at the Fair Grounds, in Savannah, Georgia, at 1:00 P. M. The Negroes will be taken to the grounds two days previous to the Sale, so that they may be inspected by prospective buyers.

On account of the low prices listed below, they will be sold for cash only, and must be taken into custody within two hours after sale.

No.	Name	Age	Remarks	Price
1	Lunesta	27	Prime Rice Planter,	$1,275.00
2	Violet	16	Housework and Nursemaid,	900.00
3	Lizzie	30	Rice, Unsound,	300.00
4	Minda	27	Cotton, Prime Woman,	1,200.00
5	Adam	28	Cotton, Prime Young Man,	1,100.00
6	Abel	41	Rice Hand, Eyesight Poor,	675.00
7	Tanney	22	Prime Cotton Hand,	950.00
8	Flementina	39	Good Cook. Stiff Knee,	400.00
9	Lanney	34	Prime Cottom Man,	1,000.00
10	Sally	10	Handy in Kitchen,	675.00
11	Maccabey	35	Prime Man, Fair Carpenter,	980.00
12	Dorcas Judy	25	Seamstress, Handy in House,	800.00
13	Happy	60	Blacksmith,	575.00
14	Mowden	15	Prime Cotton Boy,	700.00
15	Bills	21	Handy with Mules,	900.00
16	Theopolis	39	Rice Hand, Gets Fits,	575.00
17	Coolidge	29	Rice Hand and Blacksmith,	1,275.00
18	Bessie	69	Infirm, Sews,	250.00
19	Infant	1	Strong Likely Boy	400.00
20	Samson	41	Prime Man, Good with Stock,	975.00
21	Callie May	27	Prime Woman, Rice,	1,000.00
22	Honey	14	Prime Girl, Hearing Poor,	850.00
23	Angelina	16	Prime Girl, House or Field,	1,000.00
24	Virgil	21	Prime Field Hand,	1,100.00
25	Tom	40	Rice Hand, Lame Leg,	750.00
26	Noble	11	Handy Boy,	900.00
27	Judge Lesh	55	Prime Blacksmith,	800.00
28	Booster	43	Fair Mason, Unsound,	600.00
29	Big Kate	37	Housekeeper and Nurse,	950.00
30	Melie Ann	19	Housework, Smart Yellow Girl,	1,250.00
31	Deacon	26	Prime Rice Hand,	1,000.00
32	Coming	19	Prime Cotton Hand,	1,000.00
33	Mabel	47	Prime Cotton Hand,	800.00
34	Uncle Tim	60	Fair Hand with Mules,	600.00
35	Abe	27	Prime Cotton Hand,	1,000.00
36	Tennes	29	Prime Rice Hand and Coachman,	1,250.00

There will also be offered at this sale, twenty head of Horses and Mules with harness, along with thirty head of Prime Cattle. Slaves will be sold separate, or in lots, as best suits the purchaser. Sale will be held rain or shine.

An 1852 public notice announces the sale of thirty-six African Americans in Savannah, Georgia.

choice, first rate, young hands from 14 to 25 years of age (buying no children or aged negroes)." Whatever the slaves' age, sales were a human tragedy that disrupted established patterns of life almost as severely as had the original forced passage from Africa. "My dear wife," a Georgia slave wrote in 1858, "I take the pleasure of writing you these few [lines] with much regret to inform you that I am sold. . . . Give my love to my father and mother and tell them good bye for me, and if we shall not meet in this world I hope to meet in heaven. My dear wife for you and my children my pen cannot express the grief I feel to be parted from you all. I remain, your truly husband until death, Abream Scriven." In the early days of Reconstruction, thousands of freedmen and -women seeking to locate family members from whom they had been separated while in slavery would place advertisements in newspapers and solicit aid from the Freedmen's Bureau, a federal agency established in 1865 to offer relief to destitute southerners, promote education and health care among the freedmen, secure equal justice in southern courts, and in other ways oversee the transition from slavery to freedom.

Even though the law did not recognize the right of slaves to own property, many in fact acquired possessions by selling produce raised "on their own time," sometimes in garden plots assigned to them by their owners. "All the slaves on the place," one Mississippi slave later recalled, "had patches of land . . . to work as their own." On Sundays, a white visitor to Natchez observed, slaves would "leave their plantations and come into town to dispose of their produce and lay in their own little luxuries." In Charleston and Savannah, slave women dominated trading in the official town markets. Other slaves received payments from their owners as a reward for good behavior, or to induce them to labor for longer hours than tradition had established. Slaves who accumulated property passed it on to their descendants, thus strengthening family ties. Evidence of the strong sense of property that developed in some parts of the South may be found in petitions filed by former slaves with the Southern Claims Commission, a government agency established after the war to reimburse loyal southerners for wartime property losses. "My old parents used to raise poultry and pigs etc and they gave me some," one claimant told the commission. "That is how I got a start." The experience of working under their own direction and of marketing produce they had grown as slaves helped to prepare African Americans for involvement in the market economy during Reconstruction.

In some ways, gender roles under slavery differed dramatically from those in the larger society. Slave men and women experienced, in a sense, the equality of powerlessness. The nineteenth century's "cult of domesticity," which defined the home as a woman's proper sphere, did not apply to slave women, many of whom regularly worked in the fields and were unable to devote much time to child rearing. Slave men were not the economic providers for their families, nor could they protect their families from physical or sexual abuse by owners and overseers, or determine when and under what conditions their children worked.

In other ways, however, more conventional gender roles prevailed. When working "on their own time," slave men chopped wood, hunted, and fished, while women washed, sewed, and assumed primary responsibility for the care of children. But whatever its structure or internal arrangements, the slave family was central to the African American community, allowing for the transmission of values, traditions, and survival strategies—in a word, of slave culture—from one generation to the next. And when freedom came for slaves, legalizing their marriages and consolidating their families were among their highest priorities.

A second pillar of slave life was religion. Slaves developed a distinctive version of Christianity that would play a crucial role in the Reconstruction era and, indeed, down to the present day. Some blacks, free and slave, had taken part in the religious revivals of the colonial era known as the "Great Awakening," and even more were swept into the South's Baptist and Methodist churches during the Second Great Awakening of the late eighteenth and early nineteenth centuries. As one preacher recalled of the great camp meeting that drew thousands of worshipers to Cane Ridge, Kentucky, in 1801, no distinctions were made "as to age, sex, color, or anything of a temporary nature; old and young, male and female, black and white, had equal privilege to minister the light which they received, in whatever way the Spirit directed." Imbued with devotion inspired by the Second Great Awakening, many owners welcomed missionaries who preached to slaves; some even built chapels on their plantations and encouraged slaves to worship there. White ministers brought by owners to preach to the slaves usually invoked biblical passages enjoining servants to obey their masters. One slave later recalled being told in a sermon "how good God was in bringing us over to this country from dark and benighted Africa and permitting us to listen to the sound of the gospel." Especially in cities, slaves also worshiped in biracial congregations headed by white ministers, where they generally were required to sit in the back pews or upstairs.

An engraving entitled Family Worship in a Plantation in South Carolina, *published in a British illustrated weekly during the Civil War, depicts the scene in a "rude chapel" of a Port Royal, South Carolina, plantation.*

Nonetheless, much of slave religion flourished outside the owner's oversight. Before the Civil War, urban free blacks established their own churches. These institutions, at which many slaves as well as free blacks worshiped, became training grounds for postwar black leadership and schools, in a sense, of self-government. At the First African Baptist Church of Richmond, Virginia, a committee of deacons judged and disciplined members for breaches of church rules and immoral behavior such as adultery, and settled disputes over issues such as disputed debts. The church "court" was the only place where African Americans administered justice among themselves, without the intervention of an owner or the law. Most of the leaders of the Richmond church were free blacks, but in 1848, thirty congregants petitioned for a change in the constitution of the church to allow all male members, including slaves, to vote in the selection of the pastor and deacons.

The heart of slave religion lay in the secret religious gatherings where slave ministers preached a gospel of endurance and transcendence in the face of hardship, and hope for liberation from bondage. Even though it was illegal for slaves to gather without a white person being present, every plantation had its black preacher, usually a slave with little formal education but rhetorical ability and familiarity with the Bible. A blending of African traditions and Christian belief, slave religion was practiced in "praise meetings" that were replete with shouts, dances, and frequent emotional interchanges between preacher and congregation.

Slaves adopted those parts of Christianity that spoke most directly to their own experiences and aspirations. They rejected the fundamentalist doctrine of original sin, and saw God as a personal presence in the world, who promised eventual deliverance from bondage. Central to slave Christianity was the compelling biblical story of Exodus, in which a chosen people suffers a long period of bondage only to be released through the intervention of providence. (Hence, Georgia slaves understanding General Sherman to be a divinely appointed savior.) Their preachers emphasized other biblical stories as well that depicted the weak defeating the strong or triumphing over adversity—David and Goliath, Daniel escaping from the lion's den, Jonah and the whale, Samson destroying the temple (even though he perished in the process). When they sang, "I'm bound for the land of Canaan," slaves meant not only relief from worldly toils in an afterlife but also escaping to the North or, in God's time, the breaking of slavery's chains.

In the slaves' "gospel of freedom," prayers for an end to slavery were ever present. One former slave, Alice Sewell, later recalled typical secret religious gatherings: "We used to slip off in the woods in the old slave days on Sunday evening way down in the swamps to sing and pray to our own liking. We prayed for this day of freedom. We come from four and five miles to pray together to God that if we didn't live to see it, to please let our children live to see a better day and be free." At the end of the service, Sewell continued, "we used to sing 'We walk about and shake hands, fare you well my sisters, I am going home.' "

A desire to read the Bible was one reason a number of slaves secretly, and in violation of southern law, learned to read. Others recognized in literacy an element of liberation. Frederick Douglass was one who taught himself to both read and write. "From that moment," he later wrote, he understood that knowledge was "the pathway from slavery to freedom." The thirst for education so prominent among former slaves during Reconstruction originated during slavery.

"Freedom," a black minister declared, "lived in the black heart long before freedom was born." If masters devised an elaborate ideology defending slavery as a benign, paternalist system that served the best interests of white and black alike, slaves developed their own worldview, centered on their desire for liberation. Even the most ignorant slave, observed Solomon Northup, could not "fail to observe the difference between their own condition and the meanest white man's, and to realize the injustice of laws which place it within [the owner's] power not only to appropriate the profits of their industry, but to subject them to unmediated and unprovoked punishment without remedy."

The world of most rural slaves was bounded by their local communities and kin. They became extremely familiar with the local landscape, crops, and population, and gathered with slaves from nearby farms and plantations to celebrate marriages, attend funerals, and for Christmas and Fourth of July celebrations. Most, however, had little knowledge of the larger world.

Nonetheless, slaves could not remain indifferent to the currents of thought unleashed by the American Revolution, or to the language of democracy and liberty that suffused the society around them. Slaves, as Garrison Frazier remarked during the Colloquy, appreciated that slavery was, at base, a system of coercion in which one group appropriated the labor of another. ("We raise the bread / They give us the crust," declared one slave song; another told how the slaves "make the cotton and corn / And the white folks gets the money.") Their "grapevine telegraph" brought fragments of news about national and even international events, from American presidential elections to the revolutions of 1848 in Europe. They listened to political discussions among their owners and Fourth of July orations in southern towns. They learned that African Americans in the North lived as free men and women, not slaves, and that a conflict over slavery was disrupting national politics. Robert Smalls, later a major political leader during Reconstruction, recalled how as a boy on a South Carolina plantation he heard of Frederick Douglass from a literate slave who managed to acquire a copy of one of Douglass's speeches. Slaves adopted the nation's democratic and egalitarian rhetoric as their own. "I am in a land of liberty," wrote Joseph Taper, a Virginia slave who escaped to Canada around 1840. "Here man is as God intended he should be . . . not like the southern laws which put man, made in the image of God, on a level with brutes."

During Reconstruction, the semi-independent institutions of the slave quarters and the distinctive beliefs slaves had developed would blossom in the emergence of black schools, churches, benevolent societies, and political institutions. Former slaves would stake a claim to the rights of American citizens they had long been denied. The social and political agenda that African Americans would articulate during Reconstruction—civil and political equality, the strengthening of the black community, and autonomy in their working lives—flowed directly out of their experience in slavery.

Before the Civil War, however, confronted by federal, state, and local authorities committed to maintaining the stability of slavery, and outnumbered by white southerners, slaves had little opportunity to express their desire for freedom through outright rebellion. Generally, resistance to slavery had to take other forms. Most common was "day-to-day resistance"—feigning illness, doing poor work, abusing animals, breaking tools. "They break and destroy more farming utensils," one planter complained, "ruin more carts, break more gates, spoil more cattle and horses, and commit more waste than five times their number of white laborers do." One overseer on a Maryland plantation complained that slaves under his direction "get much more dissatisfied every year and troublesome for they say that they ought all to be at their liberty and they think that I am the cause that they are not."

Then there were the unknown number of slaves who ran away, either to the North, to southern cities, or to isolated rural areas such as the Great Dismal Swamp of Virginia or the Florida Everglades. Running away was a constant feature of slavery from its earliest days in America. Colonial and nineteenth-century newspapers were filled with advertisements for fugitive slaves. These notices described the appearance and skills of the fugitive and included such comments as "ran away without any cause," and "he has great notions of freedom." The difficulties of escape were enormous, but the number of runaways was significant enough by 1850 for southern congressmen to secure passage of the Fugitive Slave Act, which made the federal government responsible for returning escaped slaves to their masters. The passage of the law greatly exacerbated tensions between North and South. Many northerners who did not consider themselves abolitionists reacted with disgust when federal marshals entered their communities to seize fugitive slaves and return them to the South.

Most escapees were young men without wives or children; for women, escaping accompanied by a child was nearly impossible, and leaving children behind was a step that few were willing to contemplate. Some fugitives were aided by sympathetic abolitionists organized into a loose organization—the Underground Railroad. Most, like Douglass, who borrowed the papers of a free black sailor, or the light-skinned William and Ellen Craft, who impersonated a sickly owner traveling with a slave, escaped on their own initiative, with little assistance other than from free blacks or other slaves. A few courageous individuals made forays into the South to liberate slaves. The best known was Harriet Tubman. Born in Maryland in 1820, Tubman escaped to Philadelphia in 1849 and during the next decade risked her life by making numerous trips back to her state of birth to lead relatives and other slaves to freedom.

Despite enormous obstacles, slave rebellions sometimes disturbed slavery's outward face of tranquility. In 1800, Gabriel, a Virginia slave blacksmith, with his brother Martin, a preacher, devised a plan whereby armed slaves would march on Richmond, massacre most of the white population, and possibly sail to Haiti, where a slave insurrection in the 1790s had liberated the black population there. The plot was discovered, and the leaders arrested. Like other Virginians, participants in Gabriel's conspiracy spoke the language of liberty forged in the American Revolution. They even planned to carry a banner emblazoned with a version of Patrick Henry's famous slogan: DEATH OR LIBERTY.

Twenty-two years later, another slave conspiracy was uncovered, this time led by a free African American, Denmark Vesey of Charleston. Vesey's outlook reflected the varied sources of black ideology. He was fond of quoting the Bible to condemn slavery; he also drew on the Declaration of Independence, and carefully followed debates in Congress between 1819 and 1821 over the admission of Missouri to the Union as a slave state. The best-known slave rebel was Nat Turner, a slave preacher in Southampton County, Virginia, who in 1831 led a band that marched through the countryside and killed some sixty whites until subdued by the militia. When asked after his capture to admit that he had been "mistaken," Turner replied: "Was not Christ crucified?"

All these rebellions, and, indeed, rumors of insurrection in many other years, were greeted by widespread panic among southern whites, brutal

retribution against African Americans, and the tightening of laws and
patrols policing the slave system. In the aftermath of the Turner rebellion,
for example, the Virginia legislature, fearing, as one member put it, that "a
Nat Turner might be in every family," briefly debated a plan for gradual
emancipation. The lawmakers decided instead to strengthen the militia and
bar blacks from acting as preachers. As the sectional controversy accelerated, the South turned in upon itself. It suppressed any sign of dissention
among whites and imposed new restrictions on both the slave and free
black populations. The prospects for rebellion became more and more
remote. The balance of power in the South would have to change dramatically before slaves could frontally challenge the system. That would not
happen until the Union army entered the South during the Civil War.
When it did, blacks by the tens of thousands would abandon the plantations, fatally undermining the peculiar institution.

For some decades, it appeared that slaves and free blacks were nearly
the only Americans willing to challenge slavery. After the antislavery
impulse spawned by the American Revolution died out, the slavery question faded from national life. Those whites willing to contemplate an end
to bondage almost always coupled calls for abolition with the suggestion of

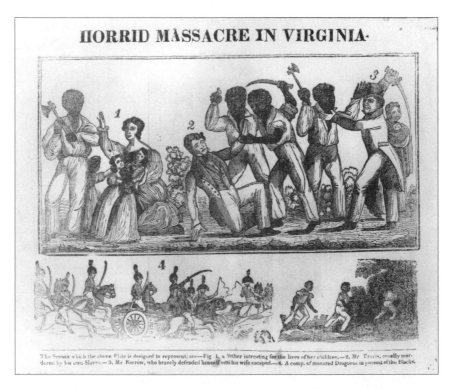

A woodcut published in an 1831 account of the Nat Turner uprising

colonization—the deportation of the black population to Africa, the Caribbean, or Central America. Colonizationists accepted the premise written into the Naturalization Act of 1790 (and reaffirmed as the law of the land by the Supreme Court in the Dred Scott decision of 1857) that the United States was a political community of whites, and that no black person could be a citizen.

It was the rise of the abolitionist movement in the late 1820s and 1830s that put the slavery question back on the national agenda. Abolitionism was only one of the era's numerous efforts to improve American society. Reformers established organizations that worked to prevent the manufacture and sale of liquor, improve conditions in prisons, expand public education, uplift the condition of wage laborers, and reorganize society on the basis of cooperation rather than competitive individualism. Nearly all these groups worked to convert public opinion to their cause. They sent out speakers, gathered signatures on petitions, and published pamphlets.

Many of these reform movements drew their inspiration from the Second Great Awakening. God, the revivalist preachers maintained, had created man as a "free moral agent." Sinners could not only reform themselves but also remake the world. The revivals popularized the outlook known as "perfectionism," which saw both individuals and society at large as capable of infinite improvement. Under the impact of the revivals, older reform efforts moved in a new, radical direction. Temperance (which literally means moderation in the consumption of liquor) was transformed into a crusade to eliminate drinking entirely. Criticism of war became outright pacifism. And critics of slavery now demanded not gradual emancipation but immediate and total abolition.

Beginning with the appearance in 1829 of the free black writer David Walker's *Appeal*—a stirring call for emancipation—and the publication two years later of the first issue of *The Liberator,* edited by William Lloyd Garrison, a new, militant abolitionist movement burst onto the national scene. Walker's condemnation of slavery cited the Bible and the Declaration of Independence, but he went beyond these familiar arguments to call on blacks to take pride in the achievements of ancient African civilizations and to claim all their rights as Americans. "Tell us no more about colonization," Walker wrote, addressing white readers, "for America is as much our country as it is yours. . . . We have enriched it with our *blood and tears.*"

Like Walker, the new generation of abolitionists insisted that blacks were Americans, entitled to all the rights of free citizens. It was their anti-colonization position as much as their attack on slavery that won them widespread support among northern free blacks. Indeed, the first national black convention, held in Philadelphia in 1817, was convened explicitly to

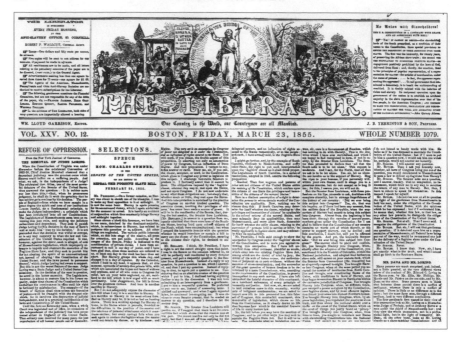

The masthead of The Liberator

repudiate the doctrines of the American Colonization Society, founded a few months earlier by a group of prominent political and social figures from both North and South, and to claim all the rights of citizenship for African Americans. "We have no wish to separate from our present homes," the convention's resolutions declared. In the years that followed, a number of black organizations removed the word *African* from their names, hoping to eliminate a possible reason for American-born blacks' being deported from the land of their birth.

The abolitionist movement engaged the energies of thousands of northern women, who circulated petitions, distributed literature, and, in some cases, broke with the prevailing assumption that they should remain in the "private" sphere by delivering public lectures on the evils of slavery. Some of these women found in abolitionist doctrines a challenge to their own subordinate status in American society. "Since I engaged in the investigation of the rights of the slave," wrote Angelina Grimké, the daughter of a South Carolina slaveowner who converted to Quakerism and abolitionism while living in Philadelphia, "I have necessarily been led to a better understanding of my own; for I have found the Anti-Slavery cause to be . . . the school in which human rights are more fully investigated, and better understood and taught, than in any other [reform] enterprise. . . . Here we are led to examine why human beings have any rights. . . . Now it naturally occurred to me, that if rights were founded in moral being, then the circumstance of sex could not give to man higher rights and responsibilities, than to woman." Abolitionist women such as Grimké and her sister, Sarah, helped launch the long struggle for equal rights for American women.

Thus, the contest over slavery gave new meaning to such core ideas of American political culture as personal liberty, political community, and the rights attached to American citizenship. The abolitionists put forward notions widely condemned in the 1830s, but that three decades later would be incorporated into the laws and constitutional amendments of the Reconstruction era—that any person born in the United States should be entitled to American citizenship and that all citizens should be accorded equal rights before the law, regardless of race.

In contrast to the official definition of nationhood bounded by race, abolitionists insisted on the "Americanness" of slaves and free blacks. Lydia Maria Child's popular 1833 treatise, *An Appeal in Favor of That Class of Americans Called Africans,* insisted that blacks were fellow countrymen, not foreigners or a permanently inferior caste. They should no more be considered Africans than whites were Englishmen. Thus, the movement challenged not only southern slavery, but the racial proscription that confined free blacks in the North to second-class status. (Between 1800 and 1860, every free state that entered the Union, with the sole exception of Maine, restricted suffrage to white males, and New York and Pennsylvania, home to significant free black communities, took away the voting rights that African Americans had once enjoyed.)

Many white abolitionists shared, to some degree, the racial prejudices of their era. But what is remarkable is how many were able to rise above them. "While the word 'white' is on the statute-book of Massachusetts," declared Edmund Quincy, an active associate of William Lloyd Garrison, "Massachusetts is a slave state." Abolitionists' battles for northern blacks' right to vote, to enjoy access to education and public accommodation, and to serve in the militia achieved only a few successes, such as the integration of the Massachusetts public schools, ordered by the legislature in 1855. But these campaigns helped to lay the legal and political groundwork for the campaigns for equal rights that were central to the politics of Reconstruction.

Most adamant in contending that the struggle against slavery required a redefinition of the nation as a whole were black members of the abolitionist crusade. "He who has endured the cruel pangs of slavery," wrote Douglass in 1847, "is the man to advocate liberty." Black abolitionists developed an understanding of freedom that went well beyond the usage of their white contemporaries. "The real battleground between liberty and slavery," wrote black editor Samuel Cornish, "is prejudice against color." More than white abolitionists, as well, black abolitionists identified the widespread poverty of the free black population as a consequence of slavery, and insisted that freedom meant some form of economic autonomy. It must be part of the "great work" of the antislavery crusade, insisted Charles L. Reason, "to abolish not only chattel slavery, but that other kind of slavery, which, for generation after generation, dooms an oppressed people to a condition of dependence and pauperism." Dozens of black abolitionists would move south after the Civil War to take part in Reconstruction, bringing with them the experience of long years of struggle for equal rights and economic opportunity.

Black abolitionists, and free blacks generally, repudiated the nation's self-definition as a land of liberty. Indeed, to counter what they viewed as the hypocrisy of Independence Day celebrations, they developed an alternative calendar of celebrations, centered on August 1, the anniversary of emancipation in the British West Indies in 1833. (This carried the disturbing implication that Britain, not the United States, now represented liberty on the world stage.) But even as they condemned the hypocrisy of a nation that proclaimed belief in freedom yet daily committed "practices more shocking and bloody" than any other, in Douglass's words, abolitionists laid claim to the founders' legacy. By abolishing slavery, Douglass proclaimed, the United States could reinvigorate the promise of the Declaration of Independence and recapture the country's original mission as an asylum of liberty. In his autobiography *My Bondage and My Freedom*, Douglass claimed as forebears not only the founding fathers but slave rebels such as Gabriel, Denmark Vesey, and Nat Turner. In their desire for freedom, he seemed to argue, the slaves were truer to the nation's underlying principles than the white Americans who annually celebrated the Fourth of July.

The abolitionists never constituted more than a small portion of the northern population. Indeed, in the 1830s, their activities were greeted with as much hostility in the free states as in the slave South. Initially, abolitionist meetings were broken up by mobs, a number of their presses were destroyed, and Congress refused to receive their petitions. Slowly, however, the abolitionists succeeded in shattering the conspiracy of silence that sought to preserve national unity (and the profits derived from slave labor) by excluding slavery from political debate.

Since the Constitutional Convention, slavery had occasionally emerged as a point of contention in American politics. Generally, it became a political issue when territorial acquisitions raised the question of whether the peculiar institution would be permitted to continue its westward expansion,

This print depicts a July 1835 nighttime anti-abolitionist raid on the Charleston, South Carolina, post office. The crowd broke into the building, removed antislavery mail, and burned it in the street.

thus affecting both the balance of power between North and South and the prospects for free citizens migrating to new lands. Missouri's request to be admitted to the Union as a slave state had inspired a controversy that was settled by the Missouri Compromise in 1821, which barred slavery from expanding into most of the remainder of the Louisiana Purchase territory. In the 1840s, as a result of the Mexican-American War, a vast new area was added to the United States, and the question of slavery's status again came to the fore. The lead was taken by politicians speaking the language of "free soil" for settlers desiring to move to the West, rather than the moral vocabulary of the abolition movement. But the growing desire among northerners to restrict slavery's expansion reflected how abolitionist petitions, speeches, and publications had begun to affect public opinion.

Once again, compromise settled the slavery issue. In 1850, Congress admitted California as a free state, decreed that local inhabitants could decide whether or not to permit slavery in the rest of the land recently acquired from Mexico, and enacted a stringent new fugitive slave law that made the federal government, not the states, responsible for apprehending and returning runaways. Harriet A. Jacobs, one of the few female slaves to publish a narrative of her experiences, recalled how the new law inspired "a reign of terror to the colored population" of the North, who feared that, even if born free, they might be improperly swept up by its draconian provisions, which did not allow the accused fugitive to testify in his or her own behalf. In New York City, "many families, who had lived in the city for twenty years, fled from it now," while others, such as Jacobs herself, "seldom ventured into the streets." Several thousand northern blacks sought safety in Canada. The sight of so many refugees seeking liberty in a foreign land cast an ironic light on the familiar image of the United States as an asylum for freedom. Some African American leaders, such as Martin R. Delany, later dubbed the "father" of black nationalism, concluded that the black population should emigrate en masse, to find a homeland in Africa or the Caribbean where they could become part of "the ruling element of the country" and enjoy the equality that seemed ever more remote in the United States.

The political peace ushered in by the Compromise of 1850 lasted exactly four years. When Congress in 1854 approved the Kansas-Nebraska Act, repealing the Missouri Compromise and opening a vast new area in the nation's heartland to slavery, party lines shattered and a new organization, the Republican Party, rose to prominence on a platform of stopping

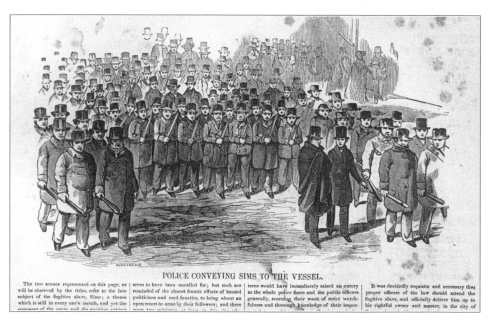

POLICE CONVEYING SIMS TO THE VESSEL.

The two scenes represented on this page, as | seem to have been uncalled for; but such are | irons would have immediately raised an outcry | It was decidedly requisite and necessary that
will be observed by the titles, refer to the late | reminded of the almost frantic efforts of heated | at the whole police force and the public officers | proper officers of the law should attend the
subject of the fugitive slave, Sims; a theme | politicians and mad fanatics, to bring about an | generally, scorning their want of strict watch- | fugitive slave, and officially deliver him up to
which is still in every one's mouth, and yet the | open resort to arms by their followers; and there | fulness and thorough knowledge of their impor- | his rightful owner and master, in the city of

Fearing resistance from abolitionists, on April 15, 1851, three hundred armed Boston police and federal marshals escorted fugitive slave Thomas Sims to a Navy ship that returned him to slavery in Georgia.

slavery's expansion once and for all. In the new party, belief in the superiority of the "free labor" system of the North and the incompatibility of "free society" and "slave society" coalesced into a comprehensive worldview. Republicans saw slavery's expansion as an obstacle to progress, opportunity, and democracy.

No one expressed this vision more eloquently than Abraham Lincoln. Having served a number of terms in the Illinois legislature and two years in Congress in the 1840s, Lincoln had retired from active political involvement in 1849. He was swept back into politics by the Kansas-Nebraska Act. His career illustrated how much northern public opinion had changed regarding slavery and race, and how far it still had to go.

Lincoln was not an advocate of immediate emancipation. He revered the Union and the Constitution and was willing to compromise with the South to preserve them. His speeches combined the moral fervor of the abolitionists with the respect for order and the Constitution of more conservative northerners. "I hate it," he said in 1854 of the prospect of slavery's expansion, "because of the monstrous injustice of slavery itself. I hate it because it deprives our republican example of its just influence in the world—enables the enemies of free institutions, with plausibility, to taunt us as hypocrites—causes the real friends of freedom to doubt our sincerity." If slavery were allowed to expand, he warned, the "love of liberty" would be extinguished and with it America's special mission to be a symbol of democracy for the entire world.

Lincoln once remarked that he "hated slavery, I think as much as any abolitionist." Yet he shared many of the era's racial prejudices, affirming in 1858 that he did not favor blacks' voting or holding office in Illinois, and frequently speaking of colonizing African Americans outside the country. In this, he represented the mainstream of northern opinion, by now convinced that slavery posed a threat to "free society," but still convinced of the inherent inferiority of African Americans. Only during the Civil War, under the impact of the disintegration of slavery and the service of black soldiers in the Union army, would Lincoln begin to envision the United States of the future as a biracial society.

Nonetheless, Lincoln maintained that slavery violated the essential premises of American life—personal liberty, political democracy, and the opportunity to rise in the social scale. "I want every man to have the chance," he proclaimed, "and I believe a black man is entitled to it, in which he *can* better his condition." Like Garrison Frazier in the Colloquy with General Sherman several years later, Lincoln declared that the slave was, in essence, a laborer illegitimately deprived of the fruits of his labor.

Blacks, Lincoln added, might not be equal to whites in all respects, but in their "natural right" to the fruits of their labor, they were "my equal and the equal of all others."

The rise of the Republican Party greatly heightened sectional tensions. These were further exacerbated in October 1859, when the abolitionist John Brown led a band of twenty-two men in an assault on the federal arsenal at Harpers Ferry, Virginia. A deeply religious man long associated with the abolitionist cause, Brown had been persuaded by reading the Old Testament that God intended to inflict His punishment on a society blighted by the sin of slaveholding. He himself would be the instrument of divine wrath, by sparking a slave insurrection that would sweep away the peculiar institution.

Militarily, Brown's plot made little sense. Most of his men were killed or captured, and Brown himself, convicted of treason against Virginia, was executed. More significant was the response to his raid. In the South, Brown inspired a reaction bordering on hysteria, even though not a single slave (of whom, in fact, there were very few in the vicinity of Harpers Ferry) had joined him. In the North, Brown became a martyr, a symbol of selfless devotion to a moral cause. To blacks, especially, he long remained a hero. One black woman, Frances Ellen Watkins, wrote to Brown before his execution, "Your martyr grave will be a sacred altar upon which men will record their vows of undying hatred to that system which tramples on man and bids defiance to God." The response to Brown's actions suggested that more and more Americans had come to believe that the slavery question would never be settled except through violence.

A recently discovered daguerreotype portrait taken in 1847 by African American photographer Augustus Washington shows John Brown before he grew his famous beard.

A little less than a year after Brown's execution, Abraham Lincoln was elected the nation's first Republican president. In the eyes of many white southerners, Lincoln's victory placed their future at the mercy of a party avowedly hostile to their region's values and interests. Those who advocated secession feared that Lincoln's election heralded a fundamental shift in national power, in which the slaveholding states, which had dominated American politics since the adoption of the Constitution, would henceforth find themselves in a shrinking minority. Lincoln had not received a single vote in most of the South. His victory demonstrated that a united North now possessed the power to determine the nation's future. During the late 1850s, southern leaders had bent every effort to strengthen the bonds of slavery. "Slavery is our king," declared a South Carolina politician in 1860. "Slavery is our truth, slavery is our divine right." Rather than accept minority status in a nation governed by their opponents, Deep South political leaders boldly struck for their region's independence.

In the wake of Lincoln's election, seven states of the Deep South seceded from the Union and formed the Confederate States of America. South Carolina's "Declaration of the Immediate Causes of Secession" placed fear for the future of slavery at the center of the crisis: experience, it proclaimed, had shown "that slaveholding states cannot be safe in subjection to non-slaveholding states." On April 12, 1861, Confederate batteries fired on Fort Sumter, an enclave of Union control in Charleston Harbor, inaugurating the Civil War. At the outset, President Lincoln insisted that the administration's aim was to preserve the Union, not to abolish slavery. To the slaves, however, the outbreak of war heralded the long-awaited day of Jubilee. Acting on this conviction, African Americans now took actions that propelled a reluctant white America down the path to emancipation.

TRUE LIKENESSES

What does a portrait tell you?

According to Nathaniel Hawthorne, nothing much: "There is no such thing as a true portrait," he declared as he sat for one in 1850. "They are all delusions and I never saw any two alike."

But in the portrait-crazed early nineteenth century, there was more involved than unhappy portrait sitters dubiously eyeing the accuracy of their rendered faces. Formerly the luxurious possession of the affluent, the portrait became a commodity that most Americans could possess—thanks to the work of itinerant "limners" stalking the countryside and, after 1839, photographers setting up daguerreotype studios in major urban thoroughfares. And while the personal photographic portrait soon graced many a parlor, a market for the faces of the illustrious and notorious proliferated in the new visual industry of inexpensive prints and illustrated magazines and books that swept the nation in the 1840s and 1850s.

When it came to those famous faces, more was at stake than merely a "true likeness." These portraits were public performances: in their stern countenances and distant gazes, they demonstrated leadership, dependability, virtue, and vision. In the form of inexpensive prints, such portraits decorated many a home, their visages offering moral guidance to impressionable youth. But were such messages necessarily what the famous portrait subjects had in mind when they sat for the painter or struck a pose for the photographer? No one knew better how often these public portraits were beyond the control of the subject than that most photographed of antebellum African Americans, the former slave and brilliant abolitionist orator Frederick Douglass.

In Douglass's view, the simplest portrait could have a deleterious impact; even the work of allies could cause damage. In 1849, he greeted the long-anticipated publication of *A Tribute for the Negro,* a 564-page compendium of African and African American achievement compiled by the Quaker abolitionist Wilson Armistead, with an acerbic comment about "the superior portraits referred to in the title page. . . . The book would have been better without them."

What could have provoked such criticism? The book's portrait of the young Douglass at first glance seems at worst uninspired. To Douglass, though, it was a misrepresentation:

"[I]t has a much more kindly and amiable expression, than is generally thought to character-ize the face of a fugitive slave."

Douglass saw his portrait, like his writing, as a critical weapon in the aboli-tionist cause. His very appearance repre-sented the abolitionist movement, and amiability was not the message he wished to convey. Douglass lauded the daguerreo-type over the painted portrait, believing he could better control the face captured in the new medium of photography. Cer-tainly, it was preferable to the arbitrary skills and sensibilities of a portrait artist—whose numbers in antebellum America included few black practitioners.

"Negroes can never have impartial portraits, at the hands of white artists," Douglass wrote in his newspaper, *North Star,* in April 1849:

It seems to us next to impossible for white men to take likenesses of black men, without most grossly exaggerating their distinctive features. And the reason is obvious. Artists, like all other white persons, have adopted a theory respecting the distinctive features of Negro physiognomy. We have heard many white persons say, that "Negroes look all alike," and that they could not distinguish between the old and the young. They associate with the Negro face, high cheek bones, dis-tended nostril, depressed nose, thick lips, and retreating foreheads. This theory impressed strongly upon the mind of an artist exercises a powerful influence over his pencil, and very naturally leads him to distort and exaggerate those peculiari-ties, even when they scarcely exist in the original.

Frederick Douglass was not alone among abolitionists in viewing the public portrait—and the burgeoning visual culture—as a resource in the fight against slavery. "[W]e regard anti-slavery prints," declared the southern-born, white antislavery activist Sarah Grimké in 1837, "as powerful auxiliaries in the cause of emancipation, and recommend that these 'pictorial representations' be multiplied a hundred fold; so that the speechless agony of the fettered slave may unceasingly appeal to the heart of the patriotic, the philanthropic, and the Christian."

One of the most famous antislavery visual documents of this era was a painting commis-sioned by the influential black Philadelphia abolitionist Robert Purvis to champion the repatri-ation of a group of captive West Africans who had taken over the Spanish slave ship *Amistad.*

Led by Sengbeh Pieh, a Mendi from Sierra Leone (whose name was foreshortened to Cinqué by American friends and foes), the enslaved Africans had killed the *Amistad*'s captain and ordered the Spanish owners to return the ship to their African homeland. Instead, the *Amistad* was taken on a meandering course until waylaid by a U.S. Navy ship in July 1839. The Africans were charged with murder and jailed in New Haven, Connecticut. Abolitionists came to their support, including ex-president John Quincy Adams, who represented them in court. While awaiting a decision by the U.S. Supreme Court, Robert Purvis came up with the pictorial strategy and hired the New Haven painter and ardent abolitionist Nathaniel Jocelyn to celebrate the *Amistad* revolt's leader.

"His dauntless look, as it appears on canvas," declared a letter published in the antislavery newspaper the *Pennsylvania Freeman* after the painting was rejected from the annual exhibition of the Philadelphia Artists' Fund Society, "would make the souls of slaveholders quake. His portrait would be a standing anti-slavery lecture to slaveholders and their apologists." Here—dressed in a toga and grasping a staff that linked Cinqué to classical republicanism and religious prophecy—was an image of a man that not only boldly contradicted notions of African savagery; it also challenged the standard American abolitionist symbol: the supplicant slave, which had been adopted from the seal of the British Society for the Abolition of the Slave Trade, created by Josiah Wedgwood in 1787.

Despite his sharp criticism of portraiture, Douglass was one of the many admirers of this subversive painting. Duplicated in a copperplate print by Philadelphia engraver John Sartrain, the portrait was disseminated across the country by the *Amistad* defense committee. While we don't know if the picture influenced the Supreme Court's 1841 decision to free the "mutineers" (the following year Cinqué and his compatriots returned to Africa), we do know that it inspired at least one other act of slave resistance. Purvis himself briefly sheltered a fugitive slave named Madison Washington. Washington was eventually recaptured and returned south, but he retained the memory of the painting hanging in his Philadelphia Underground Railroad haven. In the fall of 1841, he was dispatched from Hampton, Virginia, on the slave ship *Creole,* bound for New Orleans, where he was to be resold. Reenacting the *Amistad* incident, Washington and his fellow captives sawed through their chains and took over the ship. They sailed the *Creole* to Nassau and, under British law, were granted asylum and freedom.

However, the power of antislavery images was little match for a white supremacist visual order that was all the more insidious for its nonchalance and casual cruelty. P. T. Barnum's mid-1830s exhibition of Joice Heth, an elderly African American slave, epitomized this cruelty. Leasing Heth from her Kentucky owner, Barnum claimed she was 161 years old and the nursemaid of the young George Washington. After distributing her crude woodcut portrait—showing a wizened face above talonlike hands—in advertisements, posters,

and pamphlets, Barnum exhibited Heth in person in taverns, museums, railway houses, and concert halls in cities and towns across the Northeast. When his "greatest natural and national curiosity of the day" suddenly died, in February 1836, an autopsy revealed that Heth was no more than eighty.

But the hoax continued long after Heth's death. In different versions of his autobiography, Barnum alternated claims of Heth's feebleness from old age with counterclaims of her alcohol-driven collaboration in the deception. Either version, playing on contemporary anxieties about confidence schemes and false

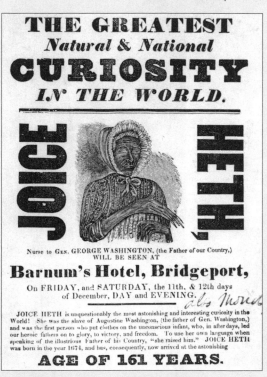

THE GREATEST
Natural & National
CURIOSITY
IN THE WORLD.

JOICE HETH

Nurse to GEN. GEORGE WASHINGTON, (the Father of our Country,)
WILL BE SEEN AT
Barnum's Hotel, Bridgeport,
On FRIDAY, and SATURDAY, the 11th, & 12th days
of December, DAY and EVENING.

JOICE HETH is unquestionably the most astonishing and interesting curiosity in the World! She was the slave of Augustine Washington, (the father of Gen. Washington,) and was the first person who put clothes on the unconscious infant, who, in after days, led our heroic fathers on to glory, to victory, and freedom. To use her own language when speaking of the illustrious Father of his Country, "she raised him." JOICE HETH was born in the year 1674, and has, consequently, now arrived at the astonishing
AGE OF 161 YEARS.

appearances, offered a grotesque and derogatory portrait of the African American slave and helped undermine the authenticity of stories, and images, of real escaped slaves such as Frederick Douglass.

The Joice Heth hoax coincided with a new "genre" of American popular entertainment that still haunts the visual depiction of African Americans more than 170 years after its introduction. While its roots date earlier, blackface minstrelsy is said to have first appeared on the stage in1831—the same year William Lloyd Garrison founded his abolitionist newspaper, *The Liberator*—when white actor Thomas Rice, his face darkened with burnt cork, mimicked the shuffling dance step he had seen performed by a slave.

With the success of Rice's "Jump Jim Crow" performance, blackface minstrelsy became a staple of American popular entertainment. And, from the stage to sheet music covers to cartoons and other published images, white performers' comic impersonations of stock minstrel characters, such as the ragged plantation Jim Crow and foppish urban Zip

Coon, were soon the most familiar of "black" figures for white Americans.

The most vicious caricatures of the antebellum period were directed toward free African Americans living in the North. By 1830, the affluence of a significant portion of Philadelphia's black community and the prospect of— as the *Pennsylvania Gazette* warned in 1828—"sable divinities . . . attended by white coachmen and *white footmen*," unleashed a series of racist attacks on African American communities and a rash of cartoons that denigrated black aspirations.

Chief among the latter was the work of Edward W. Clay, whose popular series of individually published cartoons, *Life in Philadelphia,* mocked the purported pretensions of the city's black population using the already familiar racist visual codes, popularized on the minstrel stage, that Douglass described so well. "How you find youself dis hot weader Miss Chloe?" Clay's caricatured figure asks in tortured dialect. "Pretty well I tank you Mr. Cesar only I aspire too much!" is the buffoonlike answer.

The rise of abolitionist and other political activism twisted such visual attacks into even more virulent forms. As white women increasingly broke from contemporary gendered mores of public conduct to play active roles in the antislavery struggle—and increasingly agitated for women's rights—Clay's and

others' cartoons portrayed abolition as a plot against the sexual order. Trafficking in images of interracial sex, highlighting the brutishness of the black figures, such cartoons titillated white viewers as much as they exploited their fears of racial "amalgamation."

With a visual culture awash in such racist exaggerations, Frederick Douglass well

understood that the public portrait of an African American in the antebellum United States carried a burden unlike any other. And the portraits of himself that he carefully supervised carried an unmistakable message.

Based on a photograph, the engraved frontispiece to the 1855 edition of his autobiography *My Bondage and My Freedom* grimly stares back at the viewer, forgoing the usual illustrious head's visionary gaze beyond the camera lens. Here was no amiable fugitive, no supplicant, no feeble natural curiosity, no calculating trickster or buffoonish caricature of respectability—but, starkly, all of their counterpoints. Douglass's public face embodies the words penned by an anonymous poet in 1837 after viewing the portraits of the black abolitionist painter Robert Douglass, Jr. (no relation):

> *There, too, is many a thoughtful brow,*
> *Marked by a soul that ne'er will bow,*
> *To tyrant power.*

Privately, many free blacks in the North also sought to secure such portraits. They turned to African American daguerreotypists such as James Presley Ball in Cincinnati and Augustus Washington in Hartford, who strove to capture for their clients "true likenesses" that defied the reigning pictorial conventions of race and power.

One other set of "private" pictures reveals the stakes of portraiture in the antebellum period. In 1850, the photographer J. T. Zealy took a series of fifteen daguerreotypes in his Columbia, South Carolina, studio of African-born slaves and their descendants who lived and worked on local plantations. The pictures were taken at the behest of the Harvard scientist Louis Agassiz to substantiate the theory of the separate creation of the races, which provided a scientific rationale for racial slavery.

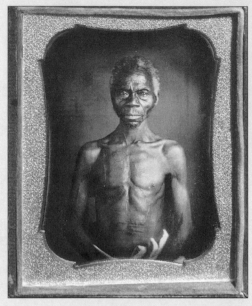

The daguerreotypes came to light only in 1975, when they were discovered in a cabinet in Harvard's Peabody Museum. We are left to ponder what impact such photographic images might have made had they been seen by antebellum Americans, black and white. Despite the coercive circumstances of the pictures' creation and the vulnerability of the nudity forced upon the subjects, the portraits dramatically contradicted Agassiz's theory. The gaze of "Renty," for example, born in the Congo and, in 1850, owned by B. F. Taylor of Columbia, South Carolina, is as direct, unrelenting, and condemnatory as any that Frederick Douglass could have wished for.

CHAPTER TWO

FOREVER FREE

IN MAY 1862, in one of the Civil War's most celebrated acts of individual daring and bravery, Robert Smalls, the slave pilot of the Confederate naval vessel the *Planter*, brought on board his family and several other slaves, disguised himself as the captain, guided the ship out of the harbor of Charleston, South Carolina, and surrendered it to Union forces. The feat won for Smalls an officer's commission in the Union navy and a reward of $1,500, which he later used to purchase land in Beaufort, South Carolina, his place of birth. During Reconstruction, Smalls would become one of the most powerful political leaders in the state. He served five terms in Congress in the 1870s and 1880s, and as late as 1913 held the position of collector of customs at Beaufort. Only when President Woodrow Wilson swept most of the remaining black appointees from office did Smalls's long political career come to an end.

ROBERT SMALLS, CAPTAIN OF THE GUN-BOAT "PLANTER."   THE GUN-BOAT "PLANTER," RUN OUT OF CHARLESTON, S. C., BY ROBERT SMALLS, MAY, 1862.

Robert Smalls and the Confederate gunboat Planter

In 1862, however, Smalls was a slave, although one whom few Confederates would suspect of having a desire to flee to Union lines, given his privileged status. Born in 1839, he was the child of an unidentified white man, possibly his owner, John McKee, and Lydia, a slave who worked in McKee's home. As a youth, Smalls was sent to live with McKee's relatives in Charleston, where he apparently taught himself to read and write. He married Hannah Jones, a slave who worked as a maid in a Charleston hotel. A sailmaker, stevedore, and harbor foreman, Smalls, like other skilled urban slaves, enjoyed the right to hire his own time and keep part of his earnings. He and his wife lived together, apart from their owners. When the Civil War broke out, Smalls had accumulated seven hundred dollars toward the purchase of his own freedom and that of his wife and daughter.

War, it has been said, is the midwife of revolution. The Civil War resulted in perhaps the most radical social and political transformation in American history—the destruction of slavery, the central institution of southern life and the greatest concentration of economic wealth and political power in the entire country. But the war did not begin as a crusade to destroy slavery. Everyone who lived through the conflict, Abraham Lincoln would remark in his second inaugural address, in March 1865, understood that slavery was "somehow" the cause of the war. For nearly two years after the war began, however, the Lincoln administration insisted that the preservation of the Union, not the abolition of slavery, was the war's goal.

Why was Smalls willing to risk his privileged status and future prospects for a Union cause that in May 1862 had not yet embraced the goal of emancipation or opened its armed forces to black participation? It was because, in a sense, the Civil War began as three overlapping but different struggles—the South's campaign to establish its independence and protect the institution of slavery; the North's battle to preserve the Union; and a new chapter in the slaves' timeless quest for freedom. Whatever politicians and military commanders might decree, slaves viewed the war through the lens of the culture they had developed in bondage. From the outset, they saw the conflict as heralding the long-awaited destruction of slavery. General Sherman later recalled encountering a Georgia slave who explained his people's outlook: "He said . . . he had been looking for the 'angel of the Lord' ever since he was knee-high, and, though we professed to be fighting for the Union, he supposed that slavery was the cause, and that our success was to be his freedom." "Let the white fight for what they want and we Negroes fight for what we want," commented another African American. "Liberty must take the day."

Long before Lincoln made emancipation a war aim, African Americans, north and south, called the conflict the "freedom war." George E. Stephens, a free black from the North who worked as a cook for the Union army early in the war, sent periodic reports to the *Weekly Anglo-African,* a black periodical published in New York. "The slaves, to a man, are on the alert," wrote Stephens during the first months of fighting. They "are watching the events of the hour, and . . . hope lights up their hearts." Robert Smalls was only one of countless slaves who, from the earliest days of the war, took enormous risks to show their support for the Union. Even before the firing on Fort Sumter, eight slaves sought refuge at Fort Pickens, a Union outpost in Florida, "entertaining the idea," wrote the fort's commander, that federal forces "were placed here to protect them and grant them their freedom." Early in the war, Harry Jarvis, a Virginia slave (who called his owner "the meanest man on all the Eastern Shore"), escaped to Fortress Monroe, which Union forces under General Benjamin F. Butler had occupied. "I went to him and asked him to let me enlist," Jarvis later recalled, "but he said *it wasn't a black man's war.* I told him it *would* be a black man's war before they got through." Two years later, Jarvis himself would enlist in the Fifty-fourth Massachusetts Infantry, one of the Union army's first black regiments.

Slaves understood that the presence of Union forces fundamentally altered the balance of power between white and black, master and slave, in the South. In 1861 and 1862, as the federal army occupied territory on the periphery of the Confederacy, first in Virginia, then Tennessee, South Carolina, Louisiana, and elsewhere, slaves by the thousands headed for Union lines. Unlike fugitives before the war, these runaways included large numbers of women, children, and elderly men, as entire families abandoned the plantations, willing, as General Daniel E. Sickles commented, to "incur any danger" in their quest for freedom. Not a few, like Smalls, passed along to Union forces valuable military intelligence and detailed knowledge of the South's terrain. "The most valuable and reliable information of the enemy's movements in our vicinity that we have been able to get," Sickles noted, "derived from Negroes who came into our lines."

All in all, the Civil War became a moment of truth, not only for the nation but also for slavery. Perceptive white southerners came to understand that their slaves' conduct during the war gave the lie to proslavery mythology. "I believed that these people were content, happy, and attached to their masters," wrote South Carolina planter A. L. Taveau shortly after the war ended, in 1865. But if this were the case, he continued, why did the slaves desert their masters "in [their] moment of need and flock to an enemy, whom they did not know?" Suddenly, Taveau understood: for generations, he concluded, African Americans had been "looking for the Man of Universal Freedom."

African Americans' determination to seize the opportunity presented by the war to escape slavery undermined the institution's stability in many parts of the South. Initially, however, it proved a burden to the Union army, which was not equipped to deal with thousands of impoverished fugitives, and an embarrassment to the Lincoln administration. Despite his antislavery convictions, Lincoln's paramount concern in the first year of the war was to keep the border slave states—Delaware, Maryland, Kentucky, and Missouri—in the Union, to build the broadest base of support in the North, and to attract wavering white southerners to the Union cause. All of these goals would, he felt, be compromised by making the destruction of slavery a war aim. When Congress assembled in special session in July 1861 to deal with the crisis of secession, one of its first acts was to pass, nearly unanimously, a resolution affirming that the war in no way endangered the South's "established institutions." In the early days of the war, Union military commanders even returned fugitive slaves to their owners (including the eight who had sought refuge at Fort Pickens). The policy raised an outcry in antislavery circles. "Massachusetts," said Governor John Andrew, "does not send her citizens forth to become the hunters of men." Many Union soldiers refused to carry out the policy.

At the outset of the war, Lincoln invoked time-honored northern values to mobilize public support. In a message to Congress, he identified the Union cause with the fate of democracy for the "whole family of man." He identified the differences between the North and the South in terms of the familiar free-labor ideology: "This is essentially a people's struggle. On the side of the Union, it is a struggle for maintaining in the world, that form and substance of government, whose leading object is to elevate the condition of men . . . to afford all, an unfettered start, and a fair chance, in the race of life." But while appealing to free-labor values, Lincoln feared that action against slavery would drive the border states, with their white population of 2.6 million and nearly half a million slaves, into the Confederacy while also alienating conservative northerners.

Yet as the Confederacy set slaves to work as military laborers and southern blacks began to escape to Union lines, the policy of ignoring slavery unraveled. By the end of 1861, the military had adopted the plan, begun at Fortress Monroe by General Butler, of treating escaped blacks as contraband of war—that is, property of military value subject to confiscation by Union forces. Butler's order gave the fortress a new name among Virginia's slaves—"Freedom Fort," and added a word to the war's vocabulary.

"Contrabands" in Cumberland Landing, Virginia, May 1862

Escaping slaves, men and women still not legally free, became known as "contrabands." They were housed by the army in "contraband camps" and educated in new "contraband schools." By the second year of the war, the Union army employed thousands of contrabands as laborers.

Even in the areas of the Confederacy far from the theater of war, the conflict disrupted and undermined the peculiar institution. Tens of thousands of slaves accompanied their owners to army camps as servants or were impressed into service to construct fortifications and do other work for the Confederate army. Fearing the impact of the war upon slavery, some masters "refugeed" their human property to Texas, as far as possible from military lines. The drain of white men into the Confederate army left many plantations under the supervision of planters' wives or elderly and infirm men, whose authority slaves increasingly felt able to challenge. On some of those plantations, slaves refused to work in the fields, devoting their time to tending their own garden plots.

When Union forces arrived in a neighborhood, slave discipline collapsed altogether. In the spring of 1862, federal forces occupied southern Louisiana, with its vast sugar estates. On Magnolia plantation, blacks refused to work, and erected a gallows in the slave quarters, claiming to have been told that they must drive off the overseer and "hang their master

and that then they will be free." The uprising ended when the owner
promised to pay the slaves for their work after the crop had been sold. Slavery, wrote a northern journalist in Louisiana in November 1862, two
months before the Emancipation Proclamation, "is forever destroyed and
worthless, no matter what Mr. Lincoln or anyone else may say on the
subject."

The need to do something more definitive about slavery became ever
more pressing now. From the outset of the war, many northerners, especially abolitionists and Radical Republicans, insisted that as the "corner-
stone" of the Confederacy (the oft-cited description by the South's vice
president, Alexander H. Stephens), slavery must become a military target.
"It is plain," declared Thaddeus Stevens, the Radical congressman from
Pennsylvania, "that nothing approaching the present policy will subdue
the rebels."

The most radical of the Radical Republicans during the Civil War and
Reconstruction, Stevens remains one of the most controversial figures in
American history. In the traditional view of Reconstruction, he was por-
trayed as the evil genius, motivated by hatred of the South. (The character

Thaddeus Stevens

of Stoneman, the vindictive "dictator" of Congress in *The Birth of a Nation*, was modeled on him.) In fact, Stevens was a lifelong defender of the rights of blacks, who saw the Civil War and Reconstruction as a golden opportunity to create a "perfect republic," shorn of racial inequality.

Born in Vermont, as a young man Stevens moved to Lancaster, Pennsylvania, where he practiced law and worked as an iron manufacturer. He served several terms in the state legislature, where he became a leading defender of free public education. A member of the convention that drafted a new state constitution in 1838, Stevens refused to sign the final document because it abrogated African Americans' right to vote. He served as a Whig in Congress from 1849 to 1853, and again from 1859 until his death, in 1868, as a Republican. Even his opponents respected his honesty, and everyone feared his quick wit. Stevens cared little about his public image. He never married, but lived for years with a black housekeeper, neither confirming nor denying rumors about their relationship. During the Civil War, he emerged as an early advocate of emancipating the slaves and enlisting blacks into the Union army. To young Georges Clemenceau, a future prime minister of France who reported on American events for a Paris newspaper, Stevens seemed the "Robespierre" of "the second American Revolution." In identifying Stevens with the most radical leader of the French Revolution, Clemenceau was also describing the monumental political and economic upheaval brought on by a war to end slavery.

Outside of Congress, few pressed the case of emancipation as adamantly or eloquently, or understood more clearly what was at stake in the war, as Frederick Douglass. From the onset of the fighting, Douglass insisted that it was futile to "separate the freedom of the slave from the victory of the Government." "There is but one effectual way to suppress and put down the desolating war," he proclaimed. "Fire must be met with water, darkness with light, and war for the destruction of liberty must be met with war for the destruction of slavery." Douglass persistently called for the Union army to begin enrolling black soldiers: "the side which first summons the Negro to its aid will conquer." Douglass's aim, however, was not simply to add to the Union's manpower, but to enable blacks to stake a claim to equal rights in the reunited nation. "Once let a black man get upon his person the brass letters U.S.," he wrote, "let him get an eagle on his button and a musket on his shoulder and bullets in his pocket, and there is no power on earth which can deny that he has earned the right to citizenship in the United States." Douglass felt certain that "the inexorable logic of events" would force "the American people and Congress" to recognize that "the war now being waged in this land is a war for and against slavery."

The arguments of men such as Stevens and Douglass won increasing support in a Congress frustrated by lack of military success. In 1862—as the disintegration of slavery continued from within, the danger of losing the border states receded, the manpower needs of the Union military continued to grow, and success on the battlefield continued to elude Lincoln's armies—pressure for emancipation mounted. In March 1862, Congress prohibited the army from returning fugitive slaves. Then came abolition in the District of Columbia and the territories, followed by the Second Confiscation Act, in July, which liberated slaves of disloyal owners in Union-occupied territory.

Almost from the beginning of the war, Lincoln had been struggling to retain control of the emancipation issue. In August 1861, John C. Frémont, commanding Union forces in Missouri, a state racked by a bitter guerilla war between pro-northern and pro-southern bands, decreed the freedom of the state's slaves. Fearful of the order's impact on the border states, Lincoln swiftly rescinded it. In November, the president proposed that the border states embark on a program of gradual emancipation, with the federal government paying owners for their loss of property. He also revived the idea of colonization. In August 1862, Lincoln invited five local black leaders to the White House for the first formal meeting of any president with African Americans. He urged them to support black emigration to Central America or the Caribbean. "There is an unwillingness on the part of our people," Lincoln told them, "harsh as it may be, for you colored people to remain among us. . . . You and we are different races. It is better for us both to be separated." The black delegation rejected Lincoln's plea. Douglass, who did not attend, said the president's remarks reflected "contempt for Negroes." Talk of colonization by men in high office, he argued, only inflamed racism and weakened the dream of a biracial American democracy. But as late as December, the president signed an agreement with a shady entrepreneur to settle former slaves on an island off the coast of Haiti.

Despite his beliefs about colonization, sometime during the summer of 1862, Lincoln concluded that emancipation had become a political and military necessity. Many factors contributed to his decision. There was the continuing lack of military success, along with the hope that emancipated slaves might help meet the army's growing manpower needs. By mid-1862, northern public opinion seemed more receptive to emancipation, and Lincoln also calculated that making slavery a target of the war effort would counteract the rising clamor in Britain for recognition of the Confederacy. But on the advice of Secretary of State William H. Seward, Lincoln delayed his announcement until after a Union victory, lest it seem an act of desperation. On September 22, 1862, five days after George B. McClellan's army

Baltimore pro-Confederate artist Adalbert Johann Volck portrayed Abraham Lincoln "Writing the Emancipation Proclamation" surrounded by symbols of Satanism, slave rebellions, and alcoholism.

forced Confederate forces under Robert E. Lee to retreat at Antietam, Maryland, Lincoln issued the Preliminary Emancipation Proclamation. It warned that unless the South laid down its arms by the end of 1862, he would emancipate the slaves.

The initial northern reaction was not encouraging. In the fall elections of 1862, Democrats made opposition to emancipation the centerpiece of their campaign, warning that the North would be "Africanized"— inundated by freed slaves competing for jobs and seeking to marry white women. The Republicans suffered sharp electoral reverses. In his annual message to Congress, early in December, Lincoln tried to calm the racial fears of northern whites, reviving the ideas of gradual emancipation and colonization. He concluded, however, on a higher note: "Fellow citizens, we cannot escape history. . . . The fiery trial through which we pass, will light us down, in honor or dishonor, to the latest generation. . . . In giving freedom to the slave, we assure freedom to the free—honorable alike in what we give, and what we preserve."

On January 1, 1863, after presiding at the annual White House New Year reception, Lincoln retired to his study to sign the Emancipation Proclamation. The first time the president attempted to affix his signature,

he stopped and laid down his pen. His hand was shaking—not from ner-
vousness, but because he was exhausted after a long day of greeting visitors. "I do not want it to appear as if I hesitated," he said. After a moment
of repose, Lincoln signed the proclamation.

The Emancipation Proclamation is perhaps the most misunderstood
important document in American history. Lincoln did not free the slaves
with a stroke of his pen. Because its constitutional legality derived from the
president's authority as military commander in chief, the proclamation
applied almost exclusively to areas under Confederate control. Thus, it had
no bearing on the nearly half a million slaves in the border slave states that
had never seceded from the Union, or on more than three hundred thousand slaves in areas of the Confederacy occupied by Union soldiers and
exempted by Lincoln from its coverage—the entire state of Tennessee and
parts of Virginia and Louisiana. On January 1, 1863, most slaves resided in
places where the proclamation could not be enforced. Thus, there was
some truth in the famous comment by the *Times* of London that the proclamation resembled a papal bull against a comet—both were acts outside the
jurisdiction of their authors.

It is not true, however, as is sometimes stated, that the proclamation
freed no slave on the day it was issued. Lincoln decided not to exempt the
Sea Islands of South Carolina, occupied since late 1861 by Union forces,
from the proclamation's purview. Here, more than ten thousand slaves did
gain their freedom with the stroke of Lincoln's pen. As to the slave population behind Confederate lines—more than three million men, women, and
children—they, declared the proclamation, "are and henceforth shall be
free." But on January 1, 1863, there was no way to enforce this edict. Their
liberation would await Union victories.

Despite its limitations, the proclamation set off scenes of jubilation
among free blacks and abolitionists in the North and contrabands and
slaves in the South. "Sound the loud timbrel o'er Egypt's dark sea,"
intoned a black preacher at a celebration in Boston. "Jehovah hath tri-
umphed, his people are free." At Beaufort, on the South Carolina Sea
Islands, more than five thousand African Americans celebrated their emancipation by singing what a white observer called "the Marseillaise [the
anthem of the French Revolution] of the slaves": "In that New Jerusalem, I
am not afraid to die; We must fight for liberty, in that New Jerusalem."
Even in areas exempted from its provisions, slaves realized that whatever
the proclamation's limitations, by making the Union army an agent of
emancipation and wedding the goals of union and abolition, it sounded the
death knell of slavery.

The Emancipation Proclamation, commented the *New York Times*, marked a watershed in American life, "an era in the history . . . of this country and the world." It altered the nature of the Civil War and the course of American history. Firing the northern war effort with moral purpose, it crystallized a new identification between the ideal of human freedom and a nation-state whose powers increased enormously as the war progressed. In a sense, the Union's war for self-preservation and the slaves' war for freedom had at last merged. "The cause of the slaves and the cause of the country," Frederick Douglass proclaimed, had become one: "Liberty and Union have become identical." The proclamation linked the national government more closely than ever with the ideal of universal freedom. For the first time, wrote the *Chicago Tribune*, the United States could truly exist as "our fathers designed it—the home of freedom, the asylum of the oppressed, the seat of justice, the land of equal rights under the law."

The proclamation also represented a turning point in Lincoln's own thinking. It contained no reference to compensation to slaveholders or to colonization of the freed people. For the first time, it committed the government to enlisting black soldiers in the Union army. Lincoln now became in his own mind the Great Emancipator—that is, he assumed the role that history had thrust upon him. In 1864, with Union casualties mounting, some northerners suggested that he rescind or modify the proclamation in order to negotiate a compromise peace. Lincoln refused to consider this. Were he to do so, he told one visitor, "I should be damned in time and eternity."

Lincoln, the moderate Illinois lawyer, had become the agent of what historians Charles and Mary Beard would later call the Second American Revolution. Begun to preserve the prewar Union, the Civil War now portended a far-reaching transformation in southern life and a redefinition of American freedom. The proclamation transformed a war of armies into a conflict of societies. In effect, it announced that Union victory would produce a social revolution within the South and a redefinition of the place of blacks in a rebuilt American life. "Up to now," wrote Karl Marx, observing events from London, "we have witnessed only the first act of the Civil War—the constitutional waging of war. The second act, the revolutionary waging of war, is at hand." By decoupling emancipation from colonization, Lincoln ensured that the emancipated slaves would become part of American society. In effect, therefore, the proclamation launched the historical process of Reconstruction. A new system of labor, politics, and race relations would have to replace the shattered institution of slavery.

Of the proclamation's provisions, few were more radical in their implications than the enrollment of blacks into military service. Since sailor had been one of the few occupations open to free blacks before the war, Secretary of the Navy Gideon Welles early in the war allowed African Americans to serve on Union warships. But as during the American Revolution, when George Washington initially excluded blacks from the Continental army, blacks in the Civil War had to fight for the right to fight on land. At the outset, Secretary of War Simon Cameron announced that federal armies would remain all white. Military recruiters turned away northern free blacks who offered themselves for service. Abolitionists vehemently attacked this policy. But the administration feared that whites would not be willing to fight alongside blacks.

By the end of 1861, however, the army did employ increasing numbers of escaped slaves as cooks, laundresses, and laborers. In 1862, as casualties mounted and enthusiasm for enlistment among whites waned, more and more northerners concluded that able-bodied blacks ought to be allowed in the Union army. Initial moves were made by Benjamin Butler, now commanding Union forces in New Orleans, who enrolled formerly free blacks under his command, and General James Lane in Kansas. In September, Edwin Stanton, now secretary of war, gave official authorization to white abolitionist Thomas Wentworth Higginson, who had once worked with John Brown, to travel to the Sea Islands to enlist slaves in the First South Carolina Volunteer Infantry.

Only after the Emancipation Proclamation, however, did the recruitment of black soldiers begin in earnest. By the end of the war, more than 180,000 black men had served in the Union army, and 24,000 in the navy. One-third died in battle, or of wounds or disease. Fifteen black soldiers and eight sailors received the Congressional Medal of Honor, the highest award for military valor. Some black units won considerable fame, among them the Fifty-fourth Massachusetts Volunteers, a regiment of free blacks from throughout the North commanded by Robert Gould Shaw, a young reformer from a socially prominent white Boston family. The bravery of the regiment in the September 1863 attack on Fort Wagner, South Carolina, where nearly half the unit, including Shaw, perished, helped to dispel widespread doubts about blacks' ability to withstand the pressures of the battlefield. (The 1989 film *Glory* popularized the exploits of Shaw and the Fifty-fourth Massachusetts.)

Unlike Shaw's unit, most black soldiers were emancipated slaves who joined the army in the South. After Union forces in 1863 seized control of the rich plantation lands of the Mississippi Valley, the disintegration of slavery accelerated. Union commanders freed the slaves, thus enforcing the Emancipation Proclamation, enlisted able-bodied black men into the army, and sent black women and children to contraband camps. In the Mississippi Valley, General Lorenzo Thomas raised fifty regiments of black soldiers, some seventy-six thousand men in all. Another large group of black soldiers hailed from the border states exempted from the Emancipation Proclamation, where enlistment was, for most of the war, the only route to freedom. Here, black military service formally undermined slavery, for Congress in March 1865 expanded the Emancipation Proclamation to liberate all black soldiers and their families.

The fate of slavery in the border states offers only one illustration of the way black military service powerfully affected race relations. The Union navy dealt with black sailors pretty much the same as it did their white counterparts. Conditions on ships made racial segregation impossible. Black and white sailors lived and dined together in the same quarters. They received equal pay and had the same promotion opportunities. The Union army, however, organized black soldiers into segregated units under sometimes abusive white officers. Initially, black troops received lower pay (ten dollars per month, compared with sixteen for white soldiers).

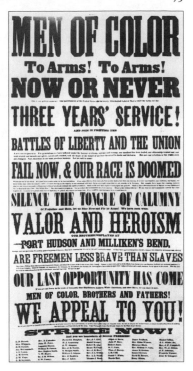

An 1863 recruiting poster signed by Frederick Douglass and other prominent black abolitionists was directed to free African Americans in Pennsylvania.

They were disproportionately assigned to labor rather than combat, and, until the very last days of the war, could not rise to the rank of commissioned officer. If captured by Confederate forces, black Union soldiers faced the prospect of sale into slavery or immediate execution. In a notorious incident in 1864, 200 of 262 black soldiers died when Confederate troops under the command of General Nathan B. Forrest (later a founder of the Ku Klux Klan) overran Fort Pillow in Tennessee. Some of those who perished were killed after surrendering.

Nonetheless, black soldiers played a crucial role not only in winning the Civil War, but also in defining the war's consequences. More than any other single development, military service, as Frederick Douglass had anticipated, placed the question of black citizenship on the national agenda. As an inevitable consequence of enrolling black men in the Union army, one U.S. senator observed in 1864, "the black man is henceforth to assume a new status among us." For black soldiers themselves, military service proved to be a liberating experience. "This was the biggest thing that ever happened in my life," one black veteran later recalled. "No negro who has ever been a soldier," wrote a northern official in 1865, "can again be imposed upon; they have learned what it is to be free and they will infuse their feelings into others."

George W. Hatton, a sergeant in the First Regiment, U.S. Colored Troops, agreed: "Though the government openly declared that it did not want the Negroes in this conflict," he noted in 1864, "I look around me and see hundreds of colored men armed and ready to defend the government at any moment; and such are my feelings, that I can only say, the fetters have fallen—our bondage is over." A month later, Hatton witnessed a remarkable reversal of power relations. Near Jamestown, Virginia, his unit captured a slaveholder who had recently administered a severe whipping to several black women. One of the man's former slaves, now a soldier, tied him to a tree and whipped him; then the women were allowed to "give him a like number." "They were no longer his," Hatton concluded.

Service in the Union army offered access to education ("the cartridge box and spelling book are attached to the same belt," wrote one observer) and established men as community leaders, opening a door to political advancement. Out of the army came many of the leaders of the Reconstruction era. At least 130 former Union soldiers served in political office after the Civil War. They included Martin F. Becker, a veteran of both the army and navy, who held a number of positions in South Carolina; Josiah T. Walls, later a congressman from Florida; and Prince Rivers, a slave coachman who ran away in 1862 to enlist in Higginson's South Carolina regiment and later won election to the state legislature.

"*Assault of the Second Louisiana (Colored) Regiment on the Confederate Works at Port Hudson, May 27, 1863*"

"Suppose you had kept your freedom without enlisting in this army," Private Thomas Long, a member of the First South Carolina Volunteers, mused during the war. "Your children might have grown up free, and been well cultivated so as to be equal to any business, but it would have been always flung in their faces—your father never fought for his freedom— and what could they answer. Never can say that to this African race any more." In time, black military service would fade from white America's collective memory. Of the hundreds of Civil War monuments that still dot the northern landscape, fewer than a dozen contain an image of a black sol- dier. But the contribution of black soldiers to Union victory remained a point of pride in black communities. "They say," an Alabama planter reported in 1867, "the Yankees never could have whipped the South with- out the aid of the Negroes." Well into the twentieth century, black families throughout the United States would recall with pride that their fathers and grandfathers had fought for freedom.

Near the end of the war, the Confederates' own growing shortage of white manpower eventually led authorities to a decision no one could have foreseen when the conflict began: to arm slaves to fight for the South. As early as September 1863, a Mississippi newspaper had argued for freeing and enlisting able-bodied black men. "Let them," it wrote, "be declared free, placed in the ranks, and told to fight for their homes and country." But many slaveholders fiercely resisted this idea, and initially, the Confederate senate rejected it. "I do not want independence if it is to be won by the help of the Negro," declared General Clement H. Stevens. Not until March 1865, after General Robert E. Lee had endorsed the plan, did the Confeder- ate congress authorize the enlistment of slaves.

The war ended before the South's recruitment of black soldiers began. But the Confederate army, as noted earlier, did employ numerous slaves as laborers. This later led to confusion over whether blacks actually fought for the Confederacy. Apart from a handful who "passed" for white, none in fact did. But the South's decision to begin raising black troops illustrates how the war transformed the struggle for Confederate independence. The war undermined not only slavery, but the pro-slavery ideology. "The day you make soldiers of them is the beginning of the end of the revolution," declared Howell Cobb, a Georgia planter and politician, in January 1865. "If slaves make good soldiers, our whole theory of slavery is wrong."

Thanks in part to black military service, many Republicans in the last two years of the war came to believe that emancipation must bring with it equal protection of the laws regardless of race. The issue of unequal pay galvanized black soldiers to demand equal treatment. "Are we soldiers, or are we laborers?" James Henry Gooding, a black soldier, wrote directly to

President Lincoln. "We are fully armed and equipped, and have . . . done a soldier's duty. Why can't we have a soldier's pay?" One of the first acts of the federal government to recognize the principle of equal rights before the law came early in 1865, when Congress granted retroactive equal pay to black soldiers. The war, wrote George William Curtis, the editor of *Harper's Weekly*, had transformed a government "for white men" into one "for mankind."

Racism, however, hardly disappeared from national life. In July 1863, the introduction of the military draft provoked four days of rioting in New York City. A mob composed largely of Irish immigrants assaulted symbols of the new order being created by the war—draft offices, the mansions of wealthy Republicans, industrial establishments, and the city's black population. Black men, women, and children were lynched on the streets of the nation's commercial metropolis. Many black New Yorkers fled to New Jersey and Brooklyn or took refuge in Central Park. Only the arrival of Union troops, some direct from the Gettysburg battlefield, quelled the uprising, but not before more than one hundred persons had died. A year later, while in Philadelphia for repairs to the *Planter*, Robert Smalls was evicted from a city streetcar by a conductor.

Yet the aftermath of these two events showed that something had indeed changed. A year after the draft riots, a regiment of black troops

The lynching of a black man on Clarkson Street during the 1863 New York Draft Riot

received an enthusiastic send-off by large crowds of New Yorkers, an "astonishing" change, noted a local newspaper, from the days only eight months earlier when "the African race in this city were literally hunted down like wild beasts." Smalls's travail regarding the streetcar, which would have passed unnoticed before the war, prompted a protest meeting and the integration of Philadelphia's transport system. Early in 1865, the same Supreme Court that eight years earlier, in the Dred Scott decision, had excluded blacks from the family of American citizenship, admitted the first black lawyer, John S. Rock, of Massachusetts, to practice before it.

The service of black soldiers affected Lincoln's own racial outlook as well. He insisted that black troops must be treated the same as white troops when captured, and he suspended prisoner-of-war exchanges when the Confederacy sought to limit such exchanges to whites. In 1864, Lincoln, who before the war had never supported suffrage for African Americans, urged the governor of Union-occupied Louisiana to work for the partial enfranchisement of blacks, singling out soldiers as especially deserving. At some future time, he observed, they might again be called upon to "keep the *jewel of Liberty* in the family of freedom."

Other factors as well affected the evolution of Lincoln's racial views away from his earlier racism. During the war, probably for the first time in his life, the president came into contact with educated, articulate black men. He developed a friendly relationship with Frederick Douglass, who visited the White House a number of times, and sought Douglass's advice on the progress of the war. Their first meeting had come in 1863, when Douglass urged the president to accelerate the enlisting of black troops and raised the issue of equal pay. Lincoln at first defended his gradualist approach to the issues of emancipation and black military service, speaking of the necessity of "preparation of the public mind" for radical departures in policy.

In August 1864, with the war apparently stalemated and Lincoln worried about his prospects for reelection, the president again invited Douglass to the White House. He asked the former slave's advice about ways to "get more of the slaves within our lines" so that their freedom would be guaranteed if the war ended and the military necessity that had justified the Emancipation Proclamation lapsed. Douglass responded by drawing up a plan, reminiscent of some of John Brown's ideas, by which a "band of scouts" would assist slaves in escaping to Union lines.

A decade after Lincoln's death, Douglass would call him "the white man's president." Blacks, he added, "were only his stepchildren." Yet Douglass also recalled that in their meetings, Lincoln "treated me like a man, he did not let me feel for a moment that there was any difference in the color of our skin." Throughout the war, Douglass insisted that from emancipation must follow the end to all color discrimination, the establishment of equality before the law, and black voting—the "full and complete adoption" of blacks "into the great national family of America." Lincoln never embraced so sweeping a vision of equality. No one knows how he would have approached the issues of Reconstruction had he not been assassinated, but it is clear that his racial views at the time of his death were far different from the ones he held when the war began.

The service of black soldiers was only one of many developments during the Civil War that helped to shape the political and social agenda of postwar Reconstruction. In September 1862, even before the issuance of the Emancipation Proclamation, a black Californian foresaw a new day for his people: "Our relation to this government is changing daily. . . . Old things are passing away, and eventually old prejudices must follow. The revolution has begun, and time alone must decide where it is to end."

One of the earliest chapters of that revolution took place in those parts of the Confederacy that were the first to come under Union control. Nowhere during the Civil War did a clear blueprint emerge for the postwar South. But in South Carolina, Louisiana, and other areas occupied earliest by Union soldiers, federal authorities found themselves presiding over the transition from slavery to freedom. Here, issues were debated—access to land, control of labor, the new structure of political power—that would carry over into the postwar world. Differences emerged between emancipated slaves, southern whites, northern businessmen, and government officials that offered a preview of conflicts that would shape Reconstruction. The merger of the "cause of the slave" with the cause of the Union did not produce a unified approach to the consequences of emancipation.

The most famous "rehearsal for Reconstruction" took place on the Sea Islands, just off the coast of South Carolina. The war was only a few months old when, in November 1861, the Union navy occupied the islands. Nearly the entire white population fled, leaving behind some ten thousand slaves. Sea Island blacks formed a unique community. Here, African carry-overs—in artistic, religious, and other cultural practices, and the local Gullah dialect—were far more prevalent than in the rest of the South. In addition, with plantations organized on the task system of labor, in which slaves were assigned daily to largely unsupervised tasks—the completion of which left them free to cultivate their own crops and market them in nearby towns—blacks enjoyed an unusual degree of day-to-day autonomy.

The Union navy was soon followed by other northerners—army officers, Treasury agents, prospective investors in cotton land, and a group of black and white reformers and teachers known as Gideon's Band—committed to uplifting the freedpeople. Each of these groups, in addition to the islands' black population, had distinctive views on how the transition to freedom should be organized. And journalists reported every development on the islands to an eager reading public in the North.

Convinced that education offered the key to making self-reliant, productive citizens of the former slaves, northern-born teachers such as Charlotte Forten, a member of one of Philadelphia's most prominent black families, and Laura M. Towne, a white native of Pittsburgh, devoted themselves to educating the freedpeople. Both had been active in the abolitionist movement and both were impressed by the progress of their black pupils. "I never saw children so eager to learn," Forten commented. Towne, who in 1862 helped to establish Penn School on St. Helena Island, remained there as a teacher until her death, in 1901. Like many of the Gideonites,

Abolitionist Laura M. Towne, shown here with three of her students on St. Helena Island, South Carolina

Towne and Forten brought from the North the assumption that blacks needed outside guidance to truly understand and embrace freedom. But despite a certain paternalism, they sympathized with the freedpeople's aspirations, central to which was a desire to own land.

When the planters fled, slaves had destroyed cotton gins and commenced planting food crops for their own families. They were imbued with the idea, one northern observer wrote, of never "planting cotton for white folks again." The former slaves insisted that the government should assist them in obtaining title to the land they and their forebears had worked for generations. Many northerners, however, believed that the transition from slave to free labor meant not giving blacks land but enabling them to work for wages in more humane conditions than under slavery. Indeed, it was an article of faith in the antislavery North that with emancipation, freed blacks would become more productive cotton laborers than slaves. Former slaves on the islands, however, preferred to grow food for their families rather than to plant cotton under white supervision. But while some black families acquired land at auctions organized by the Treasury Department or private owners during the war, and others simply became squatters on abandoned plantations, most land went to northern investors bent upon demonstrating the superiority of free wage labor, and turning a tidy profit at the same time. Edward Atkinson, who represented several Massachusetts textile factories on the islands, insisted that blacks acquire land though "the ordinary workings of our system of land tenure," not government largesse. By working for wages and slowly accumulating the funds to purchase land, they would internalize a market orientation, become used to growing cotton as free laborers, and form a "large new market" for northern manufactured goods.

By the end of the war, the Sea Island Experiment, as it was called, was widely held to be a success. Black families were acquiring education, working the land, and enjoying better shelter and clothing and a more varied diet than they had under slavery. But the experiment also bequeathed to postwar Reconstruction the contentious issue of whether a free-labor system could be devised that satisfied both the Republican North and the desire of the former slaves for land of their own.

A very different rehearsal for Reconstruction took place in Louisiana and the Mississippi Valley, involving a far larger area and population than that on the Sea Islands. In April 1862, Union forces took control of New Orleans, the South's largest city, as well as the nearby sugar region. In the following year, with the capture of Vicksburg, Mississippi, the entire Mississippi Valley came under Union control. As on the Sea Islands, the issue of the transition to free labor immediately came to the fore. Under General Benjamin Butler and his successor, Nathaniel Banks, the Union army established regulations for plantation labor. Hoping to stop the flight of slaves from the plantations, and to secure a labor force for planters who took an oath of loyalty to the Union and northern investors who leased lands abandoned by Confederates, military authorities insisted that the emancipated slaves must sign labor contracts or be deemed vagrants. But, unlike before the war, they would be paid wages and provided with education, their families were not subject to disruption, and corporal punishment would be prohibited.

Neither side was satisfied with the new labor system. Blacks resented having to resume working for whites and being forced to sign labor contracts, a requirement not applied to poor whites. Planters complained that their workers were insubordinate, spending more time on their own garden plots than on cotton land. Without the whip, they insisted, discipline could not be enforced. "They work less," one planter complained, "have less respect, are less orderly than ever." Every payday brought disputes with the labor force. The problems of the system, dubbed by critics "compulsory free labor," offered a glimpse of the bitter conflicts over land and labor that would spread throughout the South once the war had ended.

Only occasionally did army officers seek to implement a different vision of freedom. At Davis Bend, Mississippi, an eleven-thousand-acre site on which stood the cotton plantations of Confederate president Jefferson Davis and his brother Joseph, General Ulysses S. Grant decided to establish a "negro paradise." Here, rather than being forced to work for white owners, the emancipated slaves saw the land divided among them, to be worked collectively by self-selected groups. By 1864, three thousand former slaves were laboring at Davis Bend; the following year, with the price of cotton having risen to unprecedented heights because of the war, they earned a profit of $160,000. In addition, former slaves at Davis Bend were allowed to elect their own judges and sheriffs, a small preview of how southern governments would open up to black participation during Reconstruction.

Indeed, as the Civil War progressed, the future political status of African Americans emerged as a key dividing line in public debates. Events in Louisiana made this issue the subject of national attention. Hoping to establish a functioning civilian government in the state, Lincoln in 1863 announced his extremely lenient "Ten Percent Plan" of Reconstruction. Essentially, he offered amnesty and full restoration of rights, including property except for slaves, to nearly all white southerners who took an oath affirming loyalty to the Union and support for emancipation. When one-tenth of a state's voters of 1860 had taken the oath, they could elect a new state government. This government would be required to adopt a state constitution abolishing slavery, but otherwise would be allowed to adopt regulations regarding blacks "consistent . . . with their present condition as a laboring, landless, and homeless class."

Lincoln's plan offered no role for blacks in shaping the post-slavery order. He seems to have assumed that many former slaveholders would accept his terms. Rather than a blueprint for the postwar South, however, Lincoln's announcement, more correctly viewed, was a device for shortening the war and further spurring the process of emancipation. If 10 percent of the adult white men in a southern state took an oath of loyalty to the Union, endorsed emancipation, and detached their state from the Confederacy, it would certainly be a triumph for the Union and the overall cause of freedom.

Louisiana, which already had a large group of Unionist sugar planters thankful to the federal government for tariffs that protected them from competition from West Indian growers, and many merchants and immigrants in New Orleans who had never been happy about secession, seemed a promising place for Reconstruction to begin. But another group now stepped onto the political stage—the city's free black community. In wealth, social standing, education, and history, the free blacks of New Orleans were unique in the South. Many spoke only French and educated their children in Paris. On the eve of the Civil War, they dominated skilled crafts such as bricklaying, carpentry, and cigar making. A few owned slave plantations. Although they believed they had little in common with the mass of enslaved African Americans, they saw the Union occupation as a golden opportunity to press for equality before the law and a role in governance for themselves. Their complaints at being excluded under Lincoln's Reconstruction plan won a sympathetic hearing from Radical Republicans in Congress. By the summer of 1864, congressional dissatisfaction with events in Louisiana helped to inspire the Wade-Davis Bill, which required a majority of white male southerners to pledge support for the Union before Reconstruction could commence in any state, and guaranteed equality before the law, but not suffrage, for blacks. The bill passed Congress, only to die when Lincoln refused to sign it as Congress adjourned.

Despite their differences, however, Lincoln and the Radicals cooperated, in January 1865, in obtaining congressional approval of the Thirteenth Amendment, which irrevocably abolished slavery throughout the Union, and in so doing, introduced the word *slavery* into the Constitution for the first time. In March, in his second inaugural address, Lincoln called for reconciliation: "with malice toward none, with charity for all . . . let us . . . bind up the nation's wounds." Yet he also leveled a harsh judgment on the nation's past. "This terrible war," the president declared, was God's punishment for the sin of slavery. And if God willed that it continue until all the wealth created by the slaves' "two hundred and fifty years of unrequited toil" had been destroyed, and "every drop of blood drawn with the lash shall be paid by another drawn with the sword," this too would be an act of justice. Lincoln, in essence, asked Americans to confront unblinkingly the consequences of slavery, ensuring the right to the fruits of one's labor and acknowledging slavery's brutality. What are the requirements of justice in the face of this historical reality? Lincoln seemed to be asking.

As the Civil War drew to a close, it became clear that while slavery was dead, no consensus existed as to what social and political system should take its place. Events of 1864 and early 1865 hinted at battles ahead over Reconstruction. In October 1864, a national black convention gathered in Syracuse, New York, to demand complete abolition, equality before the law, and the right to vote. The delegates included Frederick Douglass, who wrote the convention address, and individuals who would become prominent leaders of Reconstruction—Richard H. Cain (a future congressman from South Carolina), Francis L. Cardozo and Jonathan C. Gibbs (later state officials in South Carolina and Florida, respectively), and Jonathan J. Wright, the only black to serve on a state supreme court during Reconstruction (in South Carolina).

Three months later, in January 1865, the Equal Rights League, representing the free black leaders of New Orleans, held a mass meeting to demand black suffrage in Louisiana. For the first time, the free blacks reached out to the state's far larger population of ex-slaves. "It was the first political move ever made by the colored people of the state acting in a body . . . ," observed the *New Orleans Tribune,* the nation's first daily black-

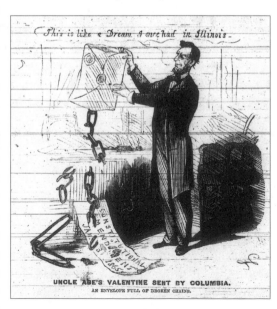

A February 1865 cartoon entitled "Uncle Abe's Valentine Sent by Columbia" celebrates the Thirteenth Amendment, which abolished slavery throughout the United States.

run newspaper. "There, were seated side by side the rich and the poor, the literate and educated man, and the country laborer, hardly released from bondage, distinguished only by the natural gifts of mind. . . . All classes were represented and united in a common thought: the actual liberation from social and political bondage." Differences between the free and the freed were hardly eliminated. The "country delegates," the *Tribune* noted, were "more radical than most of the city delegates," especially, one may surmise, on the question of land. Former slaves, many of them Union army veterans, now came to the fore, some of them destined to play important roles in Reconstruction. But the convention also offered a preview of the considerable political unity that would mark the black community after the Civil War.

Also in January 1865, General Sherman responded to the black delegation's plea for land during the Savannah Colloquy by issuing his famous Field Order 15, which set aside a large swath of land along the South Carolina and Georgia coasts for the settlement of black families on forty-acre plots. He also offered black farmers broken-down mules that the army could no longer use. Sherman aimed primarily to relieve his army of the burden of caring for thousands of black refugees, not to frame a social revolution. The order left unclear whether the land grants were permanent or temporary. But in Field Order 15 lay the origins of the phrase "forty acres and a mule," which would reverberate across the South in the next few years, and continues to echo today in debates over reparations for slavery.

By June 1865, General Rufus Saxton, who administered the land grants, estimated that some forty thousand freedmen had been settled on four hundred thousand acres of "Sherman land." One thousand of them made up a colony led by Ulysses L. Houston, one of the ministers at the Colloquy, who in April had established a self-governing black community on Skidaway Island, Georgia. Meanwhile, Congress in March had established the Freedmen's Bureau. One provision of the law empowered the bureau to divide abandoned and confiscated land into forty-acre plots, for rental and eventual sale to the former slaves. Together with Sherman's order, the measure convinced many former slaves that the federal government had assumed the responsibility of providing them with land. Allan C. Izard, a South Carolina rice planter, noted that his former slaves were "incredulous as to *his* ownership of the land. . . . That feeling of security and independence," Izard concluded, "has to be eradicated. . . . The first thing to do is to get solid and safe possession of the land." Who would actually own southern land remained unresolved as the Reconstruction era dawned.

As the war drew to a close, the freedpeople found many ways to act out their new freedom. When Sherman's army entered South Carolina, "perfect anarchy and rebellion" reigned in his path. More than in any other part of the South, the accumulated resentments of slavery burst forth in violence. Slaves ransacked Chicora Wood, the home plantation of Robert W. Allston, who, before his death in 1864, was one of South Carolina's wealthiest slaveowners. "The conduct of the negroes in robbing our house, store room, meat house, etc. and refusing to restore anything," commented Allston's widow, "shows you they *think it right* to steal from us, to spoil us, as the Israelites did the Egyptians." Charles Manigault, a wealthy rice planter, complained that slaves "broke into our well furnished residences on each plantation and stole or destroyed every thing therein." Paintings taken from the big house were "hung up in their Negro houses, while some of the family portraits (as if to turn them into ridicule) they left out, night and day, exposed to the open air." "Frederick (the Driver)," Manigault reported, "was ringleader. . . . He encouraged all the Negroes to believe that the farm, and everything on it, now since emancipation, belonged solely to him, and that their former owners had no rights, or control there whatever."

In February, Union forces, including the all-black Fifty-fifth Massachusetts singing "John Brown's Body," entered Charleston, South Carolina, where the Civil War had begun. One elderly black woman was astonished by the sight of the black unit—she "got so happy," reported one observer, "that she threw down her crutch and shouted that the year of the jubilee had come." A few weeks later, the city's black community held a massive parade in celebration, complete with a giant banner: WE KNOW NO MASTER BUT OURSELVES. In April, the *Planter*, captained by Robert Smalls, returned to the city for a ceremony to mark the end of the war.

On April 2, Grant's army finally broke through Lee's lines at Petersburg, forcing the army of Northern Virginia to abandon the city and leaving Richmond defenseless. The following day, Union soldiers occupied the southern capital. At the head of one black army unit marched its chaplain, Garland H. White, a former fugitive from slavery. Called upon by a large crowd to make a speech, White, as he later recalled, proclaimed "for the first time in that city freedom to all mankind." From a Richmond jail, imprisoned slaves could be heard chanting, "Slavery chain done broke at last!" Then, recalled Garland, the "doors of all the slave pens were thrown open and thousands came out shouting and praising God, and Father, or Master Abe." A few hours later, White was reunited with his mother, whom he had not seen for twenty years.

On April 4, heedless of his own safety, Lincoln walked the streets of Richmond accompanied only by a dozen sailors. At every step he was

The Fifty-fifth Massachusetts Colored Regiment sings "John Brown's Body" in the streets of Charleston, February 12, 1865.

besieged by former slaves, some of whom fell on their knees before the embarrassed president, who urged them to remain standing. Realizing that further resistance was useless, Lee surrendered at Appomattox Court House, Virginia, on April 9. Although some Confederate units remained in the field, the Civil War was over.

Lincoln did not approach the postwar world with a fixed plan for the South. Indeed, in his final speech, in early April 1865, faithful to his evolving point of view, he cautiously proposed that some blacks ought to have the right to vote. He singled out not only the "very intelligent"—the free blacks—but "those who serve our cause as soldiers" as most worthy. Although hardly an unambiguous embrace of equality, it was the first time an American president had publicly endorsed any kind of political rights for black Americans. Lincoln was telling the country that the service of black soldiers, inaugurated by the Emancipation Proclamation, entitled these black men to a political voice in the reunited nation. Four days later, he was dead, the victim of an assassin's bullet.

"The one question of the age is settled," a Republican political leader had commented when Congress ratified the Thirteenth Amendment, irrevocably abolishing slavery. Yet the political, civil, and economic status of the former slaves—and, therefore, the very nature of the reunited republic—remained undetermined. "Verily," as Frederick Douglass remarked, "the work does not end with the abolition of slavery, but only begins."

VISUAL ESSAY

RE-VISIONS OF WAR

Few moments in history have witnessed as rapid and surprising a change in the way a people have been visually depicted as the four years that spanned the American Civil War. Usually such shifts occur after a regime has been toppled and a new government's individuals and version of events replaces that of the former rulers. While the defeat of the Confederacy was the long-term means to the transformation of the image of African Americans, the shift occurred almost wholly in the North (southern printing capabilities were limited during most of the war and nonexistent by its end). Moreover, it was the unfolding of events and, in particular, the actions of the subjects—southern slaves and free blacks in the North— that propelled a new vision on the part of the artists, engravers, photographers, and editors who created and disseminated topical and news images.

No one predicted this outcome. Indeed, at the start of the conflict, slaves and free blacks were assigned a side role in the pictorial reporting of the escalating hostilities. But, as a war to preserve the Union became a war to end slavery, the bit players defied their restrictions, tested the limits of representation, and, finally, seized center stage, altering the way white Americans saw, and thus in many ways understood, the war and its shifting goals.

When the war began, the recently launched national pictorial press was reluctant to embrace the northern war effort fully, especially regarding how the conflict was depicted in weekly news illustrations. With a combined circulation of more than four hundred thousand nationwide, the three New York–based papers eagerly dispatched artist-correspondents to accompany federal troops and report on the war, but they also harbored lingering illusions about maintaining a southern readership (or rapidly reengaging it at the end of what was projected initially to be a short war). *Harper's Weekly, Frank Leslie's Illustrated Newspaper,* and the *New York Illustrated News* refrained from presenting news pictures that might be construed as critical of slavery.

In the early stages of the war, when Union forces occupied parts of the Carolina coast and liberated the slave population there, the pictorial press seemed more interested in the behavior of the newly freed men, women, and children than in the workings of the institution that had kept them in bondage. The childlike frivolity that slavery's apologists had for decades proclaimed as the essence of the African American character was resurrected for northern readers, but now within a frightening framework of chaos.

The scene in the mansion parlor of recently departed Beaufort, South Carolina, planter Robert W. Barnwell, recorded (or imagined) in early 1862 by *Harper's Weekly* special artist Theodore Davis, conveys the plantation slaves' joyous appropriation of their former master's privileges and property. But the donning of fine clothes over rags, the feet propped on furniture, the abuse of the piano, and the books scattered over the floor also suggests that freed slaves too readily demonstrated their ignorance and lack of discipline.

Such depictions of wild abandonment, moreover, contributed to the view of many in

the North that African Americans were benefiting from the war at the expense of white troops, who were fighting and dying for the Union. Although abolitionists and free African Americans lobbied the Lincoln administration to recruit black soldiers, the pictorial version of current events often depicted blacks as opportunistic bystanders. "Yah! Yah!" jeered the flamboyantly dressed "Gentleman of Color" cradling a mint julep in a July 1862 cartoon in the satirical weekly *Vanity Fair*. As white troops marched to battle, the seemingly carefree figure reveals a more exploitative motive (declared in the usual caricatured dialect): "Darkey hab de best ob it now. Dat's de white man's draff, and here's de niggah's!"

Not all news images reaching home-front and military readers in the early days of the war were unsympathetic to African Americans. Nevertheless, enslaved blacks were usually portrayed as a problem for the North—notably in their potential to be used as cannon fodder for the Confederate war effort. In that role, they often assumed the familiar part of hapless victim.

This illustration from a May 1862 issue of *Harper's Weekly* depicts one way that

the institution of slavery contributed to the Confederacy's cause—to the decided detriment of slaves. According to the description that accompanied the engraving, the artist, a Union soldier who contributed his eyewitness sketches to the newspaper, observed this "struggle between two Negroes and a rebel captain" through a telescope. The officer "insisted upon

their loading a cannon within range of [Union] Sharpshooters. . . . [He] succeeded in forcing the Negroes to expose themselves, and they were shot, one after the other."

Other reports suggested that slaves recruited to do southern frontline labor were victims who willingly worked against their own long-term interests. Offering an illustration of slaves dispatched from South Carolina seacoast plantations to construct Confederate army fortifications in Savannah, Georgia, the *Illustrated London News* observed: "There seems little reason to doubt that the negroes work contentedly enough at the task of riveting their fetters still more tightly upon themselves." Noting the slaves' singing as they built the earthworks, the paper's artist-reporter Frank Vizetelly concluded, "As a rule, the negroes appear to be the most contented labourers at this and similar work imaginable." Vizetelly closed his report with the usual refrain that "what with their singing and constant chattering, [the

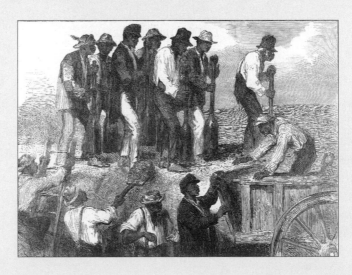

slaves] do as little for their living as any class of men I ever saw." His observation unknowingly revealed that, even when forced to support the Confederate war effort, slaves found ways to undermine the southern cause.

After May 1861, a new dimension was added to the visual representation of slavery— the contraband. As northern forces entered the South, tens of thousands of slaves voted with their feet and, with their few possessions in tow, sought the protection of the Union army. These "contrabands of war" posed an immediate logistical and political dilemma for the Lincoln administration—and clear evidence to artists and photographers accompanying federal troops that the issue of slavery needed to be represented in their illustrations of the war effort.

Frank Leslie's artist Edwin Forbes sketched this scene of a family of Virginia slaves entering the Union camp near Hanover Town, Virginia, in May 1864. Throughout the war, such scenes, documenting both the huge flood of refugees and the surprise of many northern soldiers at this collective African American search for sanctuary, were frequently depicted in newspaper engravings, prints, and photographs.

While artists and photographers tended to render sympathetic pictorial accounts of this exodus, it was also the source of derision and skepticism. The contraband "question," provoked by the actions of slaves, elicited an ambivalent if not wholly confused response— sometimes within the same publication. *Frank Leslie's Illustrated Newspaper* presented its readers with compelling illustrations (some based on photographs taken by Mathew Brady's corps of battlefield photographers) of slaves fleeing to freedom, but it also could propose—as in Frank Bellew's October 1861 cartoon, "Dark Artillery; or How to Make the

Contrabands Useful"—whimsical but cruel solutions that trafficked in all-too-comfortable racial stereotypes of African American gullibility and stupidity.

The contraband problem also starkly revealed to the northern public a pictorial record of slavery often etched, literally, on the bodies of its workforce. Pictured in a *carte de visite* ("calling card") distributed in the North, Wilson Chinn, a former slave on Volsey B. Marmillion's sugar plantation near New Orleans, displayed disciplinary devices for disobedient slaves. But his skin also offered damning pictorial evidence: Marmillion, *Harper's Weekly* reported, "was accustomed to brand his negroes, and Wilson has on his forehead the letters 'V.B.M.' Of the 210 slaves on this plantation, 105 left at one time and came into the Union camp. Thirty of them had been branded like cattle with a hot iron, four of them on the forehead, and the others on the breast or arm." In engravings, prints, and photographs, artists constructed a graphic physical map of slavery's cruelty that helped fuel northern homefront support for the increasingly bloody and costly conflict.

WILSON CHINN, a Branded Slave from Louisiana.
Also exhibiting Instruments of Torture
used to punish Slaves.
Photographed by KIMBALL, 477 Broadway, N.Y
Entered according to Act of Congress, in the year 1863. by
GEO. H. HANKS, in the Clerk's Office of the United States for
the Southern District of New-York.

The image of the contraband also began to shift subtly as former slaves, though still barred from service as Union soldiers, took on the arduous and dangerous work of frontline labor. *Harper's Weekly* "special artist" Winslow Homer's painting *The Bright Side* dates from 1865 but suggests how the pictorial terrain was unmistakably shifting by 1863. Based on Homer's wartime sketches, the painting depicts black teamsters relaxing in a Union campsite. At first glance, the picture seems merely to reiterate, albeit without the usual

physical stereotypes, the caricature of the lazy southern black. But, while the teamsters are shown resting, the supply wagons and mules in the background remind the viewer of the crucial role African Americans played in supplying ammunition and food to northern forces, and suggest that their relaxation was well earned. Few contemporary images were as subtle—indeed, many of Homer's other wartime illustrations slid into the stereotypic.

The real transformation of the figure of the black man in the pictorial record of the Civil War came with the Massachusetts Fifty-fourth Regiment's assault on Fort Wagner in Charleston Harbor on July 18, 1863—and the myr-

iad of drawings, prints, and paintings that the heroic if futile attack inspired. The recruitment and training of black Union army soldiers had been the object of acclaim but also much cruel comedy. The bravery and sacrifice exhibited by black troops in combat inspired even the most weary and cynical of war artists, and radically altered their vision of African Americans.

No longer subject to invidious comparisons with brave white troops, black soldiers saw their exploits, daring, and, inevitably, their suffering rendered in lines and tones that broke out of the tried-and-true conventions of the visual depiction of race. To be sure, the

image was no less simplified than before in that now the once craven, lazy, or victimized African American had become the epitome of the stalwart and heroic fighter. But in its implicit rejection of long-standing racist pictorial traditions, the new figure of the black American soldier suggested, for the first time, that a new way of seeing the nation and its peoples might emerge from the Civil War.

Nevertheless, many young African Americans turned to local photographers to commemorate their personal roles in the struggle for freedom, as if to ensure that their sacrifice not be left to an uncertain posterity. Such personal expressions made sense in a world that in one breath—or magazine page—extolled the black soldier and in another vilified his race. *Harper's Weekly* readers buying Christmas presents during the 1864 holiday season could still choose between pictures of battle and bloodshed and those of the "Automaton Negro Dancer," for example, that "imitates the motions of a living negro, affording infinite amusement to both old and young."

SANTA CLAUS
Automaton Negro Dancer (patented Sept. 27, 1864) imitates the motions of a living negro, affording infinite amusement to both old and young—price $2. Also Tool Chests, kitchen toys, made of strong tinned iron; box of 10 articles for $1 75; 20 or more, $3 to $5. Magic apple-parer, the best in the market, all cast iron, $1 50. ANY toy furnished at the lowest possible price. Orders with *Cash* will receive prompt attention.
  Dealers supplied on the most favorable terms.
  Berendsohn Bros., 103 Beekman Street, New York.

Despite this continuing ambivalence, and despite reversions to previous racist beliefs and invidious conventions of presentation, at the close of the Civil War the pictorial landscape was quite different than it was at the outset. Even when news images of African Americans included exaggerated physical features, as in this illustration from a March 1865 *Frank Leslie's* showing the men, women, and children who followed the campaign of Sherman's army through Georgia, their way of seeing transcended the limited vision or range of technique of the particular artist. This engraving's significance lies in its unmistakable message about slaves' utter hatred of slavery. "The oft expressed fallacy that they preferred slavery to freedom," ran the picture description, ". . . [has been] 'crushed to earth,' . . . never to rise again."

CHAPTER THREE

❦

THE MEANINGS OF FREEDOM

I N OCTOBER 1865, General O. O. Howard, head of the Freedmen's
Bureau, embarked on one of the most painful journeys of his life.
Howard had lost an arm at the Civil War battle of Fair Oaks, Virginia,
in 1862, and was known as "the Christian general" because of his close ties
to northern philanthropic societies that dispatched aid to the freedmen during the war. He took command of the bureau in March 1865 deeply committed to using the agency to protect freedpeople from violence, accord them
equality before the law, and establish schools for them in the South. Assuming that most former slaves would end up working for fair wages on land
owned by whites, Howard did not envision a massive redistribution of land
in the South. But he hoped that land that came into the bureau's possession
could be distributed to black families, and that those who had been settled
on land under General Sherman's Field Order 15 would retain ownership.

During the summer of 1865, however, as part of his plan of Reconstruction, President Andrew Johnson ordered nearly all the plantation lands
restored to their former owners. To Howard fell the task of informing the
freedpeople that they must either sign labor contracts to work for planters,
or be evicted. He brought this message to South Carolina in October,
where, on Edisto Island, one of the most poignant encounters of the entire
Reconstruction era took place. Here, according to a Freedmen's Bureau
agent, former slaves in the summer of 1865 had not only taken possession of
"Sherman land," but had established their own "simple" government, complete with "selectmen and constables elected by the people." Some two
thousand blacks gathered in a local church to be addressed by Howard.
News of his message had preceded him, and "dissatisfaction and sorrow
were manifested from every part of the assembly." Finally, as Howard later
recalled, he quieted the crowd by encouraging a "sweet-voiced negro
woman" to sing spirituals: "Nobody Knows the Trouble I Seen" and "Wan-
dering in the Wilderness of Sorrow and Gloom." When the assembly fell

silent, Howard urged them to "lay aside their bitter feelings, and to become reconciled to their old masters." Shouts from the audience continually interrupted him: "No, never." "Can't do it." "Why, General Howard, do you take away our lands?"

Howard requested that the former slaves appoint a three-man "committee in behalf of the people" to recommend ways of easing the transition when the planters returned to reclaim their property. Instead, the committee—Henry Bram, Ishmael Moultrie, and Yates Sampson—drew up petitions of protest to Howard and President Andrew Johnson. (Only for Bram does biographical information exist: evidently freeborn, he had worked in both Charleston and Boston before the Civil War, and in 1865 was farming on Edisto.) "General," began the first petition, "we want Homesteads, we were promised Homesteads by the government. If it does not carry out the promises its agents made to us . . . we are left in a more unpleasant condition than our former. . . . You will see this is not the condition of really free men." How could the government, they asked, so quickly befriend its enemies in "the war you said was over"?

To the former slaves, the war with their former masters over access to the economic resources of the South had hardly ended. The second petition reminded President Johnson that secession had been "born and nurtured" in South Carolina, and that the state's black population "have always been

Freedpeople plant sweet potatoes on Edisto Island, South Carolina, in 1862.

true to this Union." "Are not our rights as a free people and good citizens of these United States," they asked, "to be considered before those who were found in rebellion against this good and just government? . . . We look to you . . . for protection and equal rights with the privilege of purchasing a homestead—a homestead right here in the heart of South Carolina." Bram, Moultrie, and Sampson then departed to nearby islands to help coordinate black responses to the restoration of land to the planters. A few weeks later, they left Edisto Island again, this time as delegates to the statewide "Colored People's Convention," which met in Charleston.

The encounter on Edisto Island took place at an extraordinary moment in American history. In 1865, nearly four million men, women, and children, liberated from bondage, stepped onto the stage of American freedom. Despite the disappointments that followed, this generation of black Americans would always regard the moment when slavery ended as the turning point in their lives. Houston H. Holloway, age twenty in 1865, later recalled the day slaves in his section of Georgia learned they were free: "I felt like a bird out of a cage. Amen. Amen. Amen. I could hardly ask to feel any better than I did that day. . . ." Six weeks later, Holloway and his wife "received my free born son into the world." But the kind of freedom that Holloway and millions of other African Americans were to enjoy would be determined by a complex set of conflicts involving the former slaves, white southerners, and the victorious North. Each had its own understanding of the meaning of freedom.

Andrew Johnson's stern demeanor was grist for contemporary cartoonists such as Thomas Nast.

Andrew Johnson, the man who would have to respond to the Edisto petitions, was, one contemporary remarked, "the queerest character that ever occupied the White House." The man with the most humble origins of any American president (as a youth he was employed for a time as a tailor's apprentice), Johnson rose to prominence in the politics of prewar Tennessee. In 1861, he became the only United States senator from a seceding state to affirm his devotion to the Union, and thus remained in his seat in Washington. During the war, Lincoln appointed Johnson military governor of

Tennessee, and in 1864 he was nominated as vice president, to symbolize the Republican Party's intention of extending its influence into the South once the war had ended.

In prewar politics, Johnson proclaimed himself a tribune of the common man. Representing East Tennessee, where few farmers owned slaves, he spoke for the aspirations of "honest yeomen" and condemned the state's "slavocracy" as a "pampered, bloated, corrupted aristocracy" that oppressed poorer whites. Johnson, however, displayed no sympathy for the slaves. As a loyal member of the Lincoln administration, he embraced emancipation during the war and at one point even promised to be a "Moses" who would lead Tennessee's blacks to freedom. Nonetheless, racism remained deeply ingrained in his views of politics and society. His private secretary, Colonel William G. Moore, recorded in his diary that the president "has at times exhibited a morbid distress and feeling against the negroes." Blacks had no role to play in Johnson's vision of Reconstruction America.

The martyred Lincoln died without having established a coherent plan for Reconstruction. In his last speech, he had, for the first time in his life, as we have seen, publicly supported limited black suffrage in the South. This was not a position Johnson could embrace, because of his views on both race and government. Although a staunch Unionist, Johnson was also a firm defender of states' rights, and he denied that the federal government possessed the power to dictate voting requirements or other local political and social arrangements. The southern states, he insisted, had never, legally speaking, left the Union or surrendered the right to govern their own affairs. Individual traitors could be punished (and on assuming the presidency, Johnson spoke of punishing some of them severely), but in his view the problem of Reconstruction boiled down to placing the southern states under the control of loyal whites and bringing them back to their full standing in the Union as quickly as possible.

The era known to historians as Presidential Reconstruction (1865–1867) began less than two months after Lincoln's assassination. At the end of May 1865, Johnson announced his plan for Reconstruction. He offered a pardon, including restoration of property rights except for slaves, to all southern whites except Confederate leaders and wealthy planters (and most of these subsequently received individual pardons); appointed provisional governors for the ex-Confederate states; and outlined steps whereby new state governments would be created. Apart from requirements that they abolish slavery, repudiate secession, and abrogate the Confederate debt—all inescapable consequences of the South's defeat—these governments were granted a free hand in managing their affairs. Johnson appears to have assumed that ordinary white yeomen would replace in office the planters who had led the South into secession. When southern electorates disappointed his expectations by returning members of the old elite to power, Johnson did not alter his Reconstruction program. Instead, he increasingly allied himself with the South's leadership against northern Republicans. During the summer of 1865, before Howard's reluctant mission to the Sea Islands, Johnson had ordered nearly all the land in the hands of the army and the Freedmen's Bureau returned to its prewar owners, an action that solidified his support among the South's planter class.

It is not surprising, therefore, that Johnson rejected the plea of the former slaves of Edisto Island. In the waning days of 1865 and early 1866, as a result of his policy, thousands of freedpeople were displaced from land on which they had settled. Even Davis Bend, Mississippi, reverted to Joseph Davis, brother of the Confederate president. Unlike most planters, however, Davis then sold the land on long-term credit to Benjamin Montgomery, the most prominent leader of the Bend's black community, and directed his own heirs to be as generous as possible if Montgomery could not meet his payments. After his brother's death, Jefferson Davis launched a long legal battle to regain possession of the land. The Montgomery family and Joseph Davis's children fought Jefferson Davis every inch of the way. But after the end of Reconstruction and the restoration of white supremacy in Mississippi, the former Confederate president succeeded, and Montgomery was evicted, a sad end to General Grant's hope of establishing a "Negro paradise" at Davis Bend.

In a few locales, freedmen forcibly resisted eviction, until ousted by the army. In February 1866, when soldiers and Freedmen's Bureau agents arrived on Edisto Island to oversee the transfer of land ownership, freedmen wielding shovels and picks drove them away. The troops soon returned, however, and forced the former slaves to surrender their short-lived possession of the land. On the Delta plantation on the Savannah River, armed blacks initially refused to sign contracts to work as wage laborers, leave the premises, or exchange their "Sherman land" for government tracts elsewhere, as military officials proposed. "We have but one master now," they proclaimed, "Jesus Christ." Adele Allston, the widow of a prominent South Carolina planter, found the "angry, sullen" demeanor of the freedmen on another plantation a striking contrast to "the pleasant smile and courtesy or bow to which we were accustomed." At first, the freedmen refused to give her the keys to the rice and corn barns and insisted that they would allow "no white man" on the premises.

In the end, only a small number of former slaves managed to retain their land. As a result, the vast majority of rural freedpeople remained poor during Reconstruction, and for many years thereafter. In 1870, approximately thirty thousand black southerners owned some land (generally small plots), but more than four million did not. At one confrontation over land, on Jehossee Island, South Carolina, in early 1866, several freedmen told an army officer "that they knew Congress was in session and would provide for them." The government's failure to do so produced bitter disappointment and an enduring sense of betrayal. The slaves, an elderly Mississippi freedman recalled in the 1930s, "expected a heap from freedom they didn't get. . . . They promised us a mule and forty acres of land." "Yes, sir," said a Tennessee former slave, "they should have given us part of Maser's land as us poor old slaves we made what our Masers had."

The events of 1865 underscored a series of historical interconnections indispensable for understanding the social and political history of Reconstruction and, indeed, of the decades that followed. These momentous events showed how the Civil War bequeathed to the postwar world a series of explosive issues revolving around the rights of American citizens and fair access to economic resources, and how the twists and turns in national politics profoundly affected the lives of the former slaves. They also suggested how events in localities across the South interacted with and affected the decisions of policymakers in Washington. Most dramatically, they raised the central question of Reconstruction: What was the meaning of freedom, or, to put it another way, what rights and status would African Americans enjoy in postwar American society? On this question, former slaves and former slaveowners found themselves irreconcilably at odds.

Many white southerners viewed slaves as utterly unprepared for freedom. "The Negroes are to be pitied," one wrote. "They do not understand the liberty which has been conferred upon them." In fact, former slaves emerged from bondage with distinct ideas about the meaning of freedom. Some reflected aspirations widely shared in American society— self-reliance, family stability, religious liberty, economic opportunity, political participation. But for the freedpeople, these elements coalesced into a vision very much their own. Freedom meant something quite different to men and women who had long enjoyed its blessings than to those to whom it had always been denied. For white Americans, freedom was a given, a birthright to be defended. For African Americans, it was an open-ended process, a multifaceted concept that suggested a transformation of every aspect of their lives. Although the freedpeople failed to achieve full freedom as they understood it, their ongoing struggles to define the meaning of freedom did much to shape the nation's political and social agenda during Reconstruction.

"The idea of liberty," the French historian Marc Bloch once wrote, "is one which each epoch reshapes to its own liking." With the Union's triumph, freedom for the first time truly defined the nation's existence. But rather than a predetermined, clear concept, freedom during Reconstruction became a terrain of conflict, subject to multiple and competing interpretations. The legal abolition of slavery posed the definition of freedom as a concrete matter of national policy, rather than simply a philosophical problem or matter of political theory. "What is freedom?" asked Congressman James A. Garfield in 1865. "Is it the bare privilege of not being chained? If this is all, then freedom is a bitter mockery, a cruel delusion." Was freedom an individual or collective attribute? Did freedom mean simply the absence of slavery, or did it imply other rights for the emancipated slaves, and if so which ones: civil equality; suffrage; ownership of property? If freedom were to become a substantive reality, what changes were necessary in a society that had previously sanctioned slavery? Former slaves had their own answers to these questions, but their efforts to breathe meaning into their newfound freedom confronted efforts by other Americans to define freedom in very different ways.

For blacks, freedom grew out of slavery. The collective values and institutions they had nurtured in bondage now became fully visible in freedom, even as the new situation created by emancipation led to dramatic changes in the freedpeople's hopes and expectations. Both former slaves and free people of color moved to repudiate the behavior that had been expected of them before the Civil War. Black Americans in 1865 relished their ability to flaunt the innumerable regulations associated with slavery. In some cases, this meant doing what had been forbidden under slavery, in others, it meant openly practicing what had previously been forbidden and enjoyed only in secret.

Many affirmed their newly acquired freedom by physical movement, separating themselves from their former owners, if only by a few miles. "If I stay here," one freedwoman told her ex-owner, "I'll never know I am free." Thousands of blacks converged on southern towns and cities, where "freedom seemed free-er." Schools, churches, fraternal societies, offices of the Freedman's Bureau, and federal army outposts were built in cities. Between 1860 and 1870 the black population of cities such as Richmond, Virginia; Charlotte, North Carolina; Vicksburg, Mississippi; and Little Rock, Arkansas, more than doubled. Former slaves held mass meetings without the presence of whites, traveled without passes, purchased liquor and guns, and, in the case of many black women, dressed in colorful finery prohibited to them while in bondage. In Charleston, according to a disgruntled white observer, black women promenaded on King Street "arrayed in silks and satins of all the colors of the rainbow," while black schoolchildren sang

"John Brown's Body" within earshot of the tomb of John C. Calhoun, the greatest theorist of southern rights before the Civil War.

Some former slaves jettisoned the surnames of their masters and took new ones that expressed delight in freedom, pride in skill, or respect for an admired leader— names such as Deliverance, Freeman, Carpenter, Washington, and Lincoln. Many refused any longer to act in a servile manner, and insisted on being addressed as "Mister" or "Missus" instead of "boy" and "auntie." One white resident of Helena, Arkansas, was astonished in 1865 when he greeted a black man, "Howdy, uncle," only to have the former slave reply with a curse and the explanation that he did not permit non-relatives to claim him as a member of their families. Everyday encounters between the

"The negroes migrate to Louisiana and Texas in search of paying labor."

African Americans exercised their new freedom in many ways; one way was traveling where and when they chose.

races suddenly became fraught with added meaning—in a word, politicized. Violence flared over seemingly trivial incidents. A black man failing to tip his hat to a white, telling his child not to obey the orders of a former owner, or refusing to leave the sidewalk to allow white passersby to proceed could easily find himself the victim of an assault or shooting.

Underpinning such aspirations was a broader theme—a desire for independence from white control, for autonomy as individuals and as newly created communities, themselves being transformed by the process of emancipation. Central to these aims was the quest to reunite relatives separated by slavery and to consolidate long-existing family relationships. When the Union army and Freedmen's Bureau offered blacks the opportunity to legalize their marriage bonds, they responded with alacrity. "Weddings, just now, are very popular and abundant among the colored people," wrote an army chaplain as the Civil War drew to a close. "I have married during the month twenty-five couples, mostly those who have families, and have been living together for years." Once the war ended, the number of those who solemnized their unions and received marriage certificates expanded enormously. "Let the marriage bonds be dissolved throughout the state of New York today," commented one observer in 1865, "and it may be doubted if as large a proportion of her white citizens would choose again their old partners." Meanwhile, widows of black soldiers successfully claimed survivors' pensions, forcing the federal government to acknowledge the validity of prewar relationships that slavery had attempted to deny. But the process of family consolidation involved far more than gaining legal recognition for preexisting unions. Many families, divided under slavery because their members belonged to different owners, now lived together. In addition, not a few African Americans adopted the children of deceased relatives and friends. Freedmen's Bureau agents, who assumed they would have to provide for thousands of black orphans, were astonished at how many were absorbed into the black family structure.

Two years after the end of the Civil War, freedman Hawkins Wilson sought the assistance of the Freedmen's Bureau in locating family members he had not seen since being sold away from Virginia twenty-four years earlier. "I am anxious to learn about my sisters," Wilson wrote, "from whom I have been separated many years." He went on to list the names of "my own dearest relatives": his sisters, brothers-in-law, nephews and nieces, and uncles, along with their owners at the time of his sale. He also enclosed a letter to his sister Jane, in the hope that she was "still living," detailing his recent experiences. Since emancipation, Hawkins related, he had learned to read and write, secured a job in a furniture workshop, become a sexton in the Methodist Episcopal Church in Galveston, Texas, and played a leading part in mass meetings at which former slaves demanded the rights of citizenship. He had also married "a very intelligent and lady-like woman." "Thank God," Wilson added, "that now we are not sold and torn away from each other as we used to be."

The historical record does not reveal whether Hawkins Wilson located any of his kinfolk, although the odds are against it. His was one of thousands of such quests during Reconstruction. (One northern reporter encountered a freedman who had walked more than six hundred miles searching for his wife and children, from whom he had been separated by sale.) Some succeeded—such as the mother reunited in a Virginia refugee camp with her eighteen-year-old daughter, who had been sold away while still an infant—but most ended in failure. To the end of the century, black newspapers across the country carried advertisements seeking information about the whereabouts of missing loved ones. A typical one read: "Saml. Dove wishes to know of the whereabouts of his mother, Areno, his sisters Maria, Neziah, and Peggy, and his brother Edmond, who were owned by Geo. Dove, of Rockingham county, Shenandoah Valley, Va. Sold in Richmond." Nonetheless, the 1870 census reported that the large majority of African Americans lived in two-parent family households.

But while Reconstruction witnessed the stabilization of family life, freedom subtly altered relationships within the black family. Emancipation enhanced the power of black men and institutionalized the accepted nineteenth-century notion that men and women should inhabit separate "spheres." The course of Reconstruction itself, in which men but not women received the right to vote and hold office, brought men fully into the public sphere and enhanced male authority in the black community. Meanwhile, whites throughout the South complained of a "labor short-

A woman of the Sea Islands

age" caused primarily by the withdrawal of black children from the labor force in order to attend school, and of black women from the cotton fields and domestic service jobs to devote themselves to their families. Even though the ability to remain at home, outside the paid labor force, was a sign of respectability for their own families, few whites thought this ideal applicable to African Americans. Henry Watson, an Alabama planter, ridiculed freedwomen for their "desire to play the lady" rather than do the agricultural work to which they were suited. A Georgia planter complained that women with employed husbands "are not at work . . . they are as nearly idle as it is possible for them to be, pretending to spin, knit or something that really amounts to nothing."

In fact, many black women continued to do agricultural work as part of the freedpeople's household economy. They labored on garden plots and raised poultry for sale to earn extra cash for their families. Eventually, the dire poverty of the black community would compel a far higher proportion of adult women to work for wages than was the case among whites. In early Reconstruction, however, neither female field laborers nor house servants were as available to work as they had been under slavery. Many men considered it a badge of honor to see their wives remain at home—an attitude reinforced by black ministers, who generally preached a highly patriarchal vision of family life. Many women desired to devote more time to their husbands and children and to domestic responsibilities such as cooking, sewing, and cleaning than had been possible before the war. Both men and women wished, as well, to remove black women from proximity to white men in order to avoid the sexual exploitation so common under slavery. "I would rather stay here and starve and die if it comes to that," a former slave responded to his former owner's request that the family return to the old plantation, "than have my girls brought to shame by the violence and wickedness of their young masters."

Not all black women adopted the patriarchal view of the family common among men of both races. Some objected to their husbands' signing labor contracts for them, as the Freedmen's Bureau required, or holding legal title to their property and wages, as the laws mandated. A remarkable number of married freedwomen established bank accounts in their own names at the Freedman's Savings Bank, an institution established after the war to encourage "thrift" among the former slaves. But whatever the tensions in gender relations spawned by emancipation, the stability of family life was a cardinal element of African Americans' conception of freedom.

The family was only one of the institutions nourished in the slave quarters that emerged into the light of freedom, and was consolidated and changed as a result. As under slavery, the church remained a central institution of black life after the Civil War. Now, however, hundreds of thousands of blacks withdrew from existing biracial congregations to establish their own churches, preferring to worship among themselves and with ministers of their own race. Throughout the South, former slaves pooled their meager resources to construct church buildings and pay the salaries of black preachers. They challenged whites for ownership of church property that had been funded and constructed by slaves and free blacks but, as required by law, previously controlled by white trustees. When Union soldiers occupied Wilmington, North Carolina, early in 1865, the black members of the Front Street Methodist Church (who comprised two-thirds of the congregants) informed Reverend L. S. Burkhead that "they did not require his services any longer as Pastor . . . he being a rebel." They elected a black minister in his place. General John M. Schofield ordered that the spiritual day be divided between the two rival ministers. Eventually, the black worshipers withdrew and built their own Methodist church.

By the end of Reconstruction, the vast majority of black southerners had withdrawn from churches dominated by whites. Baptist churches attracted the largest number of congregants, followed closely by the African Methodist Episcopal Church. The creation of an independent black religious life was an irreversible element of freedom. Black churches were also centers of community life. They housed schools, social events, and political gatherings, adjudicated family disputes, and provided a base for the institutional infrastructure—fraternal orders, mutual aid societies, literary clubs, trade associations—that sprang up during Reconstruction. The first institution completely controlled by African Americans, the church also became a breeding ground for black leadership, and many ministers soon entered politics. At least 240 black ministers, including some who came south as missionaries after the war, held some public office during Reconstruction.

Born free in Virginia and educated in Ohio, Richard H. Cain came to Charleston for the African Methodist Episcopal Church in 1865 and reorganized the Emmanuel Church, which became one of South Carolina's largest black congregations and the base for a political career that brought Cain to the Constitutional Convention of 1868, the state senate, and two terms in Congress. "A man cannot do his whole duty as a minister except he looks out for the political interests of his people," said Charles H. Pearce, who had purchased his freedom in Maryland, come to Florida in 1865 as a religious missionary, and was subsequently elected to the Constitutional Convention and the state senate.

The "gospel of freedom," the providential view of history that had matured under slavery, strongly affected how these minister-politicians

understood the momentous events of the Civil War era. God, said one
minister, had "scourged America with war for her injustice to the black
man." He had allowed Lincoln, like Moses, to glimpse the promised land
of freedom and then removed him before he could reach "its blessed
fruitions." James D. Lynch, who came south as a missionary, took part in
the Savannah Colloquy with General Sherman, and then rose to prominence in Mississippi politics, declared the cause of the war to be America's
"disobedience," via slavery, to its divine mission to "elevate humanity"
and spread freedom all over the globe. Even among non-clerics, it was an
article of faith that, as a North Carolina speaker put it, "the negroes owed
their freedom to the courage of the negro soldiers and to God," and that
"the race have a destiny in view similar to the Children of Israel."

Also central to the meaning of freedom was access to education, so long
denied to most African Americans. As a Mississippi freedman declared, it
was "the next best thing to liberty." The thirst for learning sprang from
many sources—the recognition that learning was a form of empowerment,
a desire to read the Bible, the need to prepare one's self for the economic
marketplace, or simply a general thrust toward uplift and group advancement. As a member of a North Carolina education society established by

*Black soldiers from the Port Hudson, Louisiana, "Corps d'Afrique" pose with
textbooks in front of their school.*

former slaves put it in 1866, "he thought a school-house would be their first proof of their *independence*." But whatever the motive, white contemporaries were astonished by the former slaves' "avidity for learning." Blacks of all ages flocked to the schools established by northern missionary societies, the Freedmen's Bureau, and on their own initiative by groups of ex-slaves.

Northern journalist Sidney Andrews, who toured the South in 1865, was profoundly impressed by how former slaves in tiny towns and villages "were supporting little schools themselves," and by how much education went on outside of the classroom: "I had occasion very frequently to notice that porters in stores and laboring men in warehouses, and cart drivers on the streets, had spelling books with them, and were studying them during the time they were not occupied with their work." Children taught their parents at home after school, and farm laborers "pored over the elementary pages." In a region where state-funded public education had been all but unknown before the Civil War, the willingness of black communities to tax themselves to establish schools was a remarkable innovation, especially for a largely impoverished community. "Is it not significant," wrote a northern educator, "that after the lapse of one hundred and forty-five years since the settlement [of Beaufort, North Carolina], the Freedmen are building the first public school-house ever erected here." As in the case of ministers, black teachers quickly assumed positions of leadership, using their literacy to assist the freedpeople with labor contracts and legal matters, and often moving into politics with the advent of black suffrage. Francis L. Cardozo, a native of South Carolina who had attended the University of Glasgow before the Civil War, returned to his home state in order to train black teachers and helped establish Avery Normal Institute, in Charleston. In 1868, he was elected South Carolina's secretary of state.

But in the eyes of African Americans, freedom meant more than establishing autonomous institutions. Recognition of their equal rights as American citizens quickly emerged as the animating impulse of black politics. In a society that had made political participation a core element of freedom, the right to vote inevitably became central to the former slaves' desire for empowerment and autonomy. "Slavery," said Frederick Douglass in 1865, "is not abolished until the black man has the ballot." And throughout the South in 1865 and 1866, blacks organized Equal Rights Leagues and held local and state conventions to protest discriminatory treatment by the army, public officials, and private business, and to demand equality before the law and the right to vote. The key organizers tended to be men who had achieved positions of leadership before and during the Civil War—free blacks, skilled slave artisans and preachers, and black soldiers. While these

gatherings sometimes revealed tensions within the black community—
differences between former slaves and former free blacks over whether land
redistribution should be considered a priority, for example—participants
were unanimous in demanding equal rights and suffrage. The language of
their resolutions was respectful, but firm. "We simply ask," declared the
South Carolina Colored People's Convention of 1865 in a petition to Congress, "that we shall be recognized as men; that there be no obstructions
placed in our way; that the same laws that govern white men shall govern
black men; that we have the right of trial by jury of our peers; . . . that in
short we be dealt with as others are—in equity and justice." In Louisiana in
the fall of 1865, a Republican-sponsored "voluntary election" attracted
some twenty thousand black voters. "The whole Parish was in an uproar"
on election day, reported an army officer, with former slaves abandoning
the plantations, "stating that they were going to vote."

The political organizing of 1865 helped place the issue of black suffrage
on the national agenda, and strengthened the resolve of Radical Republicans in the North to oppose Andrew Johnson's plan of Reconstruction,
which excluded blacks from political participation. Local political action by
African Americans paved the way for the explosion of political activism in
1867, when Congress decreed that black men in the South should have the
right to vote. And it exemplified the powerful identification that blacks had
developed, thanks to emancipation and the service of black soldiers, with
the national government. In May 1865, a gathering of "colored men" in
Petersburg, Virginia, adopted a series of resolutions demanding "an equality of rights under law." They justified their claim by reference both to the
service of black soldiers and the fact that "the word white or slave is not
found in the Constitution of the United States." Many black meetings
merged the language of the Declaration of Independence with the Constitution in staking out a claim to equal rights as citizens. "We think that the
Constitution of these United States says," declared a Florida black convention, "that all its citizens shall [possess] life, liberty, and the pursuit of happiness. But we fear that we will never get justice in this country, unless it is
given by the U.S." Moving to appropriate the nation's revolutionary heritage for their own purposes, speakers pointed out that Crispus Attucks, a
man of mixed African-Indian ancestry, had shed "the first blood" in the
American Revolution. They objected to taxation without representation
and drew up "Declarations" outlining grievances and claiming their
"inalienable rights." Clearly, they had knowledge of the nation's past and a
keen sense of the historical significance of the end of slavery. As a petition
by ten Alabama freedmen, detailing violence by planters and abuses by
local authorities, put it: "This is not the pursuit of happiness."

Finally, as the battles over land underscored, economic autonomy was crucial to the former slaves' definition of freedom. Some former slaves took direct action, refusing to leave plantations or sign labor contracts, and dividing the land among themselves. "My foreman Sydney," complained a Tennessee planter, had not only taken up residence "in the rooms of my house," but claimed "the land from the lane to the river" as his own, and "planted him an orchard." Blacks deeply resented white charges that they understood freedom as idleness, or that once free they would prove unable to support themselves. When a planter berated a former slave for laziness—"You lazy nigger, I am losing a whole day's labor by you"—the freedman responded, "Massa, how many days' labor have I lost by you?" "We have been working all our lives," said a Virginia freedman, "not only supporting ourselves, but we have supported our masters, many of them in idleness." But the freedpeople remained adamant in the desire to work without the supervision of masters and overseers, to determine their own hours and pace of labor, and to receive wages commensurate with their effort. Most of all, as Garrison Frazier had explained to General Sherman during the Savannah Colloquy, genuine economic freedom could be obtained only through ownership of land, for without land, blacks' labor would continue to be exploited by their former owners. "The negroes," complained Georgia planter Charles C. Jones, Jr., toward the end of 1865, were "thoroughly demoralized. . . . Their great desire seems to be to get away from all overseers, to hire or purchase land, and work for themselves." Only land, wrote Merrimon Howard, a former slave, would enable "the poor class to enjoy the sweet boon of freedom."

When the war ended, many former slaves believed they had what one freedman, Bayley Wyat of Virginia, called "a right to the land." The belief drew not only on knowledge of Sherman's Field Order 15, but on the standards of justice nurtured under slavery, and the conviction that the nation as a whole had incurred an obligation to the newly freed slaves. (Had not Lincoln himself, in his second inaugural address, spoken of "the wealth piled by the bondsman's two hundred and fifty years of unrequited toil"?) As Wyat explained, "[O]ur wives, our children, our husbands, has been sold over and over again to purchase the lands . . . and den didn't we clear de land, and raise de crops? . . . And den didn't them large cities in the North grow up on de cotton and de sugars and de rice that we made?" Black soldiers, who accounted for over one-third of the federal forces stationed in the South in mid-1865, encouraged this belief. "The Negro soldiery here," complained a Mississippi planter, "are constantly telling our negroes that for the next year, the Government will give them land, provisions, and Stock and all things necessary to carry on business for themselves."

Blacks' determination to assert their independence in economic relationships set them on a collision course with a planter class determined to
reestablish as much of the old order as possible. Southern whites, especially
a planter class devastated by wartime destruction and the loss of their slave
property, sought to implement their own understanding of emancipation's
consequences. Bitterness and demoralization overwhelmed many a planter
in 1865. Confederate general Braxton Bragg returned from the war to his
Alabama home to find "*all, all* was lost, except my debts." Bragg and his
wife lived for a time in a slave cabin. Perhaps ten thousand slaveholders
abandoned their homes after the war to begin anew in Europe or the North,
or to reestablish plantations in Brazil, where slavery survived until 1888.
For the vast majority, who remained in the South, the adjustment to a free
labor system proved extraordinarily difficult. Most remained convinced, in
the words of South Carolina slaveholder Henry W. Ravenal, that "the old
relation of master and slave" had been "the best condition in which the two
races could live together for mutual benefit." Thus, it proved difficult to
accept the reality of emancipation. "It seems humiliating to be compelled
to bargain and haggle with our own servants about wages," wrote the
daughter of one Georgia planter.

Reared on the idea that African Americans would not work except
through physical coercion, white southerners sought ways to maintain a
disciplined labor force and revive plantation agriculture despite the end of
slavery. No less than the freedpeople, white planters quickly realized that
control of labor rested on control of land. As Allan C. Izard, a rice planter
whose former slaves claimed his plantation for themselves, wrote, "that
feeling of security and independence has to be eradicated. . . . The first
thing to do is to get solid and safe possession of the land." In effect, planters
sought to impose on blacks their own definition of freedom. In contrast to
African Americans' understanding of freedom as an open-ended ideal
based on equality and autonomy, white southerners clung to the antebellum view that freedom meant mastery and hierarchy; it was a privilege, not
a universal right, a juridical status, not a promise of equality.

Union army colonel Samuel Thomas, the director of the Freedmen's
Bureau in Mississippi, reported in September 1865 that white public sentiment had not yet "come to the attitude in which it can conceive of the negro
having any rights at all. Men, who are honorable in their dealings with their
white neighbors, will cheat a negro without feeling a single twinge of
honor. . . . And however much they confess that the President's proclamation broke up the relation of the individual slaves to their owners, they still
have the ingrained feeling that the black people at large belong to the whites
at large." Certainly, the prevailing view among white southerners was that

emancipation implied neither economic autonomy nor civil and political incorporation. "A man may be free and yet not independent," Mississippi planter Samuel Agnew observed in his diary in 1865. "A man might be free and still not have the right to vote," echoed a delegate to Virginia's Constitutional Convention two years later. The white South's general stance was summed up by a Kentucky newspaper: the former slave was "*free*, but free only to labor."

"THE POPULAR IDEA OF THE FREEDMEN'S BUREAU—PLENTY TO EAT AND NOTHING TO DO."

An 1866 cartoon lampoons "The Popular Idea of the Freedmen's Bureau—Plenty to Eat and Nothing to Do."

Rejecting the idea that emancipation implied civil and political equality or opportunities to acquire property or advance economically—rights that northerners deemed essential to a free society—most white southerners insisted that blacks must remain a dependent plantation labor force in a situation not very different from slavery. In the early days of Reconstruction, they sought to reestablish their authority over the former slaves through labor contracts. "Let everything proceed as formerly," one planter advised, "the contractual relation being substituted for that of master and slave." And contracts drawn up by planters in 1865, while providing for the payment of wages, often prescribed labor in gangs from sunup to sundown, as in antebellum days, and prohibited laborers from entertaining visitors, holding meetings, leaving plantations without the employer's permission, or even using vulgar language. Some planters still claimed the right, as under slavery, to determine whom their workers could marry. Not surprisingly, the freedpeople objected vehemently to such provisions, and these regulations generally proved impossible to enforce.

As 1865 drew to a close, rumors of an impending land redistribution swept across the rural South, animating many freedpeople and terrifying many white southerners. The "Christmas Day Insurrection Scare" that engulfed many parts of the South reflected the former slaves' continuing demands for political and economic rights, and the white South's panic at instances of black assertiveness. A federal officer who investigated reports of impending insurrection in Kingstree, South Carolina, where former slaves marched "with red colors flying" to demand better contract terms, concluded that exaggerated fears "spring from the dread on the part of the planters of the freed people asserting their rights of manhood." The fact that armed sentinels guarded many African American meetings thoroughly alarmed whites. Blacks bearing arms symbolized the social transformation brought about by emancipation.

But as it became clear that a significant change in land ownership would not be forthcoming, former slaves concentrated on other ways of asserting their economic independence and carving out day-to-day autonomy in their working lives. A long period of conflict followed on plantations throughout the South over the organization and control of labor. Disputes proliferated over the pace of work, the level of pay, the degree of oversight in daily labor, and control over the labor of children. Planters complained that agricultural workers devoted most of their time to their own garden plots, neglecting the cotton fields, and that domestic servants refused to be on call twenty-four hours a day, as before the war. Former slaves throughout the South refused to work under overseers, and frequently ignored directions from their employers. One "ploughman," reported a planter, "gets highly offended because I ask him if he has fed his oxen and does not answer the question at all, but asks me if I went in the field to see if they were fed." The early years of Reconstruction also witnessed strikes or petitions for higher wages among black urban workers as well, including Richmond, Virginia, factory laborers and Jackson, Mississippi, washerwomen. In many white-owned homes, butlers refused to cook or polish brass, and chambermaids said it was not their responsibility to answer the front door.

The postwar labor shortage, indeed, gave former slaves considerable bargaining power. If one planter's rules and regulations seemed too onerous, there was usually another planter nearby desperate for labor, and who adopted a more lenient attitude. On Laurel Hill, a Mississippi plantation, former slaves at the end of 1866 refused to sign contracts for the following year unless the owner provided education for their children and recognized the workers' right to leave the plantation at will, set their own pace of work, and have access to garden plots. White neighbors, reported the overseer, Wilmer Shields, offered the laborers "every inducement" to change jobs. One promised blacks the use of horses to ride to Natchez on Saturdays; another, according to Shields, offered "plenty of whiskey and every latitude and liberty to do as they please if they work for him." Convinced that "we are too strict and do not pay enough," Shields reported in January

1867, nearly all his laborers departed, "and we cannot blame them, in view of the tempting offers made to them." One planter placed an advertisement in a southern newspaper, offering a fifty-dollar reward for "information that will enable me to make a living . . . by the use of Negro labor."

Unable to impose their will on their former slaves, planters quickly turned for assistance to the new state governments established in 1865 under President Johnson's plan of Reconstruction. Given a free hand by the president in determining the contours of Reconstruction, nearly all of the legislatures in the former Confederate states in 1865 and 1866 enacted "Black Codes," laws that did much to undermine support in the North for Johnson's Reconstruction program. The laws recognized certain minimal elements of black freedom—they authorized the former slaves to acquire property, marry, sign contracts, and testify in court (but only in cases involving other blacks). Nonetheless, the Black Codes' provisions confirmed the observation of journalist Sidney Andrews: "the whites seem wholly unable to comprehend that freedom for the negro means the same thing as freedom for them. They readily enough admit that the Govern-

A news engraving depicts an incident involving enforcement of the Black Codes in Monticello, Florida, in late 1866, when a freedman convicted of vagrancy for not signing a labor contract was auctioned off to work for a white employer who would pay his fine.

ment has made him free, but appear to believe that they have the right to exercise the old control."

Along with denying blacks equality before the law and political rights, the Black Codes required all African Americans to sign yearly labor contracts each January. Those who failed to do so could be arrested as vagrants and fined; if they proved unable to pay, they could be auctioned off to an employer who would pay their fines, and then forced to work to reimburse him. The laws also prohibited employers from "enticing" away another employer's laborers by offering them higher wages, thus, in effect, outlawing a functioning market in labor. Several states also enacted apprenticeship laws that allowed courts to declare black parents incapable of supporting or properly raising their children, and to assign those children as uncompensated labor for white employers (with the former owner often given first preference). A direct threat to the newly won stability of black families, these laws aroused bitter complaint among the freedpeople, who deluged the Freedmen's Bureau and local courts with petitions to free their children from involuntary apprenticeships. "I think very hard of the former owners," one aggrieved parent declared, "for trying to keep my blood when I know that slavery is dead."

All these measures were enforced by a flagrantly biased political and legal system in which African Americans had no voice, and by all-white police forces and state militias (often composed of Confederate veterans still wearing their gray uniforms). No jury in Georgia, reported a Freedmen's Bureau agent, would "convict a white man for killing a freedman," or "fail to hang" a black man who killed a white in self-defense. Blacks, commented another agent, "would be *just as well* off with no law at all or no Government," as with the legal system established in the South under Andrew Johnson. "If you call this Freedom," wrote one black veteran, "what do you call Slavery?"

The real significance of the Black Codes and other measures adopted by the state governments established by Andrew Johnson lay not in their effectiveness—the law was an inefficient means of mobilizing labor, and the most onerous provisions of the codes were quickly voided by the Freedmen's Bureau—but in what they showed about the determination of the South's white leadership to ensure that white supremacy and plantation agriculture survived emancipation. In their immediate impact, the codes helped to undermine northern support for Johnson's policy. Defeated Confederates were no more able to shape the aftermath of emancipation to their own liking than were the former slaves. For a third protagonist, the victorious North, also sought to determine the meaning of freedom and the course of the transition from slavery to freedom.

Even as the war drew to a close, northerners struggled to define precisely the repercussions of the destruction of slavery. By 1865, whatever their views on black suffrage, virtually all northerners agreed that property rights in man must be abrogated, contractual relations substituted for the discipline of the lash, and the master's patriarchal authority over his former slaves abolished. In debates over the Thirteenth Amendment, one phrase was used more than any other to invoke the essential distinction between slavery and freedom—the "right to the fruits of his labor." How could this central attribute of freedom be guaranteed?

In the immediate aftermath of emancipation, the task of assisting in the birth of a free society in the South fell to the Freedmen's Bureau. The Bureau's responsibilities were, to say the least, daunting. In turn diplomat, marriage counselor, educator, sheriff, judge, and jury, the individual Freedmen's Bureau agent was supposed to establish schools, provide aid for the destitute, adjudicate disputes between whites and blacks and among the freedpeople, and secure former slaves and white Unionists equal treatment before the courts. In many areas—education and health care, for example—the bureau's achievements were indeed striking. Central to its

THE FREEDMEN'S BUREAU.—Drawn by A. R. Waud.—[See Page 807.]

An 1868 cartoon, "The Freedmen's Bureau," heralds the agency as a temporizing presence in the South. While showing the agent defending freedpeople from white aggression, the cartoon also depicts weaponry on both sides, suggesting that the Bureau was the only force preventing a southern race war.

mission, however, was the effort to establish a working system of free labor, and here the outcome proved far more problematic. The fault, however, lay not only with the bureau itself, or its limited resources (at its peak it had fewer than one thousand agents for the entire South), but with the North's free-labor ideology and the impossibility of reconciling the aspirations of former masters and former slaves.

The idea of free labor, wrote one bureau agent, was "the noblest principle on earth." Developed in the North before the Civil War and sanctified by the Union's triumph, the free-labor ideology rested on the idea that the opportunity to improve one's condition in life was a far more effective spur to efficient labor than the coercion of slavery. In the North, ostensibly, any hardworking individual could rise from the dependence of wage labor to the economic autonomy accorded by owning a farm, workshop, or business. "There is not of necessity," Lincoln had declared at the outset of the Civil War, "any such thing as a free hired laborer being fixed in that condition for life." As a result, the interests of employer and employee were harmonized, and a prosperity ensued in which all classes shared. If blacks and whites in the South abandoned ideas inherited from slavery and accepted free-labor principles, an enterprising and progressive South would rise from the ashes of slavery. To planters' complaints that without coercion— provided by the lash or the law—blacks would never work voluntarily and efficiently, bureau agents responded: "Why does the *white* man labor? That he may acquire property and the means of purchasing the comforts and luxuries of life. The *colored man* will labor for the same reason." All that was required were equitable wages and working conditions and the opportunity to improve their situation in life.

With President Johnson having rejected the idea of assisting blacks in acquiring land, however, the bureau had no alternative but to urge, and in some cases compel, former slaves to go back to work on plantations, under what it deemed equitable labor contracts. To the extent that this meant prohibiting coercive labor discipline and seeking to ensure that workers actually received their wages, the bureau reinforced the interests of the former slaves. To the extent that it helped to stabilize a chaotic plantation system, its policies coincided with the interests of the planters. In the end, the bureau's activities revealed that the free-labor outlook was not entirely applicable to an impoverished agricultural society just emerging from slavery. Far from being able to rise in the social scale through hard work, blacks were confronted by a labor market rigidly segmented along racial lines, in which black men were generally confined to unskilled and service labor, and black women to jobs in private homes as cooks, maids, and child nurses. For nearly all African Americans, especially those who labored in agriculture, wages were too low to allow for any accumulation. As former slaves and former slaveholders staked out competing definitions of freedom, the Freedmen's Bureau sought to stand, in O. O. Howard's words, as an impartial arbiter "between the two classes." But as the encounter on Edisto Island made clear, Andrew Johnson's policies made it increasingly difficult for the bureau to assist the former slaves in their struggle for genuine freedom.

Nonetheless, as the time approached for Congress to reassemble at the beginning of December 1865, events in the South had begun to undermine northern support for Johnson's Reconstruction policy. As soon as Johnson announced his plan in May 1865, Radical Republicans protested the exclusion of blacks from participation in forming the South's new governments. "I hope you will do all that can be done for the protection of the poor negroes," Senator Henry Wilson wrote to O. O. Howard, for "this nation seems about to abandon them to their disloyal masters." Initially, most northerners seemed more than willing to give Johnson's policies a chance. What turned much of the North against Presidential Reconstruction was the course adopted by the new southern governments. Alarmed by the apparent ascendancy of "rebels," northern Republicans were further outraged by the Black Codes, which flagrantly violated free-labor principles and seemed designed, as one northern observer put it, to "restore all of

President Andrew Johnson pardons Rebels at the White House.

slavery but its name." "The most favorable opportunity was afforded" to
the white South, declared the *Cincinnati Gazette* early in December 1865.
"Conventions were authorized; Constitutions were adopted; legislatures
were convened and congressmen were elected. . . . But the spirit in which
this was responded to was a rebellious one. It showed very clearly that the
people were not in a condition to be safely entrusted" with control of local
affairs. More blunt was the *Chicago Tribune,* the leading Republican newspaper of the Midwest: "We tell the white men of Mississippi that the men of
the North will convert the state of Mississippi into a frog pond before they
will allow such laws to disgrace one foot of soil in which the bones of our
soldiers sleep and over which the flag of freedom waves." Reports of violence directed against the freedpeople and northern visitors in the South
reinforced the conviction in the North that Johnson's plan had gone awry.

Thus, the immediate aftermath of slavery was both a time of profound
social conflict and a unique moment of promise in American history. On the
one hand, the aspirations of the former slaves seem in retrospect amazingly
modest. "All we ask," declared a black convention in Mississippi, "is justice,
and to be treated like human beings." Yet in a broader sense, the prospect
seemed within reach that a society of genuine interracial equality could be
constructed on the ashes of slavery. Events in 1865, especially the militancy
of former slaves in claiming substantive freedom, and the conduct of
Andrew Johnson and the state governments he set in place in attempting to
restore as much of the old order as possible, made plain that the battle over
the consequences of emancipation was far from settled. When Congress
reassembled in December 1865, the main battleground of the struggle over
the transition from slavery to freedom, and the world that would replace the
South's shattered peculiar institution, shifted to Washington.

VISUAL ESSAY

ALTERED RELATIONS

What difference can one picture make?

Frederick Douglass realized that something in America had changed after seeing a portrait published in 1870 by Louis Prang and Company, one of the nation's leading dealers in inexpensive color prints, or chromolithographs. In April of that year the firm released a print of Hiram R. Revels, the newly elected senator from Mississippi. The Revels portrait was based on a commissioned painting by the German immigrant and Union army veteran Theodore Kaufmann, which in turn was based on a photograph taken by the reigning recorder of illustrious Americans, Mathew Brady. "It strikes me as a faithful representation of the man," Douglass commented in June 1870 after Prang sent him a copy of the print. "Whatever may be the prejudices of those who may look upon it, they will be compelled to admit that the Mississippi Senator is a man, and one who will easily pass for a man among men. We colored men so often see ourselves described and painted as monkeys, that we think it a great piece of good fortune to find an exception to this general rule."

Perhaps, Douglass continued, black Americans could now benefit from the virtues of pictures already enjoyed by white citizens: "Heretofore, colored Americans have thought little of adorning their parlors with pictures. They have had to do with the stern, and I may say, the ugly realities of life. Pictures come not with slavery and oppression and destitution, but with liberty, fair play, leisure, and refinement. These conditions are now possible to col-

ored American citizens, and I think the walls of their houses will soon begin to bear evidences of their altered relations to the people about them.

"This portrait," Douglass concluded, ". . . is a historical picture. It marks, with almost startling emphasis, the point dividing our new from our old condition."

Can any one picture merit such a claim for significance? To Douglass, the quest for full citizenship for African Americans was multifaceted. He understood that it encompassed more than political rights, but extended to cultural rights as well, an expansive vision of equality that involved freedpeople's access to all forms of expression and dissemination.

Douglass was not averse to promoting the wide sale of a black statesman's portrait, but he understood that Revels's picture had a particular significance for freedpeople. For Douglass, the term *representation* had both a political and a pictorial meaning, and if the Civil War's promise of equality was to be realized, those meanings had to merge. Revels's realistic portrait embodied the myriad hopes, obstacles, and possibilities comprising Reconstruction.

Wide dissemination of such public portraits was key to the realization of this notion of equality. Despite Douglass's claims for the Prang print's particular significance, by the time he praised it, a wave of journalistic and commemorative images, published individually and in the pages of the burgeoning weekly and monthly illustrated press, had augured a new era, at least in terms of the creation of an inclusive public pictorial record. For the first time in U.S. history, in a variety of formats and publications, African Americans were demonstrably equal members in the nation's pictorial republic. At least in the short term, black Americans had at their disposal inexpensive images with which they could at last adorn the walls of their homes.

Nowhere was this more evident than in weekly illustrated newspapers such as *Harper's Weekly* and *Frank Leslie's Illustrated Newspaper.* While documenting momentous events in Washington, D.C.—such as Revels's admission to the U.S. Senate in February 1870—the press also depicted scenes of changing social relations in the South. As soon as the war had ended, the pictorial papers dispatched "special artists" on tours of the South to chart what amounted to terra incognita for most of the weeklies' readers (the vast majority of whom were northerners). The sketches and reports that veteran pictorial journalists such as Alfred R. Waud sent back in 1866 to *Harper's Weekly* often resembled an illustrated travelogue of the picturesque South, except many of the settings and

people he depicted were compelling in their intimacy, and were utterly new to northern white readers, who were most familiar with either the childish figures of romantic plantation pictures or the brutalized victims of abolitionist tracts.

After drawing a military wedding scene in Vicksburg, Mississippi, in June 1866, which subsequently was reproduced as an engraving in *Harper's Weekly,* Waud showed the sketch to a local white "lady." Her immediate response was disbelief: "the decent appearance of the party and the taste shown in the bride's apparel [was] exaggerated for the sake of appearances." This, Waud assured the incredulous woman and *Harper's Weekly's* readers in general, "was not the case; the scene is given just as it appeared." At least for some people, old habits of viewing died hard.

To be sure, the new pictorial order in the making was influenced by old pictorial conventions and modes of storytelling, and by the traditions of major northern publications and institutions. Prominent among those visions was a reform bent that framed new images in familiar paternalistic and prescriptive messages.

James E. Taylor, a former Civil War special artist dispatched by *Leslie's* to cover the South during 1866 and 1867, came across a freedman plowing his field in South Carolina. Taylor's "Plowing in South Carolina," published in October 1866, depicted a yeoman cultivating his homestead in the face of

limited resources—"the plow itself rude, the steer in the yoke clumsy and ungainly, and the whole contrivance very nearly the same that may be seen in arid Egypt or sultry Hindostan. . . ." But, in his adversity and dignity, this freedman moved from the ordinary to the symbolic, representing an African American as a quintessentially republican symbol of virtue, responsibility, and independence.

LESSON XV.

cock	wash	pig	too
crows	dawn	dig	two
food	bound	hoe	scrub
wake	clean	plow	bake
home	know	noise	eyes
cheer	knives	kneel	school

What letter is silent in hoe? in clean? Say just, not *jist*
catch, not *cotch*; sit, not *set*; father, not *fuder*.

THE FREEDMAN'S HOME.

SEE this home! How neat, how warm,
how full of cheer, it looks! It seems as
if the sun shone in there all the day long.
But it takes more than the light of the sun
to make a home bright all the time. Do
you know what it is? It is love.

This optimistic portrayal of success took its most didactic turn in the literature distributed to freedpeople. Northern reformers prepared textbooks for freedmen and -women that often contained more than practical lessons. Besides instruction in spelling, reading, and pronunciation, this page from *The Freedman's Second Reader* presents a "model" black household that does not so much depict the life of most freedpeople as propose the ideal domesticity of the northern middle-class family to which, reformers thought, the freedpeople should aspire.

More typical were news illustrations such as the *Leslie's* November 1866 picture portraying the laudable work of a Freedmen's Bureau school located in Chimborazo Hospital in Richmond, Virginia, run by the Cooke sisters. Artist James Taylor noted that "this school . . . tells its own story in the order prevailing, and the promise which it gives of permanent benefit to that colored race which could not have been so long kept in slavery if it had not likewise been kept in *ignorance*."

While the engraving contradicted popular misconceptions about the bureau's catering

to African Americans' indolence, it also reinforced familiar stereotypes in showing eager black students circled about their teachers in a traditional relationship to white benefactors.

The contrast is striking between this engraving and an illustration of the Charleston "Zion" School for Colored Children, which was based on a sketch by Alfred Waud and published almost a month later in *Harper's Weekly.* Waud reported, "It is a peculiarity of this school," organized in December 1865, "that it is entirely under the superintendence of colored teachers. . . . The children were apparently very obedient and attentive to their teach-

ers, and out of eight hundred and fifty scholars enrolled had an average daily attendance of seven hundred and twenty, the number of teachers being thirteen." Statistics aside, Waud's picture of black instructors and students situates its African American subjects as active participants in their own emancipation. Such public images of freedpeople defied popular expectations and, as a result, engendered newfound respect among white citizens for African Americans' struggles.

James Taylor and Alfred Waud both had served in the ranks of northern newspaper artists who reported the Civil War. On the other hand, in 1861 Richmond-born William Ludwell Sheppard abandoned a lucrative art career in New York City to return to his home state to fight for the Confederacy. A second lieutenant in the Richmond Howitzers, Sheppard seemingly had no trouble resuming his illustration career after the South was defeated. He quickly gained a national reputation for his postwar sketches of daily life in the South, published in many leading magazines, most of them displaying a landscape peppered by endearingly childlike "picturesque" blacks. However, even this nostalgic Confederate veteran—who later in life would design numerous monuments harking back to the glories of the South's "lost cause"—was swept up in a new way of seeing.

Perhaps more than any other contemporary image, it is Sheppard's July 1868 *Harper's Weekly* illustration, "Electioneering at the South," that best captures the exuberance of "grass roots" community politics during early Reconstruction. "The scene is wholly characteristic," the illustration description goes:

The eager attention of the listeners, and the evidently glib tongue of the speaker, reveal that remarkable adaptability and readiness so observable in the colored race. They take naturally to peaceful and lawful forms; they are naturally eloquent, and instead of scoffing loftily at them as incompetent, their white brethren will find it necessary to bestir themselves, or the "incompetent" class will be the better educated and more successful.

The patronizing tone of the text notwithstanding, such images bespoke a new public presence for freedpeople that broke from the older ways of seeing and depicting African Americans. But as much as they were powerful markers of change, these Reconstruction-era pictures also served as a red flag to those forces dedicated to halting the altered relations of life and art.

CHAPTER FOUR

AN AMERICAN CRISIS

ETWEEN 1865 AND 1868, the United States confronted one of the greatest political crises in its history: the battle between President Andrew Johnson and Congress over Reconstruction. The crisis arose from the intersection of three developments: the militancy of the former slaves in demanding substantive freedom; white southern reluctance to accept the reality of emancipation; and Johnson's intransigence in the face of growing northern concern over a series of momentous events in the South. The ensuing struggle resulted in far-reaching changes in the structure of constitutional authority and the nature of American citizenship. For the first time, the principle of equality before the law for all Americans, regardless of race, was written into the nation's laws and Constitution. For the first time, the federal government was empowered to override state actions that violated this new principle of equal civil rights. The era of Reconstruction lasted only a bit more than a decade, but the rewriting of the laws and the Constitution during those years continues to affect American life to this day. In contemporary debates over affirmative action, the rights of citizens, and the meaning of equality, Americans still confront issues bequeathed to our generation by the successes and failures of Reconstruction.

As in any historical era, unanticipated events profoundly shaped the crisis. Abraham Lincoln died without having formulated a clear Reconstruction policy. It is almost impossible to imagine Lincoln, an astute politician with a keen sense of public opinion, allowing himself to become isolated from his party and the northern electorate, as happened to his successor. It is inconceivable that Lincoln would have so alienated Congress that he would have found himself placed on trial before the Senate, coming within a single vote of being removed from office. More likely, Lincoln and the Republican Congress would have worked out a Reconstruction plan more attuned to protecting the rights of the former slaves than the one

Johnson envisioned, but less radical than the one Congress eventually adopted. Backed by a united Republican North, such a plan might have gained greater white southern acquiescence. But would a smooth transition to Reconstruction have served the nation's interests, and especially those of the former slaves? The crisis created by Johnson's intransigence and incompetence was, in a sense, the creative element of the situation. It pushed members of Congress into uncharted political waters, eventually leading them to embark on a wholly unprecedented experiment in interracial democracy.

The answers to "what if" questions, of course, are purely speculative. What is certain is that the assassination of Lincoln brought into the White House a man who lacked the personal qualities and political sagacity to provide the nation with enlightened leadership when it was most needed. Johnson was a lonely, stubborn man with few confidants, who seemed to develop his policies without consulting anyone, and then stuck to them inflexibly in the face of any and all criticism. He lacked Lincoln's ability to conciliate his foes and his capacity for growth, which was illustrated by Lincoln's evolving attitude toward black suffrage during the Civil War. Unlike Lincoln, Johnson had no real standing in the Republican Party and no sensitivity to the nuances of northern public opinion. Moreover, as noted earlier, Johnson held deeply racist views regarding blacks, and

An October 1866 Harper's Weekly *cartoon views Andrew Johnson's Reconstruction policies as a betrayal of northern sacrifices during the Civil War.*

proved unable to envision their playing any role in the South's Reconstruction, except as a dependent laboring class returning to work. "White men alone," he told one visitor to the White House, "must manage the South." Taken together, Johnson's beliefs, prejudices, and personality traits were a recipe for disaster at a time when an unprecedented national crisis put a premium on the capacity to think in new and creative ways.

The Thirty-eighth Congress adjourned in March 1865, as the Civil War hastened to its conclusion. The Thirty-ninth did not assemble until the following December. In the interim, Johnson enjoyed a free hand in shaping and implementing Reconstruction policy. He used it to set in motion Presidential Reconstruction. During the summer and fall of 1865, new southern governments were established, elected by whites alone, and Johnson ordered lands on which the army and the Freedmen's Bureau had settled former slaves returned to their former owners.

Johnson's policies initially won considerable support from a war-weary North. Not only did his promise of a quick restoration of the Union appeal to the widespread desire for a return to normality, but in support of his initiatives the president invoked traditions and beliefs deeply rooted in the American experience. Johnson's insistence that the federal government could not dictate how the states treated the former slaves appealed both to the tradition of federalism, which accorded state governments control over most local affairs, and to racism. The cry "this is a white man's government" had a potent appeal throughout the country. Moreover, businessmen anxious to invest in the South or to restore prewar connections with southern planters and merchants welcomed the prospect of quick sectional reconciliation. No one relished the prospect of a battle between Congress and the president. "We ought to do all in our power to avoid a break with him," wrote one Republican senator in November 1865. But Johnson's policies, and his unwillingness to consider any modification to accommodate criticism, would soon throw the political system into turmoil.

Events in the South in 1865 profoundly affected the political climate in the North. The freedpeople's unexpected militancy in demanding civil rights, the vote, and land appears to have thoroughly alarmed Johnson, propelling him into an alliance with the planter class he at first hoped to marginalize during Reconstruction. Reports of atrocities against the freedpeople—murders, whippings, the burning of schools and churches—and the enactment of the Black Codes by the new state governments Johnson had created led many northern Republicans to doubt whether the white South was genuinely prepared to accept the reality of emancipation.

Johnson had hoped to place southern Reconstruction in the hands of men, like him, who had always been loyal to the Union. He believed that his initial exclusion of wealthy planters from individual pardons would allow ordinary white farmers—the group for whom he considered himself a spokesman and most of whom, he believed, had been dragged unwillingly into secession—to take control of southern government. But when the South's white electorate went to the polls in the fall of 1865, as noted earlier, it filled the region's offices with former Confederate generals and public officials. William W. Holden, whom Johnson had appointed governor of North Carolina, warned the president that his "leniency" had "emboldened [the] rebellious spirits" of the South. Johnson himself worried that the elections seemed to reflect a spirit of "defiance, which is all out of place at this time." But he did not reconsider his Reconstruction policies.

Few northerners harbored vindictive attitudes toward the defeated Confederacy. Indeed, overall, Reconstruction was marked by amazing leniency. Johnson ordered nearly all confiscated property restored to its owners, and swiftly demobilized the Union army. Northern authorities arrested a handful of southern leaders, but most were quickly released. Jefferson Davis spent two years in prison but never stood trial for treason. His vice president, Alexander H. Stephens, served a brief imprisonment, returned to Congress in 1873, and died ten years later as governor of Georgia. Only one important Confederate was executed—Henry Wirz, the commander of Andersonville prison, where more than ten thousand Union prisoners of war had died.

More than 360,000 men had died fighting for the Union. It is possible to imagine a different scenario in 1865—flushed with victory and horrified by Lincoln's assassination, the North arrests and puts on trial Confederate leaders, exiles leading planters, and subjects the South to years of bayonet rule. Nothing of the sort happened, though, even after Congress supplanted Johnson's plan of Reconstruction with its own. Indeed, pro-British Loyalists during the American Revolution, many of

"Look here, Andy," says a recently reinstated southerner to Andrew Johnson poised over a basket overflowing with pardons for former Confederate officials, "if you want Reconstruction, you had better set me over the whole thing down in our state."

whom were driven from their homes and lost their property, suffered a far harsher fate than Confederates. What motivated the North's turn against Johnson's policies was not a desire to "punish" the South, but the evident inability of the region's white leaders to accept the twin realities of Confederate defeat and slave emancipation. Johnson would never quite understand that, whatever their views regarding race, most Republicans emerged from the Civil War convinced that the freedpeople had earned a claim upon the conscience of the nation.

Most adamant during 1865 in their criticism of Johnson's policies were the Radical Republicans, representatives within national politics of the antislavery impulse that had grown so markedly in the wartime North. Although they differed on many issues, such as the tariff and fiscal policy, Radicals shared the conviction that slavery and the rights of black Americans were the preeminent questions facing nineteenth-century America. Southern aggressions, they believed, had caused the Civil War, and the war's outcome presented a golden opportunity for the nation to remake itself in accordance with the principle of equal rights for all, regardless of race.

For decades, Radical leaders such as Thaddeus Stevens and Charles Sumner had defended the unpopular cause of black suffrage and equality before the law for black Americans. Now they viewed the enfranchisement of blacks as the sine qua non of a successful Reconstruction. Stevens, as we have seen, was the most outspoken Radical in the House of Representatives, an advocate of black suffrage before the war, of the arming of black soldiers during it, and of the confiscation and redistribution of planters' land in 1865. Sumner, a senator from Massachusetts, was closer to the abolitionists than any major political figure. In 1851, he had represented a black parent in Boston who unsuccessfully sued to desegregate the city's public schools. Sumner's argument—that laws requiring black children to attend separate schools were inherently unequal—anticipated by more than a century the Supreme Court's decision in *Brown v. Board of Education,* which outlawed school segregation. Without black suffrage, Sumner told Johnson soon after Lincoln's assassination, freedom for blacks "is a mockery." Sumner had little influence on the details of legislation, but his eloquent speeches advocating equality before the law attracted increasing support. "You have hundreds of believers in your doctrine in this State," a Californian wrote him, "where you had not one four years ago." More than other Republicans, as well, the Radicals embraced the expanded powers of the federal government born of the Civil War. Traditions of federalism and states rights, they insisted, must not obstruct a sweeping national effort to protect the equal rights of all citizens. The Radical vision was of citizens enjoying equal polit-

SOUTHERN CHIVALRY — ARGUMENT versus CLUB'S.

A contemporary print denounces South Carolina congressman Preston S. Brooks's assault on Massachusetts senator Charles Sumner on May 22, 1856. The attack on the floor of the Senate was in retaliation for Sumner's speech accusing South Carolina senator Andrew P. Butler (Brooks's distant cousin) of having taken "the harlot slavery" as a mistress.

ical and civil rights, secured by a powerful national state. "The same national authority," declared Sumner, "that destroyed slavery must see that this other pretension [racial inequality] is not permitted to survive."

Although hardly typical of all Radicals, Stevens was Johnson's fiercest antagonist. The floor leader of House Republicans, he was a master of parliamentary procedure and impromptu debate. The South, Stevens insisted, was a "conquered province," which Congress could govern as it saw fit. While he strongly advocated black suffrage, Stevens's most cherished goal was his proposal to divide land confiscated from disloyal planters into forty-acre plots for former slaves and northern migrants to the South. "The whole fabric of southern society," he declared, "*must* be changed, and never can it be done if this opportunity is lost. Without this, this Government can never be, as it has never been a true republic." Stevens's plan to make "small independent landholders" of the former slaves proved too radical even for most of his Radical colleagues, who remained wedded to the free-labor idea that blacks should move up the social ladder by slowly accumulating wealth while working for wages. But Stevens did shepherd to passage in the House the key legislation and constitutional amendments between 1865 and 1868.

The Radicals hardly controlled Congress, as historians hostile to Reconstruction would later claim. Nonetheless, they did enjoy considerable power. Their influence lay both in the strength of their commitment to the ideal of equal rights, and in the fact that in a time of crisis, they alone seemed to have a coherent sense of purpose. Time and again, Radicals had staked out unpopular positions only to see them vindicated by events. Uncompromising opposition to slavery's expansion, emancipation of the slaves, the arming of black troops—all these ideas were radical when first proposed, but had entered the political mainstream. The same, Radicals were convinced, would happen with black suffrage.

Occupying the political terrain between the Radicals and Johnson was the moderate majority of the Republican Party, led in Congress by senators such as Lyman Trumbull of Illinois and John Sherman of Ohio. Moderates remained unenthusiastic about black suffrage, which they viewed as a political liability in the North and an experiment whose outcome could not be predicted in the South. When the Civil War ended, only five northern states allowed blacks to vote on the same terms as whites. Indeed, in referenda in 1865, voters in Connecticut, Wisconsin, and Minnesota turned down proposals to enfranchise their states' tiny black populations (although the number of supporters, ranging from 43 to 47 percent of those voting, was far higher than in similar prewar ballots on the issue). Could the North, moderates asked, require of the South what it was not prepared to do itself? Nonetheless, moderates were fully committed to ensuring "loyal" government in the Confederate states and protecting the basic rights of the former slaves in a free-labor economy.

Moderate Republicans tended to view Reconstruction as a set of practical problems, not, as many Radicals believed, as an invitation to a social revolution. In the moderates' view, the states of the old Confederacy were neither conquered territory, as Stevens insisted, nor states retaining all their rights, as Johnson held. Having rebelled against the Union, they could temporarily be held in the "grasp of war" until the federal government decided on what terms to restore them to the full exercise of their rights and powers. In 1865, the moderates sincerely hoped to work with Johnson to devise a just and lasting plan of Reconstruction. But Johnson's policies and the actions of the state governments created under his supervision eventually drove moderates into the Radicals' arms, uniting the entire Republican Party against the president. Congress also contained a contingent of northern Democrats, but in numbers so small—in both houses Republicans outnumbered them by better than three to one—that they had no real influence on events.

When Congress assembled in December 1865, Johnson announced that

Reconstruction effectively was over. Governments led by men loyal to the Union had been established in the South, he declared, and all Congress had to do to complete "the work of restoration" was to seat their elected representatives. In response, Radicals such as Stevens and Sumner called for the abrogation of the Johnson governments and the establishment of new ones based on equality before the law and male suffrage. The more numerous moderates, however, still hoped to work with Johnson, and these proposals got nowhere. Nonetheless, the moderates were not prepared to embrace the president's Reconstruction plan without modifications. Congress refused to seat the representatives and senators elected from the southern states, many of whom had been leading officials in the Confederate government and army. It established a Joint Committee on Reconstruction, and set about debating the proper course of action.

Much of the ensuing discussion revolved around the problem, as Trumbull put it, of defining "what slavery is and what liberty is." "We must see to it," announced Senator William Stewart of Nevada, "that the man made free by the Constitution of the United States is a freeman indeed." To the Radicals, freedom was "a right so universal," in the words of another congressman, that it must apply to all Americans and no longer be limited by race. Moderate Republicans believed that further federal measures were necessary to protect blacks' civil rights. "Their present nominal freedom is nothing but a mockery," wrote Illinois Republican leader Jesse Fell shortly after Congress assembled. Equality before the law, enforced if necessary by national authority, had become the moderates' requirement for restoring the South to full participation in the Union.

In a December 1865 cartoon called "No Accommodations," a southern congressman is denied his old seat in the House of Representatives. "I am very sorry, Sir," reports the House Clerk, "but we cannot accommodate you. All the Old Seats were broken up, and are now being thoroughly Reconstructed."

Two bills reported to the Senate soon after the New Year by Lyman Trumbull, chairman of the Senate Judiciary Committee, embodied the moderates' policy of leaving Johnson's governments in place but adding federal protection of the freedpeople's rights. The first bill extended the life of the Freedmen's Bureau, scheduled to expire within a few months. The second, the Civil Rights Bill, was a far more important measure that for the first time offered a legislative definition of American citizenship. The bill declared all persons born in the United States (except Indians) national citizens, and went on to spell out the rights they were to enjoy equally without regard to race. Equality before the law was central to the measure—no longer could states enact laws such as the Black Codes declaring certain actions crimes for black persons but not white. So too were free-labor values: no state could deprive any citizen of the right to make contracts, bring lawsuits, or enjoy equal protection of the security of person and property. Although the bill addressed primarily discrimination by state officials, it also contained the intriguing word *custom*, suggesting that private acts also fell within its purview. No state law or custom could deprive any citizen of what Trumbull called the "fundamental rights belonging to every man as a free man." The bill allowed federal marshals and district attorneys to bring suit against violations—with cases to be heard in federal, not state, courts—and allowed aggrieved individuals to sue for civil damages.

In constitutional terms, the Civil Rights Bill represented the first attempt to give concrete meaning to the Thirteenth Amendment, which ended slavery, to define in legislative terms the essence of freedom. If states could deny blacks the rights specified in the measure, asked one congressman, "then I demand to know, of what practical value is the amendment abolishing slavery?" The bill said nothing of the right to vote. Nonetheless, it reflected how profoundly the Civil War had altered traditional federal-state relations and weakened traditional racism. A mere nine years earlier, the U.S. Supreme Court, in the Dred Scott decision, had decreed that no black person could be a citizen of the United States. Before the war, Congressman James G. Blaine later wrote, only "the wildest fancy of a distempered brain" could have envisioned a law of Congress according blacks "all the civil rights pertaining to a white man." Although clearly directed against the South, the bill had a national scope, and it invalidated many discriminatory laws in the North as well. "I admit that this species of legislation is absolutely revolutionary," declared Senator Lot M. Morrill of Maine. "But are we not in the midst of a revolution?"

Although most of his cabinet urged him to approve these measures, Johnson vetoed both the Freedmen's Bureau and Civil Rights bills. He insisted that Congress pass no Reconstruction legislation until the southern states were fully represented—a position, as one senator correctly predicted, that meant that "he will and must . . . veto every other bill we pass."

Scenes outside the galleries of the U.S. House of Representatives during the passage of the Civil Rights Bill

In the Freedmen's Bureau Bill veto, Johnson claimed that he, not Congress, represented the will of the people. "This is modest," one Republican remarked, "for a man made president by an assassin."

Johnson's vetoes deployed arguments opposing federal action on behalf of African Americans that have been repeated ever since, including in our own time, by critics of civil rights legislation and affirmative action. He appealed to fiscal conservatism, raised the specter of an immense federal bureaucracy trampling on citizens' rights, and insisted that self-help, not dependence on government handouts, was the surest path to individual advancement. Congress, he insisted, had neither the need nor the authority to protect the freedpeople's rights. Assistance by the Freedman's Bureau would encourage blacks to believe that they did not have to work for a living, thereby encouraging them to lead a "life of indolence." Johnson called the civil rights measure a "stride toward centralization of all legislative powers in the national Government." Although he did not use the modern term "reverse discrimination," the president somehow persuaded himself that by acting to secure the rights of blacks, Congress would be discriminating against white Americans—"the distinction of race and color is by the bill made to operate in favor of the colored and against the white race."

Johnson also delivered an intemperate speech to a crowd at the White

House in February 1866 condemning the Radicals and hinting that they were responsible for Lincoln's assassination. Singling out Stevens, Sumner, and abolitionist Wendell Phillips by name, he asked, "does not the murder of Lincoln appease the vengeance and the wrath of the opponents of this government?" But more significant than Johnson's intemperate language, his vetoes ended all chance of cooperation with Congress. Although the Senate failed by a single vote to override the Freedmen's Bureau Bill veto (another measure, enacted in July, extended the bureau's life to 1870), Congress mustered the two-thirds majority to pass the Civil Rights Act. For the first time in American history, a significant piece of legislation became law over a president's veto.

Johnson's intransigence also impelled Republicans to devise their own plan of Reconstruction, and to write their understanding of the consequences of the Civil War into the Constitution, there to be secure from shifting electoral majorities. The result was the Fourteenth Amendment, approved by Congress in 1866 and ratified two years later. It enshrined for the first time in the Constitution the ideas of birthright citizenship and equal rights for all Americans. The amendment, Stevens told the House, gave a constitutional foundation to the principle that state laws "shall operate *equally* upon all." "I can hardly believe," he added, "that any person can be found who will not admit that . . . [it] is just." Unlike the Civil Rights Act, which listed specific rights all citizens were to enjoy, the Fourteenth Amendment used far more general language. It prohibited states from abridging any citizen's "privileges and immunities" or denying them "due process" or the "equal protection of the law." This broad language opened the door for future Congresses and the federal courts to breathe meaning into the guarantee of legal equality, a process that occupied the courts for much of the twentieth century. The amendment also struck a blow against the Johnson governments in the South by prohibiting leading Confederate officials from holding office unless granted amnesty by Congress.

In this cartoon, "Extract Const. Amend.," Uncle Sam in the guise of a druggist exhorts President Johnson to accept the Reconstruction amendments: "Now, Andy, take it right down. More you Look at it, worse you'll Like it."

None of the measures of 1866 accorded black men the right to vote. The Fourteenth Amendment finessed that issue by leaving suffrage qualifications to be determined by the states but providing that if a state deprived any group of men of the franchise, it would lose some of its representatives in Congress. (The penalty did not apply, however, if the state denied women the right to vote.) The Fourteenth Amendment was a moderate measure, not a creation of the Radicals. Rather than forging a "perfect republic" from the ruins of slavery by purging American institutions of "inequality of rights," Stevens told the House on the eve of its passage, "I find we shall be obliged to be content with patching up the worst portions of the ancient edifice, and leaving it, in many of its parts, to be swept through by the storms of despotism." Nonetheless, Stevens said, he would vote for passage. Why? "Because I live among men and not among angels."

Stevens realized that whatever their limitations, the Civil Rights Act and the Fourteenth Amendment embodied a profound change in the federal system and the nature of American citizenship. The abolitionist doctrine of equal citizenship as a birthright had now been written into the Constitution. The principle of equality before the law, moreover, did not apply only to the South or to blacks. Like the Civil Rights Act, the Fourteenth Amendment invalidated many northern laws that discriminated on the basis of race. And, as one congressman noted, it affected the rights of "the millions of people of foreign birth who will flock to our shores."

With the passage of the Fourteenth Amendment, the Republican majority in Congress prepared to do battle with the president. Already thoroughly alienated from the Republican Party, Johnson found his position further weakened by incidents of violence in the South. In May, an altercation that began when two horse-drawn hacks, one driven by a white man, the other by a black, collided on a Memphis street, escalated into three days of racial violence. White mobs, aided and abetted by the city police, assaulted blacks on the streets and invaded their neighborhoods. By the time order had been restored, at least forty-eight persons, nearly all of them black, had been killed and hundreds of dwellings, schools, and churches looted or destroyed.

Three months later, another violent outbreak took place in New Orleans. Governor James M. Wells, a Johnson appointee, had become more and more alarmed at ex-Confederate control of the Louisiana legislature and local government in New Orleans. He decided to reconvene the Constitutional Convention of 1864, which had recessed but never adjourned, in order to press for black suffrage. On July 20, 1866, when the gathering was set to assemble, a white mob led by local police descended on a march of several hundred black supporters of the convention. In the melee that followed, some thirty-eight persons were killed and 146 wounded, mostly blacks. After investigating the affair, General Philip H. Sheridan called it "an absolute massacre." The New Orleans riot did more than any other single event to arouse northern public opinion against the president. The role of the city police in contributing to the violence rather than restoring order suggested that the southern governments of Presidential Reconstruction were unwilling or unable to protect the basic rights of citizens.

The events of 1866 also roused white southern Unionists to political action. Some broke with their region's racial heritage to support black suffrage. A small minority in most states, whites who had supported the Union cause during the war were numerous enough in areas such as the hill country of North Carolina, Georgia, Tennessee, and Arkansas to have hoped that Reconstruction would place them in power. Johnson's policies had dealt a severe blow to this ambition. During 1866, more and more southern Unionists gravitated to the congressional side in the Reconstruction debate. They pressed for Congress to bar leading Confederates from power, sometimes urging the wholesale disenfranchisement of "rebels."

A panoramic painting by Thomas Nast shows Andrew Johnson indifferent to the murder of freedpeople during the July 1866 New Orleans riot.

A satirical report on New Yorkers' reactions to President Johnson's visit to the city during his fall 1866 campaign tour

Some, reluctantly, began to embrace the idea of black suffrage, if only to oust ex-Confederates from power. William G. Brownlow—the "fighting parson" of the East Tennessee mountains who had been elected as the state's governor in 1865 after Johnson, then military governor, had barred supporters of the Confederacy from the polls—said "one more law" was needed to complete Reconstruction, "a law enfranchising the negroes . . . to weigh down the balance against rebeldom." The growing outspokenness of southern Unionists helped to persuade Congress that the possibility existed of creating a biracial Republican Party in the South.

The Fourteenth Amendment became the central issue in the Congressional elections of 1866. In the fall, the president broke with tradition by embarking on a speaking trip across the North, the "swing around the circle," intended to drum up support for candidates who supported his Reconstruction policies and opposed ratification of the Fourteenth Amendment. The tour was a political disaster. Johnson could not refrain from responding in kind to hecklers and launching tirades against his congressional opponents. On one occasion, he intimated that divine intervention had removed Lincoln and elevated *him*, Johnson, to the White House. In St. Louis, he compared himself to Jesus Christ, with Thaddeus Stevens as his Judas. The spectacle further destroyed his credibility and contributed to a sweeping Republican victory in the fall elections. But the main cause of the outcome was popular disaffection from Presidential Reconstruction and the widespread conviction that further steps had to be taken to protect the rights of the former slaves and place the South under the control of men genuinely "loyal" to the Union. Despite the results, however, and egged on by Johnson and the northern Democratic press, all the southern states except Tennessee refused to ratify the Fourteenth Amendment.

Once again, the intransigence of Johnson and the white South played into the Radicals' hands. When Congress reassembled in December 1866, Republicans set out to fashion a completely new plan of Reconstruction. They ignored Johnson. The president, declared the *New York Herald*, previously his supporter, "forgets that we have passed through the fiery ordeal of a mighty revolution, and that the pre-existing order of things is gone and can return no more." Numerous proposals circulated in Congress—reducing the southern states to territories, disenfranchising former Confederates, confiscating property, impeaching the president.

After much debate, Republicans coalesced around a new Reconstruction Act, passed over Johnson's veto early in March 1867. The act rested on the premise that lawful governments did not exist in the South, and that Congress could govern the region until acceptable ones had been established. It turned the political clock back to "the point where Grant left off the work, at Appomattox Court House," declared one member of Congress. The Reconstruction Act temporarily divided the South into five military districts and outlined how new governments, based on male suffrage (with the exception of leading Confederate officials, who could not vote in forthcoming elections), would be established. The southern states must

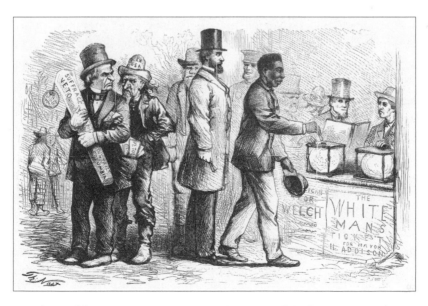

As this March 1867 cartoon shows, with his veto of the Reconstruction Act overridden by Congress, President Johnson and his southern allies angrily watch African Americans vote.

ratify the Fourteenth Amendment and adopt new constitutions embodying the principle of manhood suffrage without regard to race. Interracial democracy, the dream of abolitionists, Radical Republicans, and the former slaves, had finally come to the South. Thus began the period of Radical, or congressional, Reconstruction, which lasted until the fall of the last southern Republican governments in 1877.

The laws and amendments of Reconstruction reflected the intersection of two products of the Civil War era—a newly empowered national state and the idea of a national citizenry enjoying equality before the law. Rather than a threat to liberty, the federal government, declared Charles Sumner, had become "the custodian of freedom." What Republican leader Carl Schurz called "the great Constitutional revolution" of Reconstruction transformed the federal system, and with it, the language of rights so central to American political culture. Before the Civil War, disenfranchised groups were far more likely to draw inspiration from the Declaration of Independence than the Constitution. (The only mention of equality in the original Constitution, after all, had occurred in the clause granting each state an equal number of senators.) But the rewriting of the Constitution during Reconstruction suggested that the rights of individual citizens were intimately connected to federal power.

The Bill of Rights had linked civil liberties and the autonomy of the states. Its language—"Congress shall make no law"—reflected the belief that concentrated power represented a threat to freedom. The three Reconstruction amendments assumed that individual rights required political power to enforce them. They not only authorized the federal government to override state actions that deprived citizens of equality, but each ended with a clause empowering Congress to "enforce" the amendment with "appropriate legislation." Thus began the process—which continues to this day—by which the states have, little by little, been required to abide by the protections of civil liberties inscribed in the Bill of Rights. The Reconstruction amendments transformed the Constitution from a document concerned primarily with federal-state relations and the rights of property into a vehicle through which members of vulnerable minorities could stake a claim to substantive freedom and seek protection against misconduct by all levels of government.

It is tempting to view the expansion of citizens' rights during Reconstruction as the logical fulfillment of a vision originally articulated by the founding fathers. Yet, boundaries of exclusion—essentially, limiting the privileges of citizenship to white men—had long been intrinsic to the practice of American democracy. Reconstruction represented less a fulfillment of the Revolution's principles than a radical repudiation of the nation's actual practice of the previous seven decades. Racism, federalism, and belief in limited government and local autonomy—Reconstruction challenged these deeply rooted elements of nineteenth-century political culture. Only in an unparalleled crisis could they have been superseded, even temporarily, by the vision of an egalitarian republic embracing black Americans as well as white, and presided over by a powerful and beneficent federal government. Indeed, it was precisely because of their radicalism that the era's laws and constitutional amendments roused such bitter opposition. The underlying principles—that the federal government possessed the power to define and protect citizens' rights, and that blacks were equal members of the body politic—represented striking departures in American law. It is not difficult to understand why President Johnson, in one of his veto messages, claimed that federal protection of blacks' civil rights, together with the broad conception of national power that lay behind it, violated "all our experience as a people."

That the United States was a "white man's government" had been an article of political faith before the Civil War. "We are not of the same race," insisted Senator Thomas Hendricks of Indiana during congressional debates over Reconstruction. "We are so different that we ought not to compose one political community." Reconstruction Republicans rejected this reasoning, but their universalism, too, had its limits. In his remarkable "Composite Nation" speech of 1869, Frederick Douglass condemned prejudice against immigrants from China, insisting that America's destiny was to transcend race by serving as an asylum for people "gathered here from all corners of the globe by a common aspiration for national liberty." Any form of exclusion, he continued, contradicted the essence of democracy. A year later, Charles Sumner moved to strike the word *white* from naturalization requirements. Senators from the western states objected vociferously. They were willing to admit blacks to citizenship, but not persons of Asian origin. At their insistence, the naturalization law was amended to add Africans to the "whites" already eligible to obtain citizenship when migrating from abroad. The ban on Asians remained intact; the racial boundaries of nationality had been redrawn, but not eliminated. The juxtaposition of the Fourteenth Amendment and the 1870 naturalization law created a strange anomaly: Asian immigrants remained ineligible for citizenship, but their native-born children automatically became Americans.

Advocates of women's rights likewise encountered the limits of Reconstruction's egalitarianism. "The contest with the South that destroyed slavery," wrote the Pennsylvania lawyer Sidney George Fisher in his diary, "has caused an immense increase to the popular passion for liberty and equality." Women joined in the era's intense focus on equal rights. The

movement for women's suffrage, which had more or less suspended operations during the war to join in the fight for Union and abolition, saw
Reconstruction as a golden opportunity to claim for women their own
emancipation. Antebellum rhetoric equating the condition of women with
slavery took on new value as a vocabulary of protest. No less than blacks,
proclaimed Elizabeth Cady Stanton—who had organized the Seneca Falls
Convention to demand equal rights for women two decades earlier—
women had arrived at a "transition period, from slavery to freedom." The
rewriting of the Constitution, declared suffrage leader Olympia Brown,
offered the opportunity to sever the blessings of freedom from race and
sex—two "accidents of the body" that did not deserve legal recognition—
and to "bury the black man and the woman in the citizen." Women should
now enjoy not only the right to vote, but also the economic opportunities
of free labor. The Civil War had propelled many women into the wage
labor force and left many others without a male provider, adding increased
urgency to the argument that the right to work outside the home was essential to women's freedom. Women, wrote Susan B. Anthony, desired an
"honorable independence" no less fully than men, and working for wages
was no more "degrading" to one sex than the other.

At feminism's most radical edge, emancipation inspired demands for
the liberation of women from the "slavery" of marriage. The same "law of
equality that has revolutionized the state," declared Stanton, was "knock-
ing at the door of our homes." Property in slaves had been abolished, but
"the right of property in women" remained intact (since by law, marriage
deprived women of their independent legal identities). If "unpaid" labor
had become illegitimate on southern plantations, how could it be justified
within free households? In Stanton's writings and speeches, demands for
liberalizing divorce laws (which generally required evidence of adultery,
desertion, or extreme abuse to terminate a marriage) and recognizing
"woman's control over her own body" (including protection against
domestic violence and what later generations would call birth control)
moved to the center of feminist concerns. These questions, she found,
struck a "deeper chord" among her female audience than the right to vote.
"Women respond to my divorce speech as they never did to suffrage,"
Stanton said. "Oh! How they flock to me with their sorrows." Susan B.
Anthony, who remained unmarried her entire life, believed "an epoch of
single women" was fast approaching: "the woman who will *not be ruled*
must live without marriage."

In the end, talk of liberating women from the bonds of matrimony
found few sympathetic listeners. Former slaves, as noted earlier, rushed to
inscribe their marital status in law, and congressional Republicans saw

emancipation as restoring to blacks the natural right to family life, in which men would take their place as heads of the household and women theirs in the domestic sphere from which slavery had unnaturally excluded them. Several members of Congress explicitly rejected the idea that the Thirteenth Amendment's prohibition of "involuntary servitude" applied to relations within the family. "A husband has a right of property in the service of his wife," said one, which the abolition of slavery was not intended to destroy. Along with the right to "personal liberty," declared Republican John Kasson of Iowa, the male-headed family, embodying the "right of a husband to his wife" and of a "father to his child," comprised the "three great fundamental natural rights of human society."

When it came to the suffrage, few in Congress, even among Radical Republicans, responded sympathetically to feminists' demands. Reconstruction, they insisted, was the "Negro's hour" (the hour, that is, of the black male). "The removal of the political disabilities of race is my first desire, of sex my second," declared abolitionist Gerrit Smith. But, he claimed, pressing the latter demand would torpedo the former: "If put on the same level and urged in the same connection, neither will be soon accomplished." Therefore, Smith concluded, votes for women would have to wait. Even Charles Sumner, the Senate's most uncompromising egalitarian, feminist Francis Gage lamented, fell "far short of the great idea of liberty," so far as the rights of women were concerned.

The passage of the Fourteenth Amendment, which introduced the word *male* into the Constitution in its clause allowing states to disenfranchise women without political penalty, and of the Fifteenth, outlawing discrimination in voting based on race but not gender, produced a bitter split in feminist circles. Some leaders, such as Stanton and Anthony, denounced their erstwhile abolitionist allies and moved to sever the women's rights movement from its earlier moorings in antislavery egalitarianism. Woman, wrote Stanton, "must not put her trust in man" in seeking her own rights. In search of a new constituency outside antislavery circles, Stanton began to speak of limiting the suffrage not on the basis of gender, but by "intelligence and education," so that ignorant blacks and immigrants would not be making laws for the daughters of the native-born middle class. Other veterans of the struggle, such as abolitionist-feminist Abby Kelley, insisted that despite their limitations, the constitutional amendments were steps in the direction of truly universal suffrage and should be supported as such. The result was the creation of two bitterly divided national women's rights organizations. They would not reunite until the 1890s.

Despite its limitations, the Reconstruction Act of 1867 was indeed a radical departure in American history. A variety of motives, some

A cartoon called "The Fifteenth Amendment Illustrated" in an 1870 edition of Die Vehme (The Star Chamber), *a short-lived St. Louis satirical weekly, supports woman's suffrage at the expense of African Americans, Chinese, and illiterate immigrants.*

pragmatic, some idealistic, combined to produce the advent of black male suffrage—demands by the former slaves for the right to vote, the egalitarianism of the Radicals, disgust with Johnson's policies, the desire to fortify the Republican Party in the South, and the insistence of northerners and southern Unionists that ex-Confederates be removed from power. The effort to create an interracial democracy in the aftermath of slavery was an unprecedented experiment.

Alone among the nations that abolished slavery in the nineteenth century, the United States, within a few years of emancipation, clothed its former slaves with citizenship rights equal to those of whites. The implications of this decision were indeed profound. In a democracy, the ballot defined a collective national identity—which was why African Americans and women felt their exclusion so painfully. Therefore, the coming of black suffrage redrew the boundaries of American nationality—and raised the specter of further changes in economic, social, and political arrangements within the South. On the horizon lay further unprecedented events—the political mobilization of the southern black community, the coming to power of the Republican Party throughout the South, and efforts to build a new social order from the ashes of slavery. The era of Radical Reconstruction was at hand.

CHAPTER FIVE

THE TOCSIN OF FREEDOM

L ITTLE IS KNOWN of the antebellum life of James K. Green, a slave in Hale County, Alabama, other than that he was born in 1823 and owned by a Mr. Nelson, one of the county's largest slaveholders. But during Reconstruction, Green stepped onto the stage of history. A local political organizer and active Republican Party speaker in central Alabama, he also served as an officer of the Alabama Labor Union, a short-lived effort in the 1870s to organize black agricultural workers. Although the target of frequent threats of violence by political foes, Green helped to organize a black militia after a freedman was shot on a Greensboro street. In 1867, he was appointed a voter registrar and won election to the state constitutional convention. He served eight years in the Alabama legislature. In the 1880s, Green reflected on the remarkable trajectory of his life. Before the war, he declared, "I was entirely ignorant; I knew nothing more than to obey my master; and there was thousands of us in the same attitude . . . but the tocsin of freedom sounded and knocked at the door and we walked out like free men and . . . shouldered the responsibilities."

Like Green, thousands of former slaves "shouldered the responsibilities" of political leadership in the Reconstruction South. Indeed, no development in those years marked so dramatic a break with the nation's traditions, or aroused such bitter hostility from Reconstruction's opponents, as the appearance, a few years after the death of slavery, of large numbers of black Americans in positions of political power. The language that Democrats used to describe black officials revealed their deep sense of shock at seeing African Americans in public office. Anti-Reconstruction newspapers described constitutional conventions and legislatures with black members as "menageries" and "monkey houses." Later, some scholarly accounts echoed this feeling of outrage. "The Negroes," wrote the prominent southern historian E. Merton Coulter in 1947, "were fearfully unprepared to occupy positions of ruleship." Black officeholding, he continued, was "the most spectacular and exotic development in government in the history of white civilization . . . longest to be remembered, shuddered at, and execrated."

Before the Civil War, blacks could vote in only a handful of northern states, and black officeholding was virtually unheard of. (The first African American to hold elective office appears to have been John M. Langston, chosen as township clerk in Brownhelm, Ohio, in 1855.) But during Reconstruction perhaps two thousand African Americans held public office, from justice of the peace to governor and United States senator. Thousands more headed Union Leagues and local branches of the Republican Party, edited newspapers, and in other ways influenced the political process. African Americans did not "control" Reconstruction politics, as their opponents frequently charged. But the advent of black suffrage and officeholding after the war represented a fundamental shift in power in southern life. It marked the culmination of both the constitutional revolution embodied in the Fourteenth and Fifteenth amendments, and the broad grassroots mobilization of the black community.

The decade after the Civil War witnessed a remarkable experiment in political democracy. By the early 1870s, biracial democratic government, something unknown in American history, was functioning effectively in many parts of the South, and men only recently released from bondage were exercising genuine political power. The effort of the old white elite to substitute a legalized system of labor discipline and political subordination for the coercions of slavery had been preempted. All in all, declared a white South Carolinian in 1871, "we have gone through one of the most remarkable changes in our relations to each other, that has been known, perhaps, in the history of the world."

Never before in history had so large a group of emancipated slaves suddenly achieved civil and political rights. And the coming of black suffrage in the South in 1867 inspired a sense of millennial possibility second only to emancipation itself. Former slaves now stood on an equal footing with whites, declared a speaker at a mass meeting in Savannah; before them lay "a field, too vast for contemplation." Political mobilization, previously centered in southern cities, now swept across the plantation belt, where the majority of former slaves lived. Throughout the South, one white observer reported, the freedpeople displayed a "remarkable interest in all political information" and were "becoming thoroughly informed upon their civil and political rights." In St. Landry, Louisiana, several hundred freedmen gathered each Sunday at the offices of the local Republican newspaper to hear the weekly issue read aloud.

Traveling speakers urged former slaves to register to vote, and delivered lectures on American history, government, and citizenship. In Monroe County, Alabama, where no black political meeting had occurred before 1867, former slaves crowded around a lecturer, shouting, "God bless you." "Bless God for this." One Freedmen's Bureau official reported from Georgia that "a black man calling himself Professor J. W. Toer" was "traveling about with a magic lantern [the era's version of a slide show] to exhibit what he calls the progress of reconstruction." Toer, a Baptist minister from Florida, displayed scenes of slavery, emancipation, and the valor of black soldiers. Hearing that a black speaker had been killed in a neighboring Virginia county, the Reverend John Givens decided to "go there and speak where they have cowed the black man," and "give them a dose of my radical Republican pills and neutralize the corrosive acidity of their negro hate."

Union Leagues spread throughout the South in 1867, the year when Congress overturned Andrew Johnson's Reconstruction policies and mandated black suffrage for most of the South. The organization had originated among middle-class northerners during the Civil War, to mobilize support for the war effort and the Lincoln administration. The League established itself in the South immediately after the end of the war among upcountry white Unionists and freedmen in large cities. Now, it spread into

An African American speaker addresses a political rally in Richmond, Virginia, during the spring of 1869.

the plantation belt. At local meetings, members discussed the issue of the day and received instruction about "parliamentary law and debating," jury service, and the responsibilities of various political offices. The Union League built upon the institutional infrastructure that black communities had created since the end of slavery, although some local branches also included white members. The local leagues met in schools and churches, planned rallies and parades, and raised funds for mutual aid societies. Local leagues organized cooperative stores, advised freedmen on contract disputes with landowners, and sometimes established their own courts to deal with community disagreements.

While formal membership in the Union League was restricted to adult men, entire families, including women and children, attended league-sponsored rallies and public meetings. Indeed, even as politics came to focus on voting, officeholding, and structured party organization (all restricted to men), women continued to play an active role, expressing their political views by taking part in parades, cheering speakers, shouting slogans, and voting on resolutions passed by mass meetings. Women frequently accompanied members of their families to the polls and wore campaign buttons, even while working in white-owned homes. They publicly rebuked the small minority of blacks—generally individuals such as house servants directly dependent on the goodwill of white employers—who supported the Democratic Party. "I know women," wrote a freedman in Alabama, "who are away from their husbands today because [their husbands] voted the Democratic ticket."

African American activism in 1867 made the old rulers of the South feel all but powerless. William H. Trescot, a prominent South Carolina planter, captured something of the atmosphere in an April 1867 letter about a mass meeting in Charleston, South Carolina:

> There were about 2,000 present. The colored speakers were really admirable speakers—easy, clear, fluent. . . . But the speaker who convinced me how powerless *we* are in the hands of agitators . . . was a speech made by a former attaché of the [New York] Tribune—Solon Robinson, a tall, white bearded old man. He stepped forward to the edge of the stage and looking around exclaimed: "Will some one strike me or shake me? Will anybody wake me up? Am I dreaming—is this Charleston where I came ten years ago to see human beings sold at auction? Are you all here for sale? That is a very good looking field hand. . . . Going, going." And then he suddenly stopped and looking up to the sky pointed upward and went on, "Look yonder—do you see who is bidding for you—the soul of Abraham Lincoln is bidding you

all in for freedom. Lincoln takes the whole lot—gone!" You could feel
the effect of this speech all through the crowd. The old woman in front
of me shouted, "Yes, you old blessed man, hallelujah." What do you
suppose we can say in reply to that?

The Republican Party—the party of Lincoln, emancipation, and black
suffrage—in 1867 became as central to the black community as the church
and school. Laborers left work on Alabama cotton plantations and at Richmond tobacco factories to attend Republican Party rallies. "You never saw
a people more excited on the subject of politics than are the Negroes of the
south," wrote an Alabama overseer in the summer of 1867. "They are per-
fectly wild."

A session during the National Colored Convention in Washington, D.C., in 1869

At mass political meetings in 1867, African Americans staked their
claim to equal citizenship. Blacks, declared an Alabama gathering, deserved
"exactly the same rights, privileges and immunities as are enjoyed by white
men. We ask for nothing more and will be content with nothing less."
Blacks saw no contradiction between racial and community consciousness—taking pride in the service of black soldiers, preferring black teachers for their children and all-black churches in which to worship—and the
vision of a public sphere resting on civic equality and purged of racial dis-

tinctions. Martin R. Delany—an abolitionist known as the "father of black nationalism" because of his support before the Civil War for the emigration of blacks to Africa in order that they might enjoy freedom and political self-determination—became a Republican organizer during Reconstruction. He reported that when he tried to "speak of color" in the South Carolina countryside, he was met with "the angry rejoinder, 'we don't want to hear that; we are all one color now.'"

The political excitement of 1867 inspired direct action to remedy long-standing grievances. Hundreds of blacks took part in sit-ins that integrated public transportation in cities across the South. Individuals expressed the spirit of assertiveness in their day-to-day behavior. "I have all the rights

A composite photograph portrays the men who comprised the Republican coalition in the South Carolina legislature.

that you or any other man has, and I shall not suffer them abridged," one Alabama plantation laborer told his employer (a future governor of the state) after being evicted for attending a political meeting. As in 1865, talk abounded of confiscation and land distribution. At a mass meeting in Savannah, Georgia, Aaron A. Bradley, a former fugitive slave who had helped to organize resistance to the eviction of blacks from nearby "Sherman land," called for the division among black families of plantations belonging to "rich whites." From Virginia, a Freedmen's Bureau agent noted the former slaves' belief that "the property held by their employers has been forfeited to the Government by the treason of its owners, and it is liable to be confiscated."

In 1867, a black political leadership emerged that was far more extensive and diverse than the pioneering activists who had organized political gatherings and land protests in 1865. Resistance to their efforts had likewise become much stronger, and it took remarkable courage for men such as James K. Green to step into the political limelight. In doing so, they literally put their livelihoods and lives on the line. Some black officials prospered in office, but many suffered economic ostracism from white neighbors and sank into poverty. Jefferson Long, a black congressman from Georgia, had commanded "much of the fine custom" of Macon as a tailor before he embarked on his political career. But "his stand in politics ruined his business with the whites who had been his patrons."

Black political leaders faced the constant threat of violence, an endemic feature of post–Civil War southern society. About 10 percent of black officeholders are known to have been the victims of violent threats or assaults. Andrew J. Flowers, a justice of the peace in Tennessee, was whipped by the Klan "because I had the impudence to run against a white man for office, and beat him. . . . They said that they . . . did not intend any nigger to hold office in the United States." At least thirty-five black officials were murdered by the Ku Klux Klan or kindred terrorist organizations during Reconstruction. Richard Burke, a former slave and Baptist preacher elected to the Alabama House of Representatives in 1868, was murdered in 1870. His former owner explained that Burke had "made himself obnoxious to a certain class of young men by having been a leader in the Loyal [Union] League and by having acquired an immense influence over the people of color." But the immediate cause of his murder was that Burke had delivered a speech declaring that blacks had the same right to bear arms as whites.

Despite the danger, thousands of men stepped forward to heed what Green called the "tocsin of freedom." Some had already taken part in the conventions and other activities of 1865 and 1866. Many, like Green him-

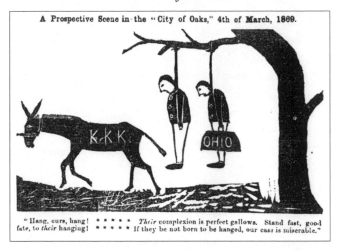

A September 1868 edition of the Democratic Tuscaloosa, Alabama, Independent Monitor—edited by the city's Grand Cyclops of the Ku Klux Klan—proposes the treatment that its Republican opponents should receive if they lose the upcoming presidential election.

self, were new to politics. Individuals of diverse talents and backgrounds, they seized the opportunity presented by Radical Reconstruction for both personal advancement and to try to better the lives of their people.

A considerable number of black political leaders had enjoyed freedom before the war, either from birth or by manumission, purchase, or escape. Some were men of remarkably broad experience. Ovid Gregory, a member of the Alabama Constitutional Convention and legislature, was fluent in Spanish and French and had traveled widely in the United States and Latin America before the Civil War. Hiram Revels, the first black United States senator, had been born free in North Carolina, attended Knox College in Illinois, and in the 1850s preached throughout the Midwest and worked briefly as principal of a black high school in Baltimore. After serving as chaplain to a black regiment during the Civil War, he came to Mississippi in 1865 to work for the Freedmen's Bureau. When Revels took his Senate seat in 1870, not a few newspapers noted the irony that the seat had been vacant since 1861, when Jefferson Davis resigned from the Senate.

Another Reconstruction leader was Mifflin Gibbs, a native of Philadelphia who was active in the antislavery movement, traveled to California in 1850 to seek his fortune in the gold rush, and went on to establish the state's first black newspaper. He subsequently moved to British Columbia (where he served on the Victoria city council), studied at Oberlin College, and eventually made his way to Arkansas, where he became a lawyer, judge,

Mifflin Gibbs in 1902

and influential figure in the Republican Party. His brother, Jonathan Gibbs, had been "refused admittance to eighteen colleges in the country because of [his] color" before finally gaining admission to Dartmouth. After graduating in 1852, Jonathan Gibbs became a Presbyterian minister in Philadelphia. He established a school for former slaves in North Carolina after the war, then moved to Florida, where he served as secretary of state and secretary of education. The Gibbs brothers were among numerous northern blacks who moved south after the end of slavery, one of the few times in American history when the region offered black men of talent and ambition greater opportunities than the North.

In Louisiana, South Carolina, and Virginia—the home of large free black populations before the war—men who had never known slavery dominated among Reconstruction officeholders. For the South as a whole, however, the black political leadership arose out of local slave communities. Some former slaves, such as Blanche K. Bruce, elected in 1875 to the U.S. Senate from Mississippi, had lived privileged lives in bondage.

Blanche K. Bruce

Possibly his owner's son, Bruce had been educated by the same tutor who instructed Bruce's legitimate half brother. Others had experienced fully the horrors of slavery. Richard Griggs, Mississippi's commissioner of immigration and agriculture during Reconstruction, had been sold eighteen times; at one point, he was owned by Nathan B. Forrest, perpetrator of the Fort Pillow Massacre discussed earlier and a founder of the Ku Klux Klan. William H. Heard, a deputy United States marshal in South Carolina, had seen his mother forced to serve as a "breeder" for her owner.

Whatever their individual histories, most former slaves who rose to prominence during Reconstruction had already established themselves as community leaders—as ministers, teachers, skilled workers, Civil War soldiers, or simply men known to possess courage and good judgment. T. Thomas Fortune, later a prominent black editor, explained how his father, Emanuel Fortune, became a member of the Florida Constitutional Convention and legislature: "It was natural for him to take the leadership in any independent movement of the Negroes. During and before the Civil War he had commanded his time as a tanner and expert boot and shoemaker. In such life as the slaves were allowed and in church work, he took the leader's part. When the matter of the Constitutional Convention was decided upon, his people in Jackson County naturally looked to him to shape up matters for them."

Hostile contemporaries portrayed black politicians as travesties of democratic government: ignorant, impoverished, dependent on white dictation, unfit for the power that had been thrust upon them. It is true that, through no fault of their own, most black political leaders had been denied access to education and governmental experience before the Civil War. But the image of the black Reconstruction politician as ignorant and impoverished distorts the historical record. The vast majority were literate, having learned to read and write in schools for free blacks, secretly as slaves, in the Union army, or in institutions established after the war to educate freedpeople. Some attended the new black universities—among them, Howard, Lincoln, Shaw, and Alcorn, established during Reconstruction—or the University of South Carolina after it was racially integrated in 1873. A number, such as Mifflin Gibbs, had studied at Oberlin, in Ohio, one of the few institutions of higher learning to admit black students before the Civil War.

The advent of black officials marked a significant change in the class composition of American government. White politicians in the South tended to be planters, lawyers, and farm owners; in the North, lawyers, professionals, farmers, and urban businessmen predominated. Among black political leaders during Reconstruction, the occupations most frequently represented were farmer, minister, teacher, skilled artisan (carpenter, blacksmith, shoemaker, and the like), storekeeper, and laborer. A few possessed substantial wealth; some held no property at all. The majority were men of modest means.

Throughout Reconstruction, black voters constituted a large majority of the southern Republican electorate. When not deterred by violence, African Americans voted in proportions approaching 90 percent of those eligible. "Irrepressible democrats," as one observer called them, they evinced an intense interest in political events throughout Reconstruction.

But in most states, black votes alone could not bring the Republican Party to power. African Americans constituted over half the population only in South Carolina, Mississippi, and Louisiana, and even there, the party hoped to attract white voters to the cause of Reconstruction. Two groups of whites formed, with blacks, the new Republican coalition; they became known as "carpetbaggers" (newcomers from the North) and "scalawags" (white Republicans native to the South). These derogatory terms, coined by their political opponents, remain an unfortunate but unavoidable part of the vocabulary of Reconstruction.

Opponents castigated carpetbaggers as representatives of the "lowest" and most dishonest class of northerners, who packed all their belongings into a soft-sided valise, or carpetbag, and ventured South to reap the spoils of office. In fact, northerners who became prominent in Reconstruction had generally moved to the region before the advent of black suffrage, when no hope existed that they could enter politics. Most carpetbaggers were Union army veterans who remained in the South after the war for the same reason millions of nineteenth-century Americans moved to the West—the hope of bettering their economic conditions. Many had been businessmen and professionals in the North. With the price of cotton at an all-time high, the region lacking in capital, and land prices having fallen precipitously, many northerners believed that by investing in cotton production they could reap a windfall and at the same time demonstrate the superiority of free labor over slave labor. One Ohioan wrote to a Cleveland newspaper in 1865 from Mississippi: "We should like to see more of our Buckeye friends here. The inducements offered far surpass anything in the west.

Southern Types— The Wolf and the Lamb in Politics.

Two of the resilient stereotypes of Reconstruction politics are portrayed in this contemporary illustration: the corrupt Radical politician and the ignorant and malleable black voter.

Fine improved plantations, convenient to the railroad, are offered from $10 to $25 an acre."

The promised windfall, however, never materialized. Not a few newcomers lost their life savings to the vicissitudes of the weather, Mississippi River flooding, and attacks of the army worm. The advent of Radical Reconstruction propelled many of them into politics—to recoup financial losses and earn a living, to help the Republican Party, or because ex-slaves frequently asked them to run for office. A few carpetbaggers were, as their opponents charged, unscrupulous men who enriched themselves through political corruption. Henry C. Warmoth, recipient of numerous bribes by railroad companies doing business with Louisiana, left that state's governorship a wealthy man and became a prominent sugar planter. More typical was Adelbert Ames, a Union army general who went on to become governor of Mississippi: Ames believed he "had a Mission with a large M" to assist the former slaves.

In states with few native white Republicans, such as Louisiana and South Carolina, northerners garnered a major share of Reconstruction offices. But "carpetbaggers" numbered only a few thousand, far too few to comprise a substantial voting bloc. Most white Republicans during Reconstruction—the so-called scalawags—were southern born. They varied enormously in background and class status. A few emerged from the prewar elite. James L. Alcorn, a native of Illinois, had married the daughter of a Mississippi planter during the 1840s and became one of the state's largest landowners. In 1867, he shocked respectable opinion by joining the Republican Party. "The 'old master,' " he bluntly informed white Mississippians, "has passed from fact to poetry." Black suffrage, Alcorn continued, was here to stay, but if men like him stepped forward to take the lead in Reconstruction, it would become a "harnessed revolution" in which blacks' rights would be respected while political power remained in white hands. In 1869, Alcorn would be elected Mississippi's first Republican governor.

The Republican Party also attracted a number of white southerners who saw the party as the best vehicle for promoting the region's economic development. Georgia's first Republican governor was Rufus Bullock, president of the Macon and Augusta Railroad and director of Augusta's first national bank. Bullock spoke of a "new era" for the state in which the plantation economy would be superseded by railroads, mines, machine shops, and cotton mills, all financed from the North. To him, "economic questions and material concerns" far overshadowed race relations or other Reconstruction issues.

Most scalawags, however, hailed not from the planter or business classes but from among the South's Unionist small farmers. Slavery had been only a minor presence in western North Carolina, eastern Tennessee, northwestern Arkansas, and other upcountry and mountainous areas of the South. Small farmers there had been skeptical about secession from the outset. As the war progressed they became bitterly disaffected from the Confederacy. Some fled the region to join the Union army; others suffered persecution at the hands of Confederate officials and armed bands of vigilantes. These areas supplied thousands of white recruits to the Republican cause.

To upcountry Republicans, the party represented an opportunity to repay those who had victimized them and their families during the war, and to ensure that "rebels" did not regain control of southern government. Others hoped to reverse prewar state policies that had favored the plantation belt over poor white counties. But more than this, to poor upcountry farmers, Republicans represented "the party of progress . . . of popular government, equal liberty, the education and elevation of the masses" as opposed to the oligarchical power structure of the prewar South. Simeon Corley, a tailor who had opposed secession, believed that Republicans spoke for the interests of "the great laboring class," white and black, and would prevent the South from falling "again under the rule of . . . traitors." Only during Reconstruction could a man such as Corley have served a term in Congress representing South Carolina.

Having matured in a slave society, most southern white Republicans shared the region's predominant racism. But they were willing to make common cause with the former slaves to fight their common foe, Confederate planters. "Let no foolish prejudice stand in the way," implored a newspaper in Rutherfordton, a white Republican stronghold in western North Carolina, in 1867. The choice lay between "salvation at the hand of the Negro or destruction at the hand of the rebels." For most scalawags, the political alliance with blacks remained a marriage of convenience, not the result of a sudden conversion to egalitarianism. Yet whatever its origins, the partnership reflected a striking change in southern political life.

Clearly, the Republican Party that came to power in the South in 1867 and 1868 faced a formidable challenge in uniting its disparate constituents—blacks, carpetbaggers, and scalawags. As party conventions gathered in 1867, many found themselves divided. "Confiscation radicals," mostly black, sought to devise policies, including land distribution, to uplift the "poor and humble" of the South. Moderates sought to ensure white control of the new party and a program of economic development more attuned to attracting capital from outside investors than to aiding the poor.

South Carolina's Republican convention, dominated by leaders from Charleston's prewar free black community, adopted a platform that summarized the radical vision of a new social order based on political and economic equality: an integrated public school system; protection of small farmers against having their homes seized for debt; government responsibility to care for "the aged, infirm, and helpless poor"; state-sponsored internal improvements, with blacks and whites enjoying "an equal and fair share" in the awarding of contracts; and heavy taxation on uncultivated land to promote "the division and sale of unoccupied lands among the poorer classes." In Louisiana, carpetbaggers, scalawags, and former free blacks united against demands for land distribution, while adopting a platform calling for "perfect equality before the law," an equal division of public offices between the races, and encouragement of northern immigrants and investment. In Texas, moderate Republicans, primarily interested in a vigorous program of railroad building, held sway.

Events in the North in 1867 and 1868 worked to strengthen the hand of moderates in the South, and dealt a final blow to blacks' hopes for land distribution. When Thaddeus Stevens once again raised the issue of confiscat-

"The operations of the registration laws and Negro suffrage in the South": a pictorial report on the changing southern political landscape in 1867

ing and redistributing the land of "rebel" planters in the spring of 1867, his plan aroused furious opposition in the northern Republican press, even among publications otherwise known for their radicalism. "To this issue," Stevens told the House of Representatives, "I desire to devote the small remnant of my life." But his efforts came at a time when labor conflict was rising in the North, with militant unions conducting strikes and demanding laws mandating an eight-hour workday, and Stevens's speeches inspired fears that the experiment of redistributing property in the South might spark unwelcome demands at home. *The Nation* remarked that for the government to give the freedpeople land would suggest that "there are other ways of securing comfort or riches than honest work." The *New York Times* not only complained that talk of confiscation deterred northerners from investing in the South, but insisted that the idea "strikes at the root of all property rights in both sections." The *Times* condemned Radicals who, it claimed, wanted "a war on property . . . to succeed the war on Slavery." Moderate Republicans were beginning to equate militant ex-slaves with labor radicals in the North.

The reaction to the land issue revealed the limits of Republican radicalism during Reconstruction. The Republican Party's free-labor ideology, so potent a weapon against slavery, envisioned a society of free individuals enjoying equal rights and competing equally in the labor market. It did not condone what *The Nation* called "special favors for special classes of people," which is what land distribution and eight-hour legislation ostensibly represented. Black suffrage in the South would prevent political power from being wielded by whites to keep blacks as a subordinate caste. But few Republicans were prepared to go beyond this. Most white Republicans believed that blacks should and would acquire land, but by working for wages and slowly accumulating savings. "Give the country reconstruction on the basis of universal suffrage," declared a writer in the *Chicago Tribune*, "and it will require but a few years to change the whole structure of society in the South, without confiscation, without vindictive measures of any kind." As for Stevens's plan, according to the *Tribune*, it was nothing more than a "grand larceny scheme."

To counteract pro-confiscation sentiment, Horace Greeley, Henry Wilson, and William D. Kelley—Republican leaders considered radical in the North—toured the South in the late spring of 1867, urging the fledgling party there to abandon hopes for land distribution. Events later that year reinforced the national drift toward moderation. Republicans suffered a series of reverses in the state elections of 1867, which moderates attributed to the "extreme theories" of Stevens and his followers and to the continuing unpopularity among many white voters of black suffrage. Although few Republicans considered abandoning Reconstruction, it was clear that the party in the North would confine itself to defending what had been accomplished, rather than pushing forward.

In the South, the fall of 1867 witnessed an entirely different electoral result. Under the terms of the Reconstruction Act, the first task of the southern states was to hold conventions to draft new state constitutions. In the first biracial elections in the region's history, most whites abstained from voting for convention delegates—an ominous indication of the difficulty of convincing the white population of Reconstruction's legitimacy. But blacks, as one Alabaman reported, "voted their entire walking strength"—their turnout ranged from 70 percent of those registered in Georgia to nearly 90 percent in Virginia. In Rapides Parish, Louisiana, according to a local newspaper, "they came from every portion of the parish and none were left home . . . all were on hand eager and panting for freedom's boon." In every state, the result was a Republican triumph.

Although blacks and whites had already sat side by side at Union League meetings, Republican Party conventions, and mass rallies, the constitutional conventions of 1867–69 were the first biracial governmental bodies in American history. Republicans made up three-quarters of the approximately one thousand delegates. Nearly half were southern whites, and one-quarter had recently arrived from the North. Around one-third of the Republican delegates, 268 in all, were black. The largest number of black representatives served in South Carolina, Louisiana, Virginia, and Florida; the smallest number in Alabama, Arkansas, North Carolina, and Texas, all states with significant cadres of white Republicanism. In South Carolina and Louisiana, the mostly freeborn black delegates formed a majority of the conventions. Elsewhere, however, a majority of the black delegates were former slaves who had emerged as local leaders through service in the Union army and participation in Union League and Republican Party organizing. Outside of Louisiana and South Carolina, most black delegates, as recently freed slaves, had little education or political experience and took little part in convention debates.

The conventions produced progressive documents that in many ways brought southern government into the nineteenth century. They forthrightly announced the principle of equality in the public sphere regardless of race—all citizens, in the words of Louisiana's constitution, would henceforth enjoy "the same civil, political and public rights and privileges, and be subject to the same pains and penalties." They established the region's first state-funded systems of free public education, and in South Carolina and Texas, they made school attendance compulsory. They mandated the establishment of new penitentiaries, orphan asylums, homes for the insane, and in some cases the provision of relief for the poor. All these were far-reaching expansions of public responsibility in a region where government had previously done little more than secure an owner's control over his slaves. The new state constitutions, moreover, abolished such archaic practices of the antebellum era as whipping as a punishment for crime, property qualifications for officeholding, and imprisonment for debt. They reduced the number of capital crimes and in some cases replaced appointive local governments with those comprising officials elected by the people. And South Carolina, for the first time in its history, authorized the granting of divorces.

Nearly all Republicans supported these measures. But the conventions revealed some of the internal divisions that would plague southern Republicanism throughout Reconstruction. The party divided over whether to restrict the voting rights of former Confederates, a step promoted most vociferously by upcountry scalawags determined to punish the "rebels." Many black delegates felt that such restrictions on the right to vote would compromise the party's commitment to universal male suffrage. Mississippi, Virginia, Alabama, and Arkansas included in their constitutions oaths and restrictions meant to bar substantial numbers of ex-Confederates from voting. These provisions, however, soon fell into disuse.

Another source of disagreement was the question of integrated education. All southern Republicans favored the establishment of state-supported public school systems. But many whites, and not a few blacks, preferred the establishment of separate schools for the two races. Most black delegates seemed more concerned with securing long-denied education for their children and employment opportunities for black teachers (who they believed white parents would never accept) than with integrating schools. No new state constitution required racially mixed education, but only Louisiana and South Carolina explicitly forbade school segregation.

As for government-sponsored land redistribution, given the outcry in the North against confiscation, the conventions shied away from that question. South Carolina took the most substantial action, authorizing its legislature to establish a state commission to purchase land for resale on long-term credit. In Louisiana, a proposal to double the tax on uncultivated lands, which some black delegates hoped would force plantation owners to rent or sell to freedmen, was opposed by Democrats and white Republicans and defeated. Generally, the new constitutions' economic provisions focused on efforts to promote railroad development and to attract investment to the impoverished region in other ways.

In the winter and spring of 1868, southerners again went to the polls to ratify the new constitutions and elect new state governments. Democrats launched a furious campaign of opposition to ratification, featuring forthright appeals to racial prejudice. In Alabama, the party sounded what one member called "the battle cry of white man's government." Such appeals often went hand in hand with overt class prejudice. The "dregs of society," complained Jonathan Worth, a North Carolina Democratic leader, were about to assume political power. Worth made it clear that he was speaking of poor whites as well as blacks. For their part, southern Republicans presented themselves as the party of economic and political progress, which would keep "aristocrats and secession oligarchs" from returning to power. Throughout the South, carpetbaggers and scalawags controlled the party machinery. To appeal to white voters, party leaders kept blacks off the state ticket in every state except South Carolina and Louisiana.

For southern Republicans, the electoral results of 1868 were mixed. The black vote remained solidly Republican. In a few states—most notably North Carolina, with its strong tradition of upcountry Unionism—thousands of whites supported the party ticket. But the Republican Party attracted almost no white voters in the Deep South. Nonetheless, the new constitutions won ratification in every state but Alabama, where a white boycott prevented approval by a majority of registered voters (a requirement Congress soon changed to a majority of those actually casting ballots), and Mississippi, where a clause disenfranchising former Confederates alienated nearly all whites. Thus, three years after the defeat of the Confederacy, Republicans came to power in most of the South.

Even as the Reconstruction process played out in the South, political turmoil continued in Washington. Early in 1868, the House of Representatives voted to impeach Andrew Johnson, who became the first president to go on trial before the Senate. The articles of impeachment charged him

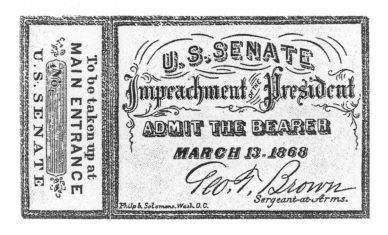

A ticket to attend the Andrew Johnson impeachment proceedings

with violating the Tenure of Office Act, passed over his veto in 1867, which barred the president from removing major officials without the Senate's consent. Johnson had ousted from office Secretary of War Edwin B. Stanton, an ally of the Radicals. Like the later impeachments of Richard Nixon (who resigned before he could be put on trial) and Bill Clinton, Johnson's raised the question of what constituted an impeachable offense—the "high crimes and misdemeanors" specified in the language of the Constitution.

By this time, Johnson had alienated the entire Republican Party. All regarded him as incompetent, stubborn, and racist. A number of moderates, however, doubted the constitutionality of the Tenure of Office Act. Others were reluctant to elevate to the presidency Benjamin F. Wade, the Radical senator from Ohio and, as president pro tem of the Senate, next in line for the White House. An outspoken defender of women's suffrage and labor rights, Wade had recently delivered a speech declaring that with slavery dead, "a more equal distribution of capital must be wrought out." The president's lawyers quietly passed the word that if acquitted, Johnson would stop trying to obstruct Congress's Reconstruction policy. In the end, seven Republicans voted for acquittal, and the margin for conviction stood at 35–19, one short of the two-thirds majority required to remove Johnson from office. Contrary to myth, the Republican Party did not drive out of its ranks the "seven martyrs" who had voted for acquittal.

Despite his acquittal, Johnson's power had been destroyed. As promised, he served out his remaining months in office without trying to interfere with Reconstruction. He was succeeded by Ulysses S. Grant, who defeated the Democratic candidate, Horatio Seymour of New York, in the presidential election of 1868. Still wary of opposition to black suffrage, the Republican platform defended Reconstruction in the South but left the issue of black voting in the North to the voters of each state. Radicals denounced this "defensive" position, but found their influence waning within the party. In August, their most illustrious spokesman, Thaddeus Stevens, died at the age of seventy-six. His wake attracted a throng of mourners to the Capitol that was second in size only to Lincoln's. His body was then transported to Lancaster, Pennsylvania, to be buried in an integrated cemetery in order, according to the epitaph he had composed, "to illustrate in my death the principles which I advocated through a long life, Equality of Man before his Creator."

In sharp contrast to these sentiments stood the language of Francis P. Blair, Jr., the Democratic vice presidential candidate, who proclaimed that a Seymour victory would restore white supremacy to the South and render the new Reconstruction governments "null and void." The Democratic campaign of 1868 was the last by a major party to use white supremacy as its national rallying cry. In campaign speeches, Blair spoke of blacks as "a semi-barbarous race" who "longed to subject the white women to their unbridled lust." In the South, the election was marked by widespread violence. The Ku Klux Klan, founded in 1866 in Tennessee, spread into nearly every southern state, launching what one Republican called a "reign of terror" against the party's rank and file and leaders. James M. Hinds, an Arkansas congressman, was assassinated during the campaign, as were three members of the South Carolina legislature and Benjamin Randolph, a black minister who had served in the state's constitutional convention. Violence was most pervasive in Louisiana and Georgia, where, as a white Republican wrote to Stevens shortly before the great Radical's death, "We can not vote without all sorts of threats and intimidations. Freed men are shot with impunity, all go off as justified homicide." Widespread reports of these atrocities in the northern press strengthened Republicans' commitment to sustain the new Reconstruction governments, lest the South fall under the control of violent ex-Confederates. Only a victory for Grant would enable a free-labor society to take root in the South.

In one respect, the election of 1868 marked a reversal of traditional political roles. Nationally, the Republican Party, for so many years the agent of far-reaching change, campaigned on a promise of order and stability, while Democrats appeared to be virtual (counter)revolutionaries. Northern businessmen feared that Democratic victory would reopen the sectional crisis and perhaps initiate another civil war. They were alarmed by the Democratic platform, which called for paying off federal bonds in paper currency rather than gold, a proposal that would work to the disadvantage of investors who had bought the bonds, since paper money had declined in value. As a result, the business community rallied as never before to the Republican Party. Grant emerged victorious, winning a sweeping majority in the electoral college. But he carried only 53 percent of the popular vote—a result whose unexpected closeness revealed that black suffrage remained unpopular among many white voters. Nonetheless, the North had once again decisively rejected Andrew Johnson's ideas about Reconstruction, now represented by the Democratic Seymour-Blair ticket. Buoyed by black votes, Republicans carried the entire South except Georgia and Louisiana, where violence had made it almost impossible for the party to campaign.

Also in 1868, Iowa and Minnesota voters approved referendums extending the right to vote to their small black male populations. Coupled with Grant's victory, these results emboldened Congress in February 1869 to approve the third and last of the era's amendments to the Constitution. The Reconstruction Act had applied black suffrage only to the South;

when ratified in 1870, the Fifteenth Amendment extended this principle to the entire nation, invalidating racially restrictive voting laws in a majority of the northern states. "[This] must be done," insisted Senator William Stewart of Nevada, the amendment's sponsor. "It is the only measure that will really abolish slavery. It is the only guarantee against . . . oppression. It is the guarantee . . . that each man shall have a right to protect his own liberty."

Even this triumph revealed the waning of the Radical impulse, however. Radical Republicans had desired a far more sweeping Fifteenth Amendment, making voting requirements uniform throughout the nation and allowing all male citizens of a certain age to vote. But many Republicans, in both sections, could not accept such a measure. Some southern Republicans did not wish to void the disenfranchisement of certain "rebels." Northern Republicans opposed surrendering their own voting requirements—a property qualification for immigrant voters in Rhode Island, and prohibitions on Chinese voting in western states such as California. Thus, the Fifteenth Amendment as ratified barred states from discriminating on the basis of race in voting rights, but left the door open to many other qualifications—property, literacy, the payment of a poll tax— that would later be employed to disenfranchise the bulk of black voters in the South.

No one in Congress, moreover, seemed willing to consider allowing women to vote, and the amendment finally severed the old abolitionist-feminist alliance. In May 1869, the Equal Rights Association, an organization devoted to black and female suffrage, debated acrimoniously a proposal to endorse the Fifteenth Amendment. Insisting on the immediate urgency of the situation confronting southern blacks, Frederick Douglass pleaded with the delegates to recognize the amendment as a step toward universal suffrage. But because the Fifteenth Amendment allowed states to continue to bar women from voting, the resolution went down to defeat, and the association disbanded.

Nonetheless, the ratification of the Fifteenth Amendment marked the culmination of the antislavery crusade. The American Anti-Slavery Society dissolved, its work, members believed, now complete. "Nothing in all history," exulted the veteran abolitionist William Lloyd Garrison, equaled "this wonderful, quiet, sudden transformation of four millions of human beings from . . . the auction-block to the ballot box." "At last," proclaimed Douglass, "the black man has a future. . . . The black man is free, the black man is a citizen, the black man is enfranchised. . . . Never was revolution more complete."

Amid the celebrations, a few dissenting voices could be heard. One was

that of the great orator Wendell Phillips, the "golden trumpet" of the abolitionist movement. As victims of "cruel prejudice" and "accumulated
wrongs" because of their enslavement, Phillips warned, the freedpeople
would continue to deserve the nation's "special sympathy," a call that
would be echoed in demands for affirmative action in the twentieth century. Most Republicans, however, believed that the nation had done as
much as could reasonably be expected for the former slaves. "The Fifteenth Amendment," declared Congressman James A. Garfield, "confers
upon the African race the care of its own destiny. It places their fortunes in
their own hands." An Illinois Republican newspaper echoed his sentiment:
"The negro is now a voter and citizen. Let him hereafter take his chances in
the battle of life."

VISUAL ESSAY

ON THE OFFENSIVE

"Here are the dreadful details! Let them aid in preventing such another calamity from falling upon the nation."

These words, by photographer Alexander Gardner, framed a stark collection of photographs of Civil War battlefield dead published in a commemorative album in 1866. During the war, however, these photographs depicting the carnage of the battlefield had transfixed the northern public in a different way. Taken by Civil War photographers Mathew Brady, Timothy O'Sullivan, and others, and displayed in the windows of city photographic salons and disseminated across the North in sets of "3D" stereograph cards, these pictures of battlefield corpses and lonely, crumpled bodies roused a popular bloodlust for vengeance that reinvigorated homeland support for the Union war effort.

No such photographic evidence exists of the atrocities perpetrated by the Ku Klux Klan and others against freedpeople in the South in the two decades after the war. Instead, Reconstruction's supporters had to rely largely on written reports and transcribed testimony both for documentation of the terror to which southern African Americans were subjected and as a means of mobilizing federal action against the violence.

There *was,* however, a different kind of pictorial record of the white southern offensive. Though prints and cartoons were not as incontestable as photographs (for those who believed that the camera didn't lie), they were numerous enough to convince later generations that, even in the face of the predominant interpretations of pro-southern Redemptionist historians, millions of Americans during the 1860s and 1870s *saw* the widespread attack on freedpeople's rights and lives.

Two countervailing visual perspectives dominated the new pictorial order of Reconstruction: the first chronicled the achievements of freedpeople since emancipation; the second told of the violence visited on African Americans in order to halt and then roll back those achievements. With few pictorial resources available in the local northern press and virtually none in the local southern press (engravings were the most practical form of pictorial reproduction in this period but were expensive and technically complicated to produce), visual documentation and commentary about the mounting offensive against freedpeople fell to the small number of national illustrated newspapers. In particular, the rise of the Ku

Klux Klan prompted critical images that recorded specific incidents and a more general sense of the terror that the organization and its kindred associations spread throughout the South.

Harper's Weekly's February 1872 "Visit of the Ku-Klux" pictured

an outrage of frequent occurrence in some of the most turbulent districts of the Southern States. The scene is the interior of a negro cabin, where the little family—fearing no evil—is gathered after the work of the day is over. Suddenly the door is opened, and a member of the Ku-Klux Klan appears, with gun in hand, to take the life of a harmless old man who sits at the fire-place, and whose only "crime" is his color. It is to be hoped that under a rigorous administration of the laws these deeds of violence will soon cease forever.

Most pictorial reportage of racist attacks dealt with the aftermath rather than with the event itself. Perhaps the intent was to spare readers' tender sensibilities, but the pictures nonetheless conveyed the gruesome results of white terror. A major episode of violence depicted in the national press came after the disputed 1872 state elections, when federal troops were sent to Louisiana to enforce a federal court decision in favor of the Republican ticket. Many whites in the state refused to accept that judicial decision. In response, they established a shadow government and organized paramilitary units known as the White League to intimidate and attack blacks and white Republicans. The worst incident of violence was the Colfax Massacre, in April 1873, in which poorly armed black citizens tried to defend the local courthouse. Seventy black men were either burned alive or shot as they tried to escape the building after white attackers set it on fire—but most were executed and thrown in the river after they surrendered. Rather than depict the courthouse battle, *Harper's Weekly* chose to show the chilling scene encountered by the commissioners dispatched by President Grant to investigate the incident, including, "[n]ear the court-

THE LOUISIANA MURDERS—GATHERING THE DEAD AND WOUNDED.—[SEE PAGE 396.]

house . . . a party of colored men and women carrying away a wounded colored man upon a sled. At a little distance in the field were the dead bodies of two colored men. About two hundred yards nearer the court-house were three dead bodies of colored men, and from that point to the court-house and its vicinity the ground was thickly strewn with dead."

Perhaps the gruesome circumstances of the Colfax Massacre dictated what aspect of the outrage was actually selected for the reading public (the vast majority of whom lived in the North). Images either allegorical or specific, which depicted or proposed armed black resistance to the violence—such as this October 1876 Thomas Nast cartoon—were rare.

One of a number of cartoons Nast published in *Harper's Weekly* in the wake of the July 1876 Hamburg, South Carolina, massacre, Nast's "He Wants a Change, Too," decried local whites' excuse for the confrontation and subsequent destruction of the black town: the participation of a black militia in an Independence Day celebration. The cartoon also denounced the continuing intimidation of South Carolina black voters in the ensuing "bloody shirt" election campaign that fall. Most unusual, however, was the

defiant figure of the armed black man standing amid the ruin of his community. Nast's cartoon was the exception to the general pictorial rule: northern white sympathizers may have denounced the victimization of southern freedpeople, but they were more comfortable with the image of the defenseless and undeserving black victim, whose traits were more akin to the abolitionist icon of the beseeching innocent slave than to a more militant and "provocative" symbol such as Nast's. While many northern commentators denounced "race war" in the South, they nonetheless were concerned that African Americans not appear to be provoking conflict, even in the name of self-defense.

The enemies of Reconstruction, however, were not reluctant to promulgate violence, and used images depicting freedpeople exercising their new rights to incite attacks on southern African Americans. Such images, in the form of racist broadsides and posters,

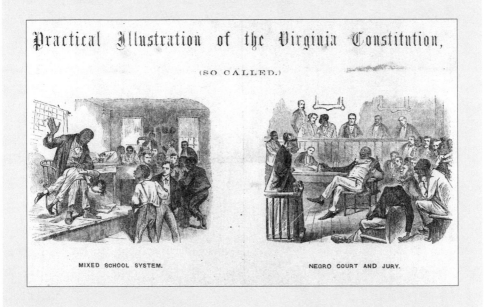

usually emerged during local political contests. With less access to the more sophisticated graphic and print resources available in the North, most of the published threats by southern whites were crudely rendered. This 1867 engraving attacking the new Virginia constitution was unusual in its professional presentation, but it still trafficked in the familiar anti-Reconstruction "bottom rail on top" message that predicted, with the codification of black rights in the Fourteenth Amendment to the U.S. Constitution and the passage of the Civil Rights Act, a reversal of racial positions in southern society.

Like the anti-abolitionist propaganda disseminated before the war, these images sought to inflame white emotions by portraying African Americans in newly privileged positions abusing their former "betters," and often also conveying an unmistakable message of sexual violation.

In tandem with the fate of Reconstruction itself, the promise of a new visual order that

emerged out of the Civil War grew increasingly hollow. Artists and publishers who had previously been allies or at least converts to emancipation's cause, rendering startling new
ways to represent freedpeople's actions and aspirations, returned to the racist conventions
of the past or created new black visual types whose antics mixed a dollop of affection with
larger quantities of condescension and derision.

Former Confederate William Ludwell Sheppard, whose sketches of black political organizing in the early years of Reconstruction had marked a significant departure from previous
depictions of African Americans, re-embraced pictorial accounts that not only romanticized
prewar plantation slavery but also erased any indication of the social revolution that had
emerged with the South's defeat. His 1870 "Merry Christmas and Christmas Gift, Ole

Massa," published in the family magazine *Every Saturday*—typical of his work for the rest of
the century—invented a plantation world in which *nothing* had changed. "This sketch," his
editor explained to the magazine's readers, "would seem to describe Christmas of years
and years ago before the war shattered the domestic institution of the South; but the
change of legal relations has in many instances left undiminished the friendly regard of the
former master and the trustful affection of the former slaves, especially the older ones, and
Christmas morning still witnesses many scenes like that so graphically and faithfully drawn
by Mr. Sheppard."

Even an ardent supporter of equal rights such as Thomas Nast began occasionally to
resort to racial stereotypes in his popular political cartoons—expanding his penchant for
cruel simian caricature that he had previously reserved for Irish Americans. Questioning the

behavior of black members of the South Carolina legislature, Nast's March 1874 "Colored Rule in the Reconstructed (?) State" showed the figure of "Columbia," symbol of the nation, chiding: "You are Aping the lowest Whites. If you disgrace your Race in this way you had better take Back Seats."

Within days of the publication of the *Harper's Weekly* cover engraving, however, Nast got a taste of his own medicine in this answering cartoon on the cover of the *New York Daily Graphic*. Neatly posing a facsimile of Nast's work within its own frame, the *Daily Graphic* cartoon quipped, "I Wonder How *Harper's* Artist Likes To Be Offensively Caricatured Him-self?" In this instance, a betrayal of the promise of a new pictorial order received a very public rebuke.

Perhaps the most durable mani-festation of any pictorial order is in its commemorative forms, with their intention to convey the significance of certain contemporary events and individuals to future generations. Immediately after Abraham Lincoln's death, plans were instituted for a national monument to emancipa-tion, a fitting tribute to the fallen president (the contemporary Lincoln Memorial was a twentieth-century creation). The monument was first financed by contributions from Afri-can Americans, particularly black soldiers. Its plans grew in ambition

and soon came under the sway of sympathetic white sponsors. The original design by New England sculptor Harriet Hosmer highlighted the African American experience from slavery to freedom, culminating with the figure of a black soldier brandishing a rifle. This concept represented a break from earlier traditions of public sculpture, offering both a powerful cel-ebration of Reconstruction and a new form of civic representation of black Americans—the first time a black figure would appear in a national monument. Plans foundered as additional funds for a more sizeable and ambitious installation in Washington, D.C., were sought and other constituencies were wooed for support. Moving through a succession of plans and artists, the designs grew more fragmented and unfocused.

Adequate funding never materialized, and a more modest monument was finally unveiled on the eastern edge of Capitol Hill on April 14, 1876, the eleventh anniversary of Lincoln's assassination. Half-clad, kneeling at the Great Emancipator's feet, the figure of the slave in Thomas Ball's *Freedmen's Memorial to Abraham Lincoln* may have offered a realis-

tic portrait of a black man (based on a photograph of a former slave named Archer Alexander), but his appearance and position offered posterity a message of subservience. In Frederick Douglass's words, overheard at the unveiling ceremony, "it showed the negro on his knee when a more manly attitude would have been indicative of freedom."

The year of this monument's unveiling, 1876, also marked the one hundredth anniversary of the nation's existence, and the celebration reflected a further eroding of the new visual order. The center of the celebration was the lavish Philadelphia Centennial Exposition, an event set forth on 450 acres of technological wonders, national resources, and achievements in art and culture. The fair was more about the future than the past, heralding the nation's triumphant recovery and dynamic growth since its bloody civil war. Although it opened in the third year of the worst economic depression in U.S. history up to that time (a shantytown outside the fairgrounds threatened to compromise the celebration until city officials tore it down), the exposition drew ten million visitors, and every pictorial publication in the nation depicted its attractions for months. But there was little either on the fairgrounds or in print that acknowledged, let alone celebrated, the very recent extraordinary experience of emancipation and Reconstruction.

The work of African American sculptor Edmonia Lewis and painter Edward Mitchell

Bannister were to be found among the fine art exhibits, but, otherwise, black Americans were notable for their absence in almost every aspect of the fair's planning and execution. The Women's Pavilion excluded black women from participation even though they had helped raise money to construct the exhibit. No black workers were hired to construct the fair's buildings, and those who were employed on the grounds during its six-month run did only menial tasks (including work in the Southern Restaurant, where, one guidebook explained, "a band of old-time plantation 'darkies' . . . sing their quaint melodies and strum the banjo").

Undaunted, many African Americans visited the Centennial Exposition, determined to participate in the national celebration. Their efforts even as eager visitors to the fair became grist for the mill of popular artists such as *Harper's Weekly*'s Sol Eytinge, Jr., whose "Blackville" series of comic illustrations offered readers across the country a continuous supply of buffoonlike portrayals of freedpeople.

One extraordinary exception to the racial divide that the Centennial marked both socially and symbolically was the statue of *The Freed Slave,* which stood in the exposition's massive Memorial Hall. Significantly, especially in light of the fate of Ball's Lincoln monument, the bold, life-size figure holding the Emancipation Proclamation aloft and breaking his own chains was not an American effort but sculpted by an Austro-Italian artist, Francesco Pezzicar, and mounted as part of Austria's contribution to the fair. It also was the focus of unusual derision by American commentators. *Atlantic Monthly* editor and later well-known novelist William Dean Howells, for example, called it "a most offensively Frenchy negro, who has broken his chain, and spreading both his arms and legs abroad is rioting in a declamation of something from Victor Hugo; one longs to clap him back into hopeless bondage."

"THE FREED SLAVE" IN MEMORIAL HALL.—From "

But as an engraving published in *Frank Leslie's Illustrated Newspaper* attested—itself a unique pictorial report on the fair—the statue was a magnet for African American visitors of all classes, a powerful visual symbol from abroad that commemorated their hard-fought achievements and, even in the face of violence and faltering federal commitment, their persistent aspirations. The statue (which was returned to Trieste, where it is now housed in the Museo Revoltella, Galleria d'Arte Moderna) was to have no counterpart in the United States for more than a generation.

CHAPTER SIX

THE FACTS OF RECONSTRUCTION

ON THE NIGHT OF October 29, 1869, some thirty disguised men appeared at the home of Abram Colby, an African American who represented Greene County in the Georgia legislature. "They broke my door open," Colby later told a congressional committee investigating the Ku Klux Klan, "took me out of bed, took me to the woods and whipped me three hours or more and left me for dead." Born a slave in Georgia, the son of his owner, Colby had been freed in 1851 and subsequently earned his living as a barber, laborer, and minister. During Reconstruction, he became one of the many thousands who "shouldered the responsibilities" of freedom, in the words of his Alabama contemporary James K. Green. He also represented the threat that freedom posed to the power structure of the Old South.

The assault on Colby took place just as biracial governments were assuming power in every state of the old Confederacy. Overall, these Reconstruction governments present a mixed picture of achievement and failure. Yet their very existence represented a radical transformation in southern life. Radical Reconstruction was a stunning experiment in the nineteenth-century world, the only attempt by a national government in league with emancipated slaves to fashion an interracial democracy from a slave society. In some ways the era's most remarkable development was how Reconstruction affected day-to-day life in local communities. In matters both prosaic and significant, the presence of sympathetic Republican officials made a real difference in the lives of former slaves. By 1870, hundreds of black men were serving as police and justices of the peace and on juries throughout the South, ensuring that whites were prosecuted for crimes against blacks and that black defendants received a modicum of fairness in court. The appearance of black sheriffs, school board officials, and tax assessors in plantation regions—sometimes former slaves evaluating the property of their former owners—symbolized the political revolution wrought by Reconstruction. The assault on Abram Colby, one of countless such incidents during Reconstruction, typified the dangers faced by politically active African Americans. The reaction against Reconstruction was so extreme because the extent of political and social change was so unprecedented.

Colby was typical of local leaders elected to political office once the South's African Americans won the right to vote. Even before the coming of black suffrage, in 1867, Colby had emerged as an outspoken advocate of his fellow freedpeople. In 1866, he organized one of the largest branches of the Georgia Equal Rights Association. On a number of occasions that year, he complained to the Freedmen's Bureau about the myriad injustices suffered by the former slaves. In one petition he asked that blacks in Greene County be empowered to settle disputes among themselves, since they did not enjoy "the most distant shadow of right or equal justice" in the courts of Presidential Reconstruction. Local whites offered him five thousand dollars to abandon his activism. "I told them," Colby related, "I would not do it if they give me all the county was worth." In 1868, Colby was elected to the Georgia legislature.

What brought down the wrath of the Klan, according to the local agent of the American Missionary Association, was that Colby had gone to Atlanta to urge the new state government to provide protection against violence for the area's African Americans, "and [they] had besides as they said, many old scores against him as a leader of the people." Among his assailants, Colby recognized some of the "first-class men in our town. One is a lawyer, one a doctor, and some are farmers." They asked him, he related, " 'Do you think you will ever vote another damned radical ticket?' I said, 'I will not tell a lie. . . . If there was an election tomorrow, I would vote the radical ticket.' They set in and whipped me a thousand licks more." Colby's wife and young daughter witnessed the entire affair. The girl, Colby told the congressional committee, was almost literally frightened to death: "She never got over it until she died. That was the part that grieves me the most."

Well into the twentieth century, historians hostile to Reconstruction castigated the era as a time of "Negro rule." The phrase captured white southerners' sense of living through a terrifying social and political revolution (one that perhaps evoked fear of another Haiti, where in the 1790s slaves had overthrown the slave system and massacred thousands of whites), but did not accurately describe the makeup of Reconstruction government. In most of the South, the reins of power remained largely in white hands. Half the black officials who served during Reconstruction lived in three states— South Carolina, Louisiana, and Mississippi, where African Americans comprised a majority of the population. In the case of South Carolina and

Louisiana, large communities of blacks who had been free before the Civil War stood ready to assume a role in Reconstruction government. Even there, however, African Americans initially accepted a smaller share of offices than their proportion of the party's electorate seemed to entitle them to.

At the top echelons of Reconstruction politics, power remained in white hands. In Alabama, Georgia, North Carolina, Texas, and Virginia, no African American held a major office during Reconstruction. Even in Louisiana, Mississippi, and South Carolina, every Reconstruction governor was white (with the brief exception of P. B. S. Pinchback, the lieutenant governor of Louisiana, who became governor for one month when his pre-

A captured member of the Ku Klux Klan poses for a Holly Springs, Mississippi, photographer after turning state's evidence in the 1871 prosecution of Klan members.

decessor was impeached), and only one, Jonathan J. Wright of South Carolina, won a seat on a state supreme court. Moreover, with white Republicans much better connected with national party leaders than African Americans, whites controlled lucrative federal patronage appointments, the oil of the nineteenth century's party machinery.

Nonetheless, the appearance of African Americans in positions of political power a few years after the end of slavery represented a truly radical transformation in southern and American history. Not only was the old ruling class stripped of political power, but most Reconstruction officeholders, whether white or black, now depended for their positions on the votes of former slaves. Many contemporary observers truly believed that they were living through a revolution.

Unprecedented challenges confronted these new Reconstruction governments. In addition to the mammoth problems of a society devastated by war and bankrupt state treasuries, the governments had to deal with the consequences of emancipation while consolidating a political party that had not even existed in the region a year or two earlier. They faced opponents who monopolized the South's remaining wealth and political experience, denied the very legitimacy of the new regimes and their black voters, and proved quite willing to resort to violence to reassert their positions of power. Given the daunting problems faced by the Reconstruction governments, their accomplishments were indeed remarkable.

Although the course of Reconstruction varied considerably from state to state, three interrelated issues dominated southern politics in these years: education, race relations, and economic policy. Schooling reflected the more general expansion of governmental activism and responsibility during Reconstruction. The creation of tax-supported public school systems in every state of the South stood as one of Reconstruction's most enduring accomplishments. Despite the immense cost of building a new system virtually from scratch and serving a newly doubled citizenry, a public system of education gradually took shape, benefiting both white children and former slaves. By 1875, in states such as South Carolina and Mississippi, half the children of both races were attending public schools. African Americans' thirst for education, so evident at the dawn of freedom, did not diminish during Reconstruction. Young and old flocked to the new schools. A northern reporter in Vicksburg in 1873 observed that "female negro-servants make it a condition before accepting a situation, that they should have permission to attend the night-schools."

Nearly all the schools established in Reconstruction were racially separate. The new state constitutions and laws did not require segregation—as they would after the end of Reconstruction—but white parents overwhelmingly refused to send their children to be educated alongside blacks. Black parents seem to be concerned more with access to the education long denied their families, an equitable division of school funds, and the employment, where possible, of black teachers than with the composition of the student body. One remarkable experiment in integrated education did take place in New Orleans, where the free-black leadership made the racial integration of all public institutions a major priority. Here, thousands of black and white children attended mixed schools by the mid-1870s. Generally, however, whether blacks or whites controlled local boards of education, the schools established during Reconstruction were segregated by race. This was also true for higher education. With the exception of the University of South Carolina, which in 1873 admitted Henry E. Hayne to its medical school (whereupon a majority of the white students withdrew, along with much of the faculty), existing colleges remained all white. These were supplemented by institutions for blacks such as Alcorn, Southern, and Fisk universities, founded by churches, northern aid societies, or the new state governments. Other state institutions also separated people by race. Even the South Carolina School for the Deaf and Blind had separate classes for whites and blacks. Thus, as one historian puts it, "color was distinguished where no color was seen."

But if black parents and leaders seem to have accepted racial segregation in schooling, they simultaneously demanded equal treatment in other realms of public life, especially transportation and public accommodation. Black officials and businessmen deeply resented their widespread exclusion from restaurants, hotels, theaters, and first-class railroad cars. As John M. Brown, a Mississippi sheriff, complained, "Education amounts to nothing, good behavior counts for nothing, even money cannot buy for a colored man or woman decent treatment and the comforts that white people claim and can obtain." Even ordinary freedpeople who could not afford to patronize a fine restaurant or hotel viewed the demeaning treatment meted out to their elected representatives as an insult to the entire black community.

Several of the new state governments outlawed racial discrimination by such businesses. These civil rights measures broke entirely new legal ground. They had no precedent in pre–Civil War American law and roused deep resentment among white Democrats. Many native-born white Republicans also insisted that "social equality" should remain a private matter, beyond the legitimate reach of government. Between 1868 and 1870, moderate Republican governors James L. Alcorn of Mississippi, Harrison Reed of Florida, and Henry C. Warmoth of Louisiana vetoed bills barring railroad companies and other businesses from discriminating against black patrons. On the other hand, South Carolina in 1869 enacted a sweeping series of laws imposing fines and prison terms on those who operated public accommodations that treated citizens unequally. As black influence in the Republican Party grew in the early 1870s, a majority of the southern states passed measures guaranteeing all citizens "full and equal rights" in access to transportation and places of public entertainment and business. Such laws proved difficult to enforce, but they reflected African Americans' vision of a color-blind society in which all citizens would enjoy the same treatment before the law and in all realms of public life.

The third preoccupation of Reconstruction politics, economic policy, revealed how much Republican rule changed southern government but also highlighted the enduring tensions within the party. For the first time in southern history, legislatures sought to bolster the economic power of

LEX AFRICANUS.

Trafficking in racist caricature, this 1874 cartoon also captures the unprecedented nature of antidiscriminatory legislation. "But I don't want to sleep with a Negro," exclaims a guest when confronted by the proprietor of a crowded hotel. "Well, it's the only double bed in the house," is the response, "and if I don't give him half of it I shall have to pay him five hundred dollars damages. You may either sleep with him or go into the street."

laborers rather than of planters. Lawmakers swept away the remnants of the Black Codes, with their coercive apprenticeship systems and limits on the former slaves' economic options. They enacted measures that gave agricultural workers, rather than other creditors, first claim on an employer's assets when payment was due. They prohibited the discharge of laborers for political reasons and required that, in the event of eviction, sharecroppers be compensated for work they had already done. "Now there is a law that allows a man to get what he works for," commented Florida black legislator Robert Meacham—quite a change from the days of slavery or even Presidential Reconstruction. "Under the laws of most of the Southern States," a South Carolina planter complained in 1872, "ample protection is afforded to tenants and very little to landlords."

When it came to the former slaves' continuing quest for land, however, Reconstruction governments took few concrete actions. South Carolina did establish a state land commission, which purchased farms for resale to black families on generous terms. By 1876, perhaps one-seventh of the state's African Americans, along with a handful of poor whites, had been settled on land of their own. But Republicans in Washington, along with many party leaders in the South, still adhered to the idea that advancement must come through individual initiative rather than governmental fiat. As a result, the hopes of the mass of the South's freedpeople for land of their own remained unfulfilled. Instead, by the early 1870s, the system of sharecropping had come to dominate agriculture in the cotton South—a system in which individual black families rented portions of a plantation and split the crop with the land-owner at the end of the year. Sharecropping offered blacks considerable day-to-day autonomy in their working and social lives. No longer did they labor under the direction of an employer or over-seer, and no longer could a white person determine whether women and children worked in the fields. Yet given the falling price of cotton and the high cost of credit from local merchants, share-cropping offered few farmers a route to land-ownership.

Rather than pursu-ing direct action to uplift the poor, Reconstruction governments invested their hopes for change in a program of regional economic development,

While many white artists dabbled in romantic visions of the rural South, Thomas Anshutz's 1879 The Way They Live *captured the hardship of subsistence farming in the post-Reconstruction South.*

with railroad construction as its centerpiece. There was nothing unusual in governmental promotion of economic activity in nineteenth-century America. Before the Civil War, state and local authorities throughout the country had helped to finance all sorts of economic enterprises. But the scope and ambition of Reconstruction aid differed markedly from prece-dents in the South. Before the war, southern railroads had served as adjuncts to the plantation system. Their primary purpose was to facilitate getting cotton to market. During Reconstruction, however, Republicans hoped to create a far larger and more integrated railroad network, to spur the emergence of a diversified economy of booming factories, bustling towns, and a diversified agriculture freed from the plantation's dominance. This, in turn, would offer black and white southerners far more opportuni-ties for economic advancement. "A free and living republic," said one Tennessee Republican, would "spring up in the track of the railroad as inevitably, as surely as grass and flowers follow in the spring."

The new state governments offered generous financial aid to railroad companies that pledged to begin construction in the South. They also used tax incentives and direct assistance to lure northern investment in factories and other enterprises. Many Democrats, who sat on the boards of regional railroad companies, supported these measures. Black lawmakers, like white, pressed for aid to projects that promised to benefit their constituents. In the end, however, the railroad program failed to fulfill its promise. Between 1868 and 1872, more than three thousand miles of track were laid in the South, but this progress was largely confined to Georgia, Alabama, Arkansas, and Texas. The other states had little to show for their generosity to railroad companies except rising debts. Overall, expenditures on economic development produced rising state budgets and tax rates and declining state credit, but few significant benefits.

The entire railroad program, moreover, was marred by corruption. The rapid growth of state budgets, because of the new school systems and economic development programs, and the benefits to be gained from state aid led to a scramble for influence that produced bribery, insider dealing, and a get-rich-quick atmosphere. Given the prevailing "social discord," commented one New Yorker, the South was "the last region on earth in which . . . a Northern or European capitalist [would] invest a dollar." With political instability deterring many northern investors (who preferred to put their capital in the more tranquil West), the South attracted marginal and often shady entrepreneurs who were willing to pay off state officials for a share of

Inspired by Mary Shelley's novel about a man-made monster, this cartoon depicts the railroad as "The American Frankenstein" trampling the rights of the American people.

governmental largesse but were prone to pocketing state aid rather than actually using it for railroad construction.

Reconstruction's opponents, and generations of subsequent historians, seized on the corruption issue to castigate blacks as "unfit" for the right to vote. Bribery and favoritism, however, were hardly confined to the Reconstruction South. This was the era, after all, of the Tweed Ring, which pillaged New York City's municipal coffers, and the Whiskey Rings, Crédit Mobilier scandal, and other frauds that brought down members of President Grant's cabinet and leading members of Congress. Moreover, if some Republicans, black and white, participated in corruption, by the early 1870s others were leading drives that cleaned up public life and effectively put an end to the program of railroad aid that had spawned the illicit gains. But corruption handed Reconstruction's opponents a way of discrediting the new southern governments, and it also drained away money that could more usefully have been spent on schools and other regional needs.

Given the unprecedented challenges and intense opposition Republican leaders faced, political unity should have been their first priority. Yet factionalism weakened the party in many states. In some cases, walkouts and fistfights marred Republican conventions. In Louisiana, the Republican legislature impeached the Republican governor; in Alabama, Governor William H. Smith and Senator George Spencer, both Republicans, headed rival factions that competed for federal patronage. Moderate Republican governors such as Robert K. Scott of South Carolina and James Alcorn of Mississippi sought to expand the party's base of support by appointing white Democrats to office, to the dismay of loyal Republicans. Scalawags complained that carpetbaggers were monopolizing important positions and connections to party leaders in Washington. The precarious economic position of most Republican leaders intensified the struggle for office. Carpetbagger, scalawag, and black alike, they depended on office for their livelihoods.

The party infighting increasingly alarmed black leaders. Although in cities such as New Orleans and Mobile considerable friction emerged between prewar free blacks and former slaves, black politicians generally seemed to place a greater premium on party unity than did their white counterparts. Nonetheless, as time went on, they became more assertive in party affairs, even if it meant offending white Republicans. At the outset of Republican rule, white leaders urged blacks to moderate their claims to office, so as not to alienate white voters. At first, black leaders heeded such pleas. In Georgia, they "went from door to door in the 'negro belt,' " seeking whites who would stand as Republican candidates. Increasingly, however, they became unwilling to accept the role of junior partners in the Republican coalition.

By the early 1870s, black leaders demanded a larger share of political power, especially in states where former slaves comprised a majority of the electorate. Of the sixteen blacks who sat in Congress during Reconstruction, most were elected during the 1870s. In South Carolina, black leaders in 1870 demanded and received half the eight executive offices. The number of black lawmakers increased steadily, until by the mid-1870s they made up a majority of the South Carolina legislature. In Mississippi, black leaders opposed to Governor Alcorn's conciliatory policy toward former Whigs like himself and to his refusal to approve civil rights legislation organized former Union general Adelbert Ames's successful run for governor in 1873. At the local level, too, blacks became dissatisfied with being used as "stepping stones to office" by whites. The growing black presence in office reflected the maturing of grassroots politics in black communities across the South. But it drove a number of white Republicans (Alcorn included) into the ranks of the Democrats.

During Reconstruction, enclaves of black political power existed throughout the South. In Edgefield County, South Carolina, blacks held the offices of sheriff, magistrate, school commissioner, and officer of the state militia. In the plantation belt along the Mississippi River, blacks by the early 1870s had taken control of county boards of supervisors. They raised taxes on plantation lands, established schools and charitable institutions, and embarked on road building and other construction projects to improve black communities. Many local black leaders were remarkably young. Most of Edgefield County's black officials had not reached the age of twenty-five when they assumed office. Indeed, by the early 1870s, a new generation of political leaders began to replace the organizers of 1865–67. In St. Landry Parish, Louisiana, for example, freedmen in 1873 for the first time outnumbered the freeborn on the Republican executive committee.

In some areas, Reconstruction altered the balance of power between laborers and employers at the local level. Planters throughout the South complained that Republican officials did nothing to discourage vagrancy and theft and that they interfered in plantation disputes on behalf of former slaves. Unlike in the days of slavery and Presidential Reconstruction, planters could not turn to the state to impose discipline on their labor force. In Terrebonne Parish, Louisiana, the parish court in 1869 ordered a sugar planter to sell his crop in order to settle back wages owed to his laborers, even if his other debts remained unpaid. Local authorities employed blacks, whites, and Chinese laborers to work repairing the Mississippi River levees. In a repudiation of previous practice, all received the same wages. As the chief engineer reported, whites "were a little disgusted at not being allowed double (colored) wages, and the Chinamen were astonished at being allowed as much and the American citizens of African descent were delighted at being '*par.*' "

One of the most compelling stories of the Reconstruction era took place in McIntosh County, Georgia. There, in the heart of the antebellum rice kingdom, the home of some of the state's wealthiest aristocrats, trial justice Tunis G. Campbell established a center of black political power that left local planters complaining of being rendered "powerless" to enforce discipline among their workers. Campbell had a long career of activism. A native of New Jersey, he had been educated in New York and worked at various times as a barber, minister, and hotel steward. He participated before the Civil War in campaigns for black suffrage, abolitionism, and temperance, and had helped to establish African American schools and churches.

Campbell came to Beaufort, on the South Carolina Sea Islands, in 1863, "to instruct and elevate the colored race," bringing with him three thousand dollars of his own money. Two years later, while employed by the Freedmen's Bureau, he organized black settlements on St. Catherine's and Sapelo islands in Georgia, complete with their own governments, militia units, and schools, and divided land among the former slaves. When the bureau dissolved his Republic of St. Catherine's, Campbell moved to the mainland, where he rented a plantation from a Unionist white landowner and leased small plots to black families. Campbell won election both as a member of the state senate from McIntosh County and as a local justice of the peace. He appointed black constables to assist him, insisted that juries include an equal number of black and white members, and ordered the arrest of employers accused of abusing or cheating their laborers.

So significant was this kind of transformation of political power at the local level that constituents invested Republican officeholders with even more authority than they really possessed. John R. Lynch—a slave in Louisiana freed by the Union army in 1864, educated in a Natchez, Mississippi, school established by northern aid societies, and appointed justice of the peace by military governor Ames in 1869—wrote about his experiences in *The Facts of Reconstruction* (1913), one of the first works to challenge the then-dominant portrayal of Reconstruction as a time of corruption and misgovernment. Lynch recalled how the former slaves "magnified" his office "far beyond its importance," bringing him cases ranging from disputes with their employers to family quarrels. Ordinary Republicans of

John R. Lynch

both races also deluged the South's new governors with letters detailing their grievances and aspirations, requesting financial assistance, and seeking advice about all kinds of public and private matters. "We consider ourselves under your protection [and] care," one family wrote to William W. Holden, the Republican governor of North Carolina. In part, such letters reflected the political inexperience of so much of the southern Republican electorate, black and white alike. But they also poignantly revealed that whatever the new governments' failures, the aspirations of the former slaves for a better life depended on the survival of Radical Reconstruction.

By the early 1870s, biracial democratic government, something unprecedented in American history, was functioning throughout the South. Grounded in the families, churches, schools, and political institutions of the black community—the institutional infrastructure originating in slavery and consolidated after emancipation—former slaves continued to evince a powerful political activism and exercised a considerable degree of political power. Meanwhile, the old planter elite had been evicted from political power.

Years later, a black Reconstruction legislator in South Carolina named Thomas Miller would recall the era's achievements: "We were eight years in power. We had built schoolhouses, established charitable institutions, built and maintained the penitentiary system, provided for the education of the deaf and dumb . . . rebuilt the bridges and reestablished the ferries. In short, we had reconstructed the State and placed it upon the road to prosperity." In enumerating Reconstruction's accomplishments, Miller failed to note its shortcomings, among them political corruption and party factionalism. Most important, former slaves by and large remained desperately poor, and their desire for land had not been fulfilled.

Yet even as Reconstruction's failures betrayed the hopes that African Americans had invested in the new governments, the very existence of this experiment in interracial democracy was anathema to those accustomed to controlling the South's destiny. Undeterred by federal and state laws and the rewritten Constitution, they launched a violent campaign to bring Reconstruction to an end.

Violence, of course, was an intrinsic element of the slave system and had been endemic in large parts of the South since 1865. In the immediate aftermath of the Civil War, it was localized and seemingly random, directed against individual freedmen who acted in ways that flouted the conventions of slavery and especially against those unwilling to work under conditions dictated by whites. Sometimes, as in the Memphis and New Orleans riots of 1866, violence swept over entire communities. But the coming to power of Republican governments stimulated its rapid expansion.

The depredations of the Ku Klux Klan and kindred groups such as the White Brotherhood and the Knights of the White Camelia were more organized and more overtly political than earlier violence, not only in the sense of aiming to influence elections and overturn Reconstruction governments, but also in seeking to affect power relations between the races throughout the South. One victim complained of a "reign of terror" in his county, and, indeed, the Klan during Reconstruction offers the most extensive example of homegrown terrorism in American history.

In 1870, the Senate and House of Representatives authorized investigations into the problem. They sent a joint committee into the South to take testimony from public officials, army officers, victims of violence, and, on occasion, Klansmen themselves. Widely reported in the press, the Ku Klux Klan hearings of 1870–71, which yielded thirteen thick volumes of firsthand testimony, revealed to the country an almost incredible campaign of criminal violence by whites determined to punish black leaders, disrupt the Republican Party, reestablish control over the black labor force, and restore white supremacy in every phase of southern life. The Klan concentrated its attacks on the individuals and institutions responsible for the dramatic changes in southern society resulting from Radical Reconstruction.

Testimony by friends of murder victims and by survivors of Klan attacks revealed the organization's methods and the kind of individuals who became its targets. Abram Colby was only one of numerous black leaders who told the investigators of having to face daily threats of violence. Scores received death threats, were driven from their homes, or were assaulted or murdered. In parts of the South, black leaders lived, as Congressman Richard H. Cain of South Carolina noted, "in constant fear."

Frequently, the Klan set out to destroy the Union League and the local Republican Party. Jack Dupree was murdered in Monroe County, Mississippi, in 1870 because he was "president of a republican club" and was known as a man who "would speak his mind." The Klan's purposes, however, were not confined to electoral politics. In a sense, the organization took on the function of the antebellum slave patrols: making sure that blacks

Members of a Senate committee hear the testimony of a New York schoolteacher who was tortured by the Ku Klux Klan.

did not violate the rules and etiquette of white supremacy. "They do not like to see the Negro go ahead," commented a white farmer from Mississippi. Frequently, blacks who had managed to acquire land became targets of reprisal, as did laborers who stood up for their rights on plantations. Victims included a black woman whipped for "laziness" and freedmen beaten for "suing white men" in court. In Noxubee County, Mississippi, according to a former Confederate officer, the Klan aimed "to keep them from renting land, so that the majority of the white citizens may control labor." In 1869, Georgia Klansmen lynched a freedman and his wife accused of "resenting a blow from their employer," and murdered a blacksmith who refused to work for a white employer until being paid for previous labor.

"There is an eternal hatred," observed a committee of Tennessee lawmakers in 1868, "existing against all men that voted the Republican ticket, or who belong to the Loyal League, or [are] engaged in teaching schools, and giving instruction to the humbler class of their fellow men." Ministers, teachers, and other African Americans who sought to uplift their people became targets of violence. In the first half of 1871 alone, Klansmen destroyed twenty-six schools in Monroe County, Mississippi. A white mob attacked the home of South Carolina freedman Thomas S. Jones and drove him to seek refuge "in swamps and woods," because, he related, "they say I shall not teach school any longer." Another group of victims were black men accused of showing disrespect for white women or, in some cases, of sexual assault (although in most instances, the latter charge was invented after the fact to justify the acts of violence).

Some locales gained a national reputation for extreme violence. One was Jackson County, in the Florida Panhandle. "That is where Satan has his seat," remarked a black clergyman; more than 150 persons were murdered in Jackson, including black political leaders and Samuel Fleischman, a Jewish merchant resented by local whites for voting Republican and dealing fairly with black customers. As Fleischman's fate demonstrates, while the large majority of victims of violence were black, whites associated with Reconstruction or deemed to have violated the Klan's definition of proper relations between the races were also terrorized. Hundreds of Republicans were whipped and saw their property destroyed in Spartanburg County, in the largely white upcountry of South Carolina. White women who violated the taboo against "miscegenation" by engaging in sexual liaisons or establishing long-term relationships with black men sometimes suffered violent reprisals. Klansmen murdered three white Republican members of the Georgia legislature and drove ten others from their homes. "They beat and cut me with knives," reported one white victim, a teacher in a black school, "for I had often spoken of the colored people of this place and said they ought to have learning the same as the whites. . . . I am in for equal rights and that was the cause they done me so."

On occasion, violence escalated from assaults on individuals to mass terrorism or even local insurrections. On the day after Republicans carried Laurens County, South Carolina, in the election of 1870, armed bands of whites scoured the countryside, driving 150 blacks from their homes and killing thirteen, including a member of the legislature. In Meridian, Mississippi, rioting in 1871 left some thirty blacks dead, including "all the leading colored men of the town with one or two exceptions." The bloodiest single act of carnage in Reconstruction took place in Colfax, Louisiana, in 1873, where fifty or more members of a black militia unit were massacred after surrendering to armed whites who had assaulted the town with a small cannon.

Klansmen frequently disguised themselves while committing illegal acts (they wore no standard costume; their familiar white robe and headdress is a twentieth-century invention). Nonetheless, like Abram Colby, many victims were able to identify their assailants. Although criminals who traveled at night tended to be mainly young single men, the Klan included many men of substance—planters, lawyers, newspaper editors, merchants, even ministers. "The most respectable citizens are engaged in it," reported an agent of the Freedmen's Bureau, "if there can be any respectability about such people." A number of former Confederate generals served as Klan

Freedpeople hiding in the Louisiana swamps

leaders, among them John B. Gordon, Democratic candidate for governor in Georgia in 1868.

Of course, most white southerners did not commit criminal acts, and some spoke out against the Klan. But the large majority of southern whites remained silent. Indeed, the Democratic Party's constant vilification of carpetbaggers and scalawags as corrupt incompetents, their insistence that blacks were unfit for equal citizenship, and their public laments about the intractability of black labor created an atmosphere that made violence seem a legitimate response in the eyes of many white southerners. Community support for the Klan extended to lawyers who represented the criminals in court, editors who established funds for their defense, and the innumerable women who sewed costumes and disguises for them. While most white southerners were law-abiding citizens, they seemed willing to forgive the Klan's excesses because they shared the organization's ultimate goal—the overthrow of Reconstruction and the restoration of white supremacy.

The widespread violence posed a difficult dilemma for Republicans, north and south. By the early 1870s, very few federal troops remained in the South—in Louisiana, for example, they numbered fewer than five hundred. In states such as Tennessee, Arkansas, and Texas, where they could draw on a considerable force of white Republicans, Reconstruction governors mobilized the militia and dealt effectively with the Klan. In some localities, blacks succeeded in banding together to fight the Klan, relying on the paramilitary organization that had sprung up around the Union Leagues. In 1868, armed members of the Union League patrolled the streets of Wilmington, North Carolina, and succeeded in enforcing order against Klan threats to disrupt the election to ratify the new state constitution.

Generally, however, the scale of violence outstripped the response of the new and weak Reconstruction governments, and of ad hoc local arrangements. Republican governors such as James L. Alcorn of Mississippi, William H. Smith of Alabama, and Henry C. Warmoth of Louisiana hoped to expand their base of support among white voters. They proved extremely reluctant to deploy a predominantly black militia, fearing this would further alienate local whites. Warmoth did create the Metropolitan Police Force, commanded by former Confederate general James Longstreet, to keep order in New Orleans, but failed to take action against violence in rural parts of the state.

Part of the problem was that blacks took democratic and legal procedures more seriously than did Reconstruction's opponents. To be sure, blacks sometimes intimidated, ostracized, or assaulted fellow freedmen who wished to vote Democratic. But no Republicans rode at night to murder their political foes. "We could burn their churches and schoolhouses," wrote one former slave from a violent section of Georgia, "but we don't want to break the law or harm anybody. All we want is to live under the law."

Increasingly, Reconstruction governors appealed to Washington for aid. Only "power from without," said one southern Republican leader, could restore order and save Reconstruction. In the early 1870s, national Republican leaders responded. "I am willing," said Senator John Sherman of Ohio, "to . . . again appeal to the power of the nation to crush, as we once before have done, this organized civil war." In 1870 and 1871, Congress enacted three Enforcement Acts, meant to suppress violence in the South. Most sweeping was the Ku Klux Klan Act of 1871, one of the most far-reaching measures of the Reconstruction era. The Fourteenth and Fifteenth amendments and the Civil Rights Act of 1866 had been directed primarily against discriminatory action by state and local governments. Now, for the first time in American history, certain crimes committed by individuals were declared offenses punishable under federal law, including conspiracies to deprive citizens of the right to vote, hold office, serve on juries, and enjoy the equal protection of the laws. The KKK Act allowed the president to suspend the writ of habeas corpus (that is, to have individuals arrested and held without charge) and use the army to suppress Klan violence.

Traditionally, private criminal acts had been punished under state law. The unprecedented expansion of the federal government's criminal jurisdiction outraged Democrats and alarmed even some Republicans in the North. The Ku Klux Klan Act, complained *The Nation*, armed the federal government with power "over a class of cases of which it has never hitherto had, and never pretended to have, any jurisdiction whatever." To most Republicans, however, the act seemed a logical extension of the expansion of national power wrought by the Civil War and already embodied in Reconstruction legislation. "If the federal government," asked former Union army general Benjamin F. Butler, now representing Massachusetts in Congress, "cannot pass laws to protect the rights, liberty, and lives of citizens . . . why were guarantees of those fundamental rights put in the Constitution at all?" Black congressmen staunchly supported the new measures. While Democrats charged Congress with violating constitutional guarantees of state autonomy, a black Republican member of the House of Representatives, Joseph Rainey of South Carolina, responded: "Tell me nothing of a constitution which fails to shelter beneath its rightful power the people of a country." Robert B. Elliott, another black congressman from South Carolina, caustically noted that Klan violence refuted southern whites' claims to superior morality and a higher level of civilization. "Pray tell me," he asked, "who is the barbarian here?"

Members of the Ku Klux Klan of Moore County, North Carolina, prepare to execute a victim in August 1871.

Employing the powers of the Enforcement Acts, President Grant in 1871 sent federal marshals into the South to crush the Ku Klux Klan. The marshals arrested hundreds of men. While most escaped punishment by promising to desist from violent activities, leaders of the organization went on trial in federal court and some received prison sentences. In South Carolina, Grant suspended the writ of habeas corpus in nine upcountry counties. Federal troops occupied the area and arrested perhaps two thousand Klansmen. A few dozen of the worst offenders were indicted; most pleaded guilty and went to prison. By 1872, the reign of terror was, temporarily at least, over. The election of that year was the most peaceful in the entire Reconstruction era. But violence had helped Democrats regain political control in Tennessee (in 1870) and Georgia (in 1871) and had destroyed the infrastructure of the Union Leagues in local communities in many parts of the South.

Even as the Grant administration acted decisively against violence in the South, it confronted new challenges in the North. With the question of Reconstruction supposedly settled, new political questions came to the fore, as industrial workers demanded that state governments enact laws guaranteeing an eight-hour workday and farmers sought state intervention to combat what they considered unfair practices by railroads. These groups in the North called on the activist state spawned by the Civil War and Reconstruction to redress their own grievances, and they sought to extend the Reconstruction principle of equality into economic relations within the North.

The rise of these issues reflected the North's own transformation during the Civil War era. Although hardly as sweeping as the destruction of slavery in the South, the North experienced an economic revolution of its own, as manufacturing output expanded rapidly and the railroad knitted the country into a single giant market. The rapid expansion of agriculture, mining, and railroad construction in the trans-Mississippi West exemplified the shift from Lincoln's America—the world of the small farm and artisan workshop—to a mature industrial society. As in the South, the sudden appearance of large corporations seeking favors from the state fueled political corruption. "The galleries and lobbies of every Legislature," one Illinois Republican complained, "are thronged with men seeking to procure an advantage" for one economic interest or another. Frequently, they were successful. Northern legislatures awarded thousands of special grants and privileges to railroad, manufacturing, and mining companies, often businesses in which key lawmakers held stock or directorships. Increasingly, the Republican Party was taking on a new identity: along with its cherished history of preserving the Union and emancipating the slaves, it developed closer and closer ties to business corporations and, through railroad land grants, high tariffs, and other largesse, sought to promote business interests and economic development.

The presidential campaign of 1872 revealed the impact of these changes on the Republican Party, and on northern perceptions of Reconstruction. A key group of party leaders was more and more estranged from the Grant administration. They included influential founders of the Republican Party such as Carl Schurz of Missouri and Lyman Trumbull of Illinois, and prominent editors and journalists such as E. L. Godkin of *The Nation* and Samuel Bowles of the *Springfield Republican*. Initially, their disaffection with the Grant administration had little to do with Reconstruction. These self-styled "best men" were alarmed by the corruption that seemed to pervade northern politics, and by what they considered the degradation of a party increasingly under the control of local political machines and bosses and susceptible to manipulation by the corporate elite. These reformers also found disturbing the rising tide of labor and farmer unrest in the North. Now that the legal framework of equality had been achieved, they insisted, the government should step back and let the economy develop according to its own internal laws. Corporate demands for land grants and high tariffs, labor's call for an eight-hour day, and laws passed by certain western states attempting to regulate railroad rates all represented, in the reformers' eyes, illegitimate examples of "special legislation"—measures that violated the principle of equality by favoring one interest in society over others.

This combination of machine politics, political corruption, and new demands on government spurred reformers to action. Some were former Radical Republicans, firmly committed to the Reconstruction agenda of equal rights for all. But by 1870, Radical Republicanism as a coherent political movement was rapidly disintegrating. Stevens had died, and veteran Radicals such as Benjamin F. Wade of Ohio and George Julian of Indiana failed to win reelection. Unlike during the battle with Andrew Johnson, divisions between Radicals and moderates no longer defined groupings within the Republican Party. More important was one's relationship to the Grant administration and attitudes toward the role of government itself.

Much of the degradation of politics, the reformers believed, resulted from the power of demagogues who thrived on corruption and played on the misguided desire of working-class voters for government action on their behalf. The solution was somehow to oust the bosses from power and place government in the hands of educated men devoted to the public good—the reformers themselves. One way to do this would be to reduce the number of those eligible to vote. "Expressions of doubt and distrust in regard to universal suffrage are heard constantly," one journalist commented. Reformers recognized that measures such as property qualifications for voting, abandoned in every state before the Civil War, stood little chance of enactment. More viable was their most cherished proposal—

eliminating party patronage by basing appointment to government posts on competitive examinations, not political connections.

Initially, the reform revolt had little to do with Reconstruction. Increasingly, however, the language in which anti-Grant Republicans condemned northern politics echoed white complaints against the new governments in the South. The alleged corruption of carpetbaggers seemed to parallel the depredations of political bosses in the North. Black demands for land seemed analogous to northern labor's pressure for legislation on its own behalf. Complaints by the South's planters, merchants, and prewar politicians that the region's "natural leaders" had been excluded from power in favor of "ignorance, stupidity and vice" (the words of a declaration by South Carolina Democrats in 1868) paralleled the reformers' sense that less-than-able men had pushed themselves to the side in the North. Violence and corruption in the South, reformers became convinced, arose from the fact that Reconstruction had not won the allegiance of "the part of the community that embodies the intelligence and the capital." By 1872, anti-Grant Republicans had concluded that new policy departures had become necessary to restore the "best men" to power in the South as well as the North.

Unable to prevent Grant's renomination in 1872, the dissidents held their own convention in Cincinnati in May, at which they nominated newspaperman Horace Greeley for president. They called themselves Liberal Republicans. Greeley's nomination resulted from behind-the-scenes maneuvering

Entitled "Clasp Hands over the Bloody Chasm," Thomas Nast's August 1872 cartoon denounces the Liberal Republican Party's presidential platform.

of the kind reformers condemned among Grant's supporters. And he was certainly an odd choice as the reformers' candidate for president. Greeley had a history of erratic judgment, such as when he supported peaceable secession in the winter of 1860–61, or tried to negotiate an end to the Civil War in 1864. Even though most Liberals favored free trade, Greeley had long supported the protective tariff, and he had never shown much interest in the reformers' pet scheme, civil-service reform. But as editor of the *New York Tribune* and a longtime foe of slavery and defender of blacks' rights, Greeley was widely respected throughout the North (even though, by 1870, he had declared that it was time to end Reconstruction: "the country is sick and tired of it," he claimed).

Realizing that the Republicans' split offered them a golden opportunity to repair their political fortunes, Democrats endorsed Greeley (a difficult decision, since he had spent much of his political career denouncing the Democratic Party). Many Democratic voters could not stomach their party's official candidate, who, at one time or another during his long career, had referred to Democrats as "murderers, adulterers, drunkards, cowards, liars, and thieves." Large numbers stayed at home, and Greeley went down to a devastating defeat. Grant carried every state north of the Mason-Dixon Line. But despite the debacle, the Greeley campaign placed on the northern agenda the one issue on which he, the reformers, and the Democrats could agree—a new policy toward the South. Opposition to Reconstruction had become linked to the crusade for political reform and good government. Greeley's campaign gave unprecedented national attention to complaints against Republicans' southern policy—that it brought corrupt government to the South and threatened to obliterate the traditional powers of the states—which within a few years would help to justify a broad northern retreat from the ideal of equality, and bring Reconstruction to an end.

VISUAL ESSAY

COUNTERSIGNS

During the last three decades of the nineteenth century, the period known as the Gilded Age, one of the most popular ways to decorate the home was by purchasing lithographic prints. Before the perfection of photographic reproduction, these prints were an attractive, affordable, and relatively accurate means of duplicating and distributing works of fine art and photographs. They also offer a revealing lens on the nation's visual culture. Lithograph houses often commissioned original works for publication, and some artists gained reputations for subjects that addressed the many different markets that comprised the picture-hungry public. There were inoffensive still lifes and landscapes for the parlor, edifying historical tableaux and portraits of the illustrious for the children's room, and genre themes, sports prints, topical illustrations, and comic cartoons—the latter three most likely destined for the kitchen or for public, and often male-oriented, venues, such as barbershops and bars.

Currier and Ives was among the nation's most successful and prolific lithography houses and, amid its multitude of themes and subjects, views of the "new" South were favorites. But, as exemplified in the 1872 "The Old Plantation Home," it was often hard to discern at what point in history the South was being depicted. There was little in these bucolic visions of a lush and languid region to distinguish scenes set before from those done

after the war and the demise of slavery. Indeed, the goal may very well have been to exploit the nostalgia of white customers for a "simpler" time, before the trauma of civil war and the turmoil of Reconstruction. In these pictures, black people become stock figures in an attractive landscape. On those rare occasions, as in this print, when blacks were featured in such compositions, they frolicked—they certainly never worked—in modest but domestic surroundings, with the big house looming benevolently in the background.

It is unlikely that many black Americans were counted among the customers for these lithographic views. But we *can* say for certain that African Americans avoided the most popular of Currier and Ives's many pictorial products—Thomas Worth's *Darktown Comics,* a long-running series of inexpensive hand-colored prints, and a mainstay of Currier and Ives's business. In fact, *Darktown Comics* probably ensured the company's financial security throughout the 1880s and into the 1890s. Each installment of the series sold quickly in the tens of thousands, and the series' ubiquity and popularity situated African Americans in the unenviable position of the nation's buffoons. Usually published in pairs, the *Darktown Comics* invariably offered before-and-after sequences in which pompous, bumbling, and grotesque black figures tried to carry out the simplest task, everyday activity, or popular sport, with disastrous consequences.

White viewers apparently found these prints highly amusing. The response of black Americans—and the casual racism of Gilded Age everyday life—is epitomized in one incident recalled by cartoonist Thomas Worth late in his life. One afternoon, co-proprietor James Ives and Worth observed "a big crowd about the front window, looking and laughing at the [latest] 'Darktown' picture." Lapsing into the racist idiom of the day, Worth noted:

There was one well-dressed darky who took exception to the Darktown part of the show and he was expressing himself most forcibly. He said "he would like to just once get hold of the fellow who drawed dem 'scanlous' pictures of de poor colored man." The quick-witted Ives took in the situation. He said to the coon he would give him an introduction to the artist "who drawed dem pictures,"—to wait a minute. He stepped back into the store and descended into the basement where the pictures were boxed to be sent away. The man who boxed the goods was a tremendous big Dutchman, a perfect Hercules. Ives explained the situation to him, and presented him to the complaining coon who took one look at him, sneaked off and vanished around the corner of Ann Street in a hurry, without getting hold of the man who "drawed dem pictures."

In contrast to cartoons, pictorial journalism still occasionally broke from grotesque caricature to depict events involving African Americans. This visual reorientation was usually spurred by actions by black Americans that seemed to take the illustrated press by surprise, disrupting the general trend toward "normalizing" race relations through invidious racial comparisons.

For example, in April 1879, *Frank Leslie's Illustrated Newspaper* took note of the ongoing migration of tens of thousands of African Americans from the lower Mississippi Valley to Kansas. Editorials expressed surprise at the so-called Exodusters' numbers and their determination to leave the South. And, while deploring the ramifications of the migration on the southern economy, *Leslie's* acknowledged the migration as evidence of the injustice and intimidation accompanying renewed Democratic Party control in the region. Moreover, when *Leslie's* published engravings in its April 19, 1879, issue showing the arrival of black migrants in St. Louis, one panoramic illustration depicted an orderly procession of homesteaders

instead of the chaos of fleeing refugees described in many press reports. The modest dress and calm demeanor of the St. Louis Exoduster procession seems unremarkable at first glance, but it stood in sharp contrast to most contemporary news illustrations of southern African American life.

Just three weeks later, *Leslie's* showed "A family of Negroes who do not favor the exodus." "Here we have a portion of a well-to-do colored family in Virginia," the weekly commented, "whose thrift, or 'good luck,' has enabled them to maintain themselves in comfort, and who, in consequence, find no occasion in their surroundings for joining in the general exodus. Contentment beams from the old folks," *Leslie's* description continues, "and positive happiness from the son and heir. Perhaps, too, there is a shade of a feeling of superiority to the average run of the Virginia negroes, such as might be justly borne by a landed proprietor of the interior, and something also of the assumptions of aristocracy."

Unlike the Exodusters, the Virginia family in this picture exuded pomposity, the now standard depiction of the buffoonery of southern blacks aspiring to rise above their appointed station. And, in this comparison, *Leslie's* also demarcated a new visual distinction between African Americans: the engraving of the migrants heralded the ambition and dignity of those who left versus the "characteristic" complacence of those who stayed behind.

The Exoduster phenomenon even affected the realm of the cartoon. The exaggerated physical traits—and some props—of racial caricature in depicting African Americans remained. But, as this cover of the weekly humor magazine *Puck* attests, the laugh was sometimes at the expense of the white Redemptionist South.

In the grand visual record of postwar national expansion, epitomized in the figures of stalwart pioneers, enterprising migrants, and rowdy cow-

THE NEW EXODUS.
SAMBO:—"Now, boss, how you like it you' self!"

boys, there was not much room for people of color. The pictorial paeans to and reporting on western settlement, railroad building, gold mining, and territorial warfare were often cruel to Native Americans, Mexicans, and Chinese immigrants—when these groups weren't completely cut out of the pictures. Similarly, African Americans who joined the trek westward were not standard subjects for pictorial journalists, cartoonists, painters, or photographers. But when black westerners did appear in pictures, their treatment was distinctive, harking back to the heroic imagery of the Civil War years.

Frederic Remington, the great chronicler and mythmaker of the late-nineteenth-century conquest of the West, was a notorious bigot who detested Italians, Jews, and other recent immigrants, whom he viewed as a "malodorous crowd of foreign trash." Remington did, however, revere soldiers, especially the troops engaged in the containment of the Plains Indians. He traveled to the western territories in the 1880s to report on their exploits for *Harper's Weekly, The Century,* and other periodicals, and in the process ended up covering four black U.S. cavalry regiments, part of the "peacetime" army established by Congress in 1866.

"Sign Language" was one of a collection of Remington's drawings that accompanied an article by him in the April 1889 issue of *The Century.* The article portrayed the exploits of a scouting party of the Tenth U.S. Cavalry "buffalo soldiers" stationed in Arizona Territory (the term *buffalo soldier* was supposedly coined by Indians who thought African Americans' hair resembled buffalo pelts). Although the party was commanded by a white officer, Remington's eye was drawn to the black troops, and the resulting pictures, like all of his drawings of the buffalo soldiers, hailed their skill and courage without relying on the sort of gross facial stereotypes that dominated most imagery of southern blacks. Whatever Remington's fasci-

nation, it was fleeting: after his spate of buffalo soldier drawings in the 1880s, he never again chose African Americans as a subject.

If the 1880s marked any significant breakthrough in the visual documentation of the African American experience, it was in the engravings showing black participation in the nation's burgeoning labor movement. To be sure, some of those pictures portrayed blacks as strikebreakers, gaining momentary eligibility for certain jobs only when employers were battling trade unions (which too often barred blacks from membership). But, increasingly faced with limited prospects in agriculture, African Americans joined the nation's growing industrial labor force and, often in concert with their white working compatriots, sometimes met with disaster.

Disaster has always been fodder for pictorial journalism. It can also be a great leveler in even the most stratified of societies. In the expanding number of industrial accidents during the Gilded Age—which accompanied the heedless accumulation of capital at the expense of safety and accountability and affected primarily railroad and mine workers—African Americans achieved equality on the common ground of tragedy.

This shared misfortune found a visual equivalent, as a February 1882 illustration in *Frank Leslie's* attested. Presenting a scene outside of the Midlothian coal mine in Chesterfield City, Virginia, shortly after an underground explosion, the illustration was distinctive in its delineation of mutual catastrophe: black and white miners and their families intermingled in the grieving and shocked crowd gathered at the mine entrance.

There were other interracial visions of labor offered to the readers of the Gilded Age press. Four years later, in 1886, *Leslie's* covered the tenth annual meeting of the Knights of Labor, the era's largest labor organization, in Richmond, Virginia, with a front-page picture showing the African American New York City delegate Frank J. Ferrell introducing Grand Master Workman Terence Powderly to the organization's General Assembly. In the wake of racial tensions provoked by the New York contingent's insistence on equal access for its black delegate to Richmond's segregated services and institutions, *Frank Leslie's,* along with Powderly, took pains to assure agitated southern whites that the Order had "no purpose to interfere with or disrupt the social relations which may exist between the different races in the various parts of the country."

Leslie's October 16, 1886, engravings of the convention chose to mark the Knights' refusal to allow the imposition of the "color line" in its own proceedings and celebrated the convention's commitment to the principle of "civil and political equality of all men" that "in the broad field of labor recognizes no distinction on account of color." In both the Midlothian

disaster and Richmond convention engravings, *Leslie's* provided its readers with images of equality rather than just black figures in a labor "landscape."

These images were framed by stories that also testified to the costs attending black aspirations and the continuing obstacles to realizing those lofty goals.

But these occasional offerings of respectful representation stoked frustration on the part of African American readers as much as they provided some respite from the overall flood of offensive and negative imagery. In the fifteen years following the Civil War, African Americans around the country founded some fifty newspapers and periodicals. None had the resources to compete with the lavishly illustrated weekly news magazines, but Indianapolis's *The Freeman*, founded in 1886, quickly gained a reputation as "A National Colored Newspaper"—or, as editor Edward E. Cooper preferred to characterize it, "the *Harper's Weekly* of the Colored Race."

The Freeman's circulation spread beyond Indianapolis to black communities all over the Midwest and South. Its popularity was in no small part a result of its weekly political cartoons, which captured many black Americans' sentiments about national politics and the "Negro Problem." The paper's first cartoonist was a former slave, a self-taught artist and engraver, and an occasional contributor to *Leslie's* and *Harper's Weekly*, Henry

Jackson Lewis. Joining *The Freeman* in 1888, Jackson helped enliven the newspaper with portraits, journalistic illustrations, and especially pointed political cartoons critical of the new Republican president, Benjamin Harrison. But cartoons such as "The National Executive Asleep"—with black figures trying to awaken an unconscious Harrison with bugles blaring the song "The Race Question"—raised the ire of local white allies of the president (Harrison had served as an Indiana senator prior to his election), who may have put pressure on the paper to squelch its critical pictorial commentary.

Whatever the exact cause, Jackson's work disappeared from the pages of *The Freeman* for the first half of 1890. His cartoons returned later that year, but the man who was the nation's first black political cartoonist died suddenly in April 1891. Jackson would therefore never witness the next betrayal that African Americans would confront in the following decade, codified into federal law and endorsed by the U.S. Supreme Court. As the United States turned its back on equality, a new pictorial order emerged to rationalize the nation's embrace of the malevolent doctrine of Jim Crow.

CHAPTER SEVEN

THE ABANDONMENT
OF RECONSTRUCTION

I N September 1877, a freedman named Henry Adams (who had
been born a slave in Georgia in 1843) drafted a letter from Shreveport,
Louisiana, to the American Colonization Society. Founded in 1816 with
the aim of settling black Americans in Africa, the society had not, either in
antebellum days or during the Civil War and Reconstruction, received much
black support. Now, however, Adams reported that he had gathered the
names of sixty thousand "hard laboring people" anxious to leave the South.
"This is a horrible part of the country," he explained, "and our race can not
get money for our labor. . . . It is impossible for us to live with these slaveholders of the South and enjoy the right as they enjoy it."

Adams had been brought to Louisiana by his owner from his birthplace
in Georgia. At the end of the Civil War, his former master urged him to
remain on the plantation and work for a share of the crop, but Adams
decided to leave. "I said if I cannot do like a white man," he later recalled,
"I am not free. I see how the poor white people do. I ought to do so too, or
else I am a slave." After witnessing many acts of violence against freedpeople in the Shreveport area, and being assaulted by thieves himself, Adams
in 1866 enlisted in the Union army, where he rose to the rank of quarter-
master sergeant and learned to read and write. After his discharge, three
years later, he worked as a plantation manager and became president of a
Shreveport Republican club and, in 1876, deputy marshal of Bienville
parish. Even before the end of Reconstruction, with violence pervasive in
his part of Louisiana, Adams formed the Colonization Council, with the
aim of obtaining for blacks "a territory to our selves," preferably in Africa,
"where our forefathers came from."

No one knows if Adams managed to emigrate to Africa. He was last
reported working in New Orleans in 1884 "for anybody I could get a job
from." He then disappears from the historical record. No doubt, his report

of sixty thousand black Louisianans ready to leave for Africa was some-thing of an exaggeration. But his letter illustrates how, by 1877, some African Americans despaired of ever achieving equality in the land of their birth.

Adams's letter came a few months after newly inaugurated Republi-can president Rutherford B. Hayes ordered federal troops to withdraw from positions at the statehouses of Louisiana and South Carolina, where they had been protecting Republican claimants to the governorships. This action (subsequently described by most historians, inaccurately, as the "withdrawal" of all federal troops from the South) marked the effective end of Reconstruction. It also represented a fundamental turning point in nineteenth-century American history, in effect announcing that the federal government would no longer intervene to protect either the political prospects of southern Republicans or the constitutional rights of black cit-izens. But Hayes's policy was not a sudden and unexpected repudiation of Reconstruction. Rather, it marked the culmination of a retreat that had gathered force since Ulysses S. Grant's reelection in 1873.

Many factors contributed to this development. In 1873, the United States, and indeed the entire Atlantic world, experienced a severe economic downturn. The failure of Jay Cooke and Company, one of the country's leading banking houses, triggered a financial panic that was soon followed by the worst depression in the country's history to that date. In the wake of factory closings, business bankruptcies, falling prices for agricultural prod-ucts, and widespread unemployment (in some cities as high as 30 percent of the workforce), economic recovery replaced Reconstruction as the main focus of national and local political debates. In the North, major cities wit-nessed demonstrations demanding government relief for the unemployed. Farmers in western states demanded that the government regulate the con-duct of railroads, whose high rates and monopolistic practices the farmers blamed for their economic plight. In the South, the price of cotton fell by half between 1873 and 1877, plunging many merchants and planters into bankruptcy, forcing indebted small white farmers to forfeit their land and become sharecroppers, and undermining progress blacks had made toward landownership. The depression destroyed whatever hope still existed that Reconstruction would usher in a modernized New South.

The economic disaster revitalized the Democratic Party. In 1874, for the first time since the Civil War, Democrats won control of the House of Representatives. Shortly before the new Congress met, Republicans enacted the last of the major Reconstruction measures—the Civil Rights Act of 1875, which prohibited racial discrimination in transportation and public accommodation. Its author, the Radical Republican senator Charles

Sumner, had repeatedly introduced the bill without success since the late 1860s; it passed, in part, as a tribute to Sumner, who had died in 1874. But the Democratic election victory meant that Congress, divided between the two parties, was essentially paralyzed. No further Reconstruction legislation or other initiatives to protect the rights of the former slaves would be forthcoming.

Growing labor unrest made many white northerners more sympathetic to white southern complaints about Reconstruction. Racial and class prejudices re-

A September 1873 cartoon, "Panic, as a Health Officer, Sweeping the Garbage out of Wall Street," offered a ghastly vision to readers of the New York Daily Graphic *while suggesting that financial disasters cleansed the economy.*

inforced one another, as increasing numbers of middle-class northerners identified what they considered the illegitimate demands of workers and farmers in their own society with the alleged misconduct of the former slaves in the South. Liberal Republican journals found a wider and wider audience for their call for a return to rule by the "best men" throughout the country. They placed the blame for Reconstruction's problems squarely on the alleged inferiority and incapacity of the South's black voters.

In 1873, *New York Tribune* editor Whitelaw Reid sent James S. Pike to South Carolina to report on conditions in the state. A Liberal Republican, Pike intended his reports to further discredit the Grant administration and to punish black voters for favoring Grant over Greeley in the previous fall's election. Pike's reports, gathered in a widely read book, *The Prostrate State,* had a powerful impact on the image of the former slaves in the North. His portrait of South Carolina was suffused with racial and class prejudice: the state, wrote Pike, "lies prostrate in the dust. . . . It is the spectacle of a society turned upside down. . . . It is the dregs of the population [dressed] in the robes of their intelligent predecessors, and asserting over them the rule of ignorance and corruption, through the inexorable machinery of a majority of numbers. It is barbarism overwhelming civilization by physical force." South Carolina's freedpeople, he added, possessed an "average of intelligence but slightly above the level of animals." Pike pointedly compared the former slaves, who allegedly refused to labor efficiently for whites and still coveted land of their own, with disaffected northern workers, who conducted strikes and called on state governments to provide jobs for the unemployed. In both cases, the lower orders sought to elevate their positions in society by interfering with the rights of property owners, rather than through thrift and hard work. Pike's book helped make South Carolina a national byword for political corruption and reinforced the idea that the cause lay in "negro government."

A "counter-revolution" was now overtaking Reconstruction, lamented Vice President Henry Wilson, a veteran Radical Republican. "Men are beginning to hint at changing the condition of the Negro." Racism, of course, had never been eliminated from northern life. As noted earlier, despite Reconstruction, the vast majority of African Americans remained trapped in poverty, confined to menial and unskilled jobs. Nonetheless, as a result of Reconstruction, the North's public life had been opened to blacks in ways inconceivable before the Civil War. In the 1860s, the Republican Party had not only given northern blacks the right to vote, but also sought to ensure their access to public schools, and in many places worked against discriminatory practices on streetcars and railroads, and in private businesses. In the economic crisis of the 1870s, however, as the nation looked for scapegoats, racism increasingly reasserted its hold on northern thought and behavior. Engravings in popular journals depicted the freedpeople not as upstanding citizens harassed by violent opponents (as had been the case immediately after the Civil War) but as little more than unbridled animals. (See "Countersigns" visual essay.) By the mid-1870s, it was quite common in the North to write, in the words of the contemporary historian Francis Parkman, of "the monstrosities of Negro rule in South Carolina." Racism in other words, offered a convenient explanation for the alleged "failure" of Reconstruction.

The idea of the natural superiority of some races to others, which before the Civil War had been invoked to justify slavery in an otherwise free society, now reemerged, cloaked in the vocabulary of modern science. The growing use of language borrowed from Charles Darwin's evolutionary theory, such as "natural selection," "the struggle for existence," and "the survival of the fittest," became part and parcel of social discourse in the North. What came to be called Social Darwinism condemned all forms

THE WORLD'S PEOPLES.

INTRODUCTORY.

The object of these pages is to furnish a brief yet comprehensive record of the nations of the world, their origin and growth, their leading characteristics, manners, and customs, together with a general review of the part they have played in the progress of civilization. To the historian belongs the task of a more extended chronicle.

It has been observed that "history is but a record of crimes," but a broader view recognizes that the true life of a people lies in its development of the arts of peace, the narrative of which more properly forms the object of historic study. In the following pages, designed to interest the popular mind, it is assumed that the reader will seek only to obtain a clear, graphic conception of the nations themselves, apart from special achievements in peace or war.

The advantages of a more accurate knowledge of the peoples of the earth can not be over-estimated by the century in which we live. The progress of Christianity has more than ever served to extend the domain of human sympathy, while the startling results of modern invention, binding, as it were, in one vast family the scattered millions of mankind and, through the medium of steam and electric intercourse, making isolation impossible, have contributed to stimulate a desire of further acquaintance with our fellow-men.

This sketch, then, is designed to portray, so far as its scope permits, the actual status of the political and social world; thus introducing its

readers to a more intimate and extended acquaintance with the nations of the earth.

The illustrations not only add pictorial interest to the work, but give a more vivid idea of the scenes and customs, as well as of national types, it is designed to impress upon the general student. Having been carefully selected, and in their details corresponding closely with the most authentic narratives of travel, they portray with fidelity the varied subjects connected with the nations to which they refer.

When we consider how comparatively small a portion of the habitable globe remains unexplored, every conquest in the realm of discovery assumes peculiar interest and importance. It is, therefore, indispensable to the student of geography that his knowledge should be abreast of the times, and that he should examine carefully the ever-extending boundaries of exploration, that the value of each successive discovery in this field may be duly understood and appreciated. The theories of speculative astronomy and the consideration of "other worlds than ours" may well engage the thoughts of philosophers; to mankind in general, life, as we know it, is related to the planet we inhabit; and, in the natural zeal of our researches, we shall not rest until we have exhausted the resources of science in establishing, not only the configuration of seas and continents, but the minutest facts connected with terrestrial history.

ORANG-UTAN, AND THE FIVE PRINCIPAL RACES OF MAN.

A—ORANG-UTAN.
D—INDIAN.
B—MALAYAN.
E—MONGOLIAN.
C—ETHIOPIAN.
F—CAUCASIAN.

An illustration in a popular late-nineteenth-century world atlas offers an ascending hierarchy of the human race, beginning with an orangutan.

of state interference with the "natural" workings of society, especially misguided efforts to uplift those at the bottom of the social order. By and large, in this view, the poor were responsible for their own conditions, and African Americans were consigned by nature itself to occupy the lowest rungs of the social ladder. Whether in the form of labor legislation or Radical Reconstruction, governmental efforts to alter the natural workings of society only impeded social progress.

If any one episode symbolized the accelerating retreat from Reconstruction, it was the collapse in 1874 of the Freedman's Savings Bank, one of the many financial institutions to succumb during the depression. Chartered by Congress in 1865 to encourage thrift among the former slaves, the bank was a private corporation, but it often shared offices with the Freedmen's Bureau and employed federal army officers to persuade freedpeople to open accounts. By 1874, when the bank collapsed, sixty-one thousand African Americans had done just that. Although President Grant called on Congress to reimburse the depositors, Congress did nothing; in the end, half the depositors received compensation for a fraction of their losses when the bank's assets were liquidated, and half received nothing at all. The biggest loser was Frederick Douglass, who had been appointed the bank's president in 1874 to shore up public confidence in the bank just before its collapse. Douglass deposited ten thousand dollars, which he never saw again. In the same year, the *New National Era,* a weekly newspaper that Douglass edited in Washington during Reconstruction, also fell victim to the depression.

The Supreme Court, it is often said, follows the election returns. And as support for Reconstruction waned in the North, the court began to emasculate the legislation and constitutional amendments of the 1860s. The first pivotal decision, in the "Slaughterhouse Cases," was announced in 1873. Allegedly to preserve the public health, Louisiana had created a corporation to monopolize the slaughter of animals in New Orleans, effectively making it impossible for many butchers to practice their traditional craft. White butchers who faced the loss of their livelihoods sued, on the grounds that their rights as American citizens under the Fourteenth Amendment had been violated. The "equal protection of the law" guaranteed by the amendment, their lawyers insisted, included "the right of free labor"—that is, the ability to follow any lawful trade without governmental interference. The court rejected their argument. Speaking for a 5–4 majority, Justice Samuel F. Miller ruled that the Fourteenth Amendment applied only to the former slaves, and that the rights it protected were only those that owed their existence to the federal government, not to the states. Miller mentioned that these federal rights included access to ports and waterways, the ability to travel abroad, and the right to run for federal office. Few of these were of pressing concern to the majority of black Americans. Otherwise, the decision continued, citizens' rights originated where they always had, with the states. Thus, in the guise of affirming the freedmen's status as national citizens, the Slaughterhouse Cases severely limited the rights for which they could claim federal protection.

Three years later came *United States v. Cruikshank,* a case that arose from the Colfax, Louisiana, massacre of 1873, discussed earlier. Here, the court not only overturned the three convictions that federal prosecutors had managed to obtain against the white perpetrators, but it went on to state that the postwar amendments empowered Washington to act only against violations of citizens' rights by the states, not by individuals—a repudiation of the expansion of federal criminal jurisdiction embodied in the Enforcement Acts. The decision made national prosecution of crimes committed against blacks almost impossible.

By the time *Cruikshank* was decided, in 1876, terrorism had again reared its head in the South. With northern commitment to Reconstruction waning and African American assertiveness rising—as evidenced by the growing number of state and local black officeholders in the Deep South—

Democrats had both the opportunity and an increased motive to move aggressively against Republican rule. Democrats in 1873 regained control of Texas, a state with a large white majority, where the party could win by mobilizing white voters, without resorting to violence. Elsewhere in the Gulf states, however, blacks represented 45 percent of the population or more, and Republicans usually would be favored in a fair and peaceful election. Thus, Democrats turned to illegal methods. In 1874, the White League was formed in Louisiana with the avowed purpose of restoring white supremacy, by violent means if necessary. On September 14, some 3,500 leaguers seized control of city hall and the statehouse in New Orleans; they withdrew only when federal troops arrived. Republicans managed to carry Louisiana in the fall elections, but were not so fortunate in Alabama, where armed bands prevented many blacks from casting ballots on election day. There, thanks to a significant falloff in Republican votes in the plantation belt, where most blacks lived, Democrats won control of the governorship and legislature.

If the dispatch of troops after the New Orleans uprising indicated that President Grant was not willing to countenance the overt overthrow of a Reconstruction government, events in Alabama suggested that he would not intervene against violence during electoral campaigns. This became abundantly clear in 1875, when, thanks to a carefully orchestrated campaign of violence, Democrats overturned the Reconstruction government of Mississippi. They mobilized nearly the entire white population of the state with appeals to white supremacy and protecting the sanctity of the white family, allegedly threatened by a recent state law banning discrimination by railroads, hotels, and places of public entertainment. (This, Democrats insisted, would result in "unnatural association" between the races and, eventually, integrated schools and interracial marriage.) But talk alone did not carry the state. As the fall legislative elections approached, armed Democratic bands terrorized black communities throughout Mississippi. In Yazoo County, several prominent black leaders were murdered, and the sheriff, Albert T. Morgan, a white Ohioan who had moved to the area after the war (and compounded his offense by marrying a black woman), was driven from the region. Democrats attacked a Republican barbecue at Clinton, and went on to murder some thirty blacks, among them schoolteachers, ministers, and local Republican organizers. In Copiah County, the sheriff reported, whites "formed themselves into military organizations . . . armed themselves with army guns and bayonets and cannon," and prevented blacks from assembling or campaigning.

Besieged by requests for protection, Republican governor Adelbert

A December 1874 illustration in Frank Leslie's Illustrated Newspaper *provides a distant and bloodless perspective on the Vicksburg, Mississippi, White League's efforts violently to unseat African American sheriff Peter Crosby. After defeating the sheriff's supporters, armed white bands terrorized the countryside, murdering hundreds of black citizens.*

Ames asked the president to dispatch federal troops. But Grant refused, and northern newspapers drew attention to one sentence in his reply: "The whole public are tired out with these annual autumnal outbreaks in the South . . . [and] are ready now to condemn any interference on the part of the government." Given this license by the president to intimidate, Democrats intensified their campaign. Moreover, unlike the Klan's depredations a few years earlier, violent bands in 1875 operated without disguise, as if to flaunt their lack of fear of legal reprisal. On election eve, armed riders warned freedmen they would be killed if they attempted to vote. The following day, whites equipped with a cannon and rifles drove black voters from the polls at Aberdeen; elsewhere, they stuffed or destroyed the ballot boxes. "The reports which come to me almost hourly are truly sickening," wrote Ames. "The government of the U.S. does not interfere."

Braving the campaign of intimidation, blacks turned out to vote in most parts of Mississippi. Where the violence was most intense, however, the Republican vote declined precipitously. In Yazoo, only seven ballots were counted for the party. In the end, Democrats swept control of the legislature, and then forced Ames to resign under threat of impeachment. "A *revolution* has taken place," Ames wrote, "by force of arms, and a race are disfranchised. They are to be returned to a condition of serfdom, an era of second slavery."

Victory did not slake the thirst for violence. On Christmas Day, a white friend invited freedman Charles Caldwell to share a drink at a store in Clinton. A blacksmith who had represented Hinds County in the constitutional convention of 1868 and the state Senate, Caldwell chaired the local Republican executive committee. "He was as brave a man as I ever knew," commented a white Republican associate. But on that day, armed men lay in hiding, and as Caldwell raised his glass, they shot him in the back.

At the 1876 national Republican convention, Frederick Douglass, who had labored tirelessly for the party during Reconstruction, pointedly asked, "Do you mean to make good to us the promises in your constitution?" By this time, most Republican leaders had concluded that the northern white public would no longer support intervention in the South on behalf of the former slaves. Their presidential candidate, Governor Rutherford B. Hayes of Ohio, pledged in his letter accepting the nomination to bring the South "the blessings of honest and capable local self government"—code words for an end to Reconstruction. The Democrats nominated Samuel J. Tilden, the governor of New York. It was quite clear that, whoever emerged victorious, Reconstruction was doomed.

In the South, Democrats redoubled their efforts to take control of states that still had Reconstruction governments. Their most strenuous effort took place in South Carolina, where they nominated former Confederate general Wade Hampton as their candidate for governor. While Hampton pledged to respect the equal rights of the state's African Americans, many of his supporters, inspired by the example of Mississippi, turned to violence to neutralize the considerable black voting majority. At Hamburg, South Carolina, where Prince Rivers, once a sergeant in Thomas Wentworth Higginson's black Civil War regiment, served as trial justice, an altercation on July 4, 1876, escalated into a battle between the black militia and armed whites under the command of former Confederate general Matthew C. Butler. In the end, the outnumbered militiamen surrendered, whereupon five were murdered in cold blood. The Hamburg Massacre demoralized many Republicans, but it spurred others to emulate their opponents. The 1876 campaign became one of the few times during Reconstruction when violence originated on both sides. Six white men were killed at Cainhoy, near Charleston, when armed blacks opened fire on a political meeting. But the campaign of intimidation launched by General Hampton's "Red Shirts" dwarfed such events. "Every Democrat must feel honor bound to control the vote of at least one Negro, by intimidation, purchase, keeping him away [from the polls] or as each individual may determine," declared the "Plan of campaign" circulated by Democratic leader Martin W. Gary. A reign of terror reminiscent of the Ku Klux Klan days spread over upcountry counties, and the election, one Democratic observer admitted, was "one of the grandest farces ever seen."

On a suspenseful election night, it became clear that the result of the

In a parody of the meaning of equality, Harper's Weekly *cartoonist Thomas Nast depicts Justice demanding white deaths to match the black victims of the July 1876 Hamburg, South Carolina, massacre.*

presidential contest hinged on the returns from Florida, Louisiana, and South Carolina, which both parties claimed to have carried. After much confusion, Congress appointed an electoral commission, composed of five representatives, five senators, and five members of the Supreme Court to adjudicate the disputed returns. By a series of 8–7 votes, strictly following party lines, the commission awarded the three contested states to the Republican, Hayes, certifying him as victor by a single electoral vote.

Even as the commission deliberated, however, behind-the-scenes negotiations were under way between national leaders of the two parties. Hayes's representatives agreed that if he became president, he would recognize Democratic control of the entire South and refrain from further intervention in southern affairs. He also pledged to place a southerner in the cabinet and to work for federal aid to the Texas and Pacific Railroad, a transcontinental line projected to follow a southern route. For their part, Democrats promised not to dispute Hayes's election and to respect the civil and political rights of blacks. Thus was concluded the Bargain or Compromise of 1877. Some of its promises were fulfilled—Hayes became president; Democrats took control of Florida, Louisiana, and South Carolina; and David M. Key of Tennessee was appointed postmaster general. Some were violated—the Texas and Pacific never got its land grant, and, most ominously, the triumphant southern Democrats would never truly recognize blacks as equal citizens.

Within two months of taking office, Hayes ordered federal troops to stop guarding the statehouses in Louisiana and South Carolina, thus allowing Democratic claimants to seize the two remaining Republican governorships. (Florida's Supreme Court had earlier declared a Democrat the victor in the 1876 gubernatorial election, although it also held that Hayes had carried the state.) "The whole South—every State in the South," commented one former slave, "had got into the hands of the very men who held us as slaves." "The long controversy over the black man," announced the *Chicago Tribune*, "seems to have reached a finality."

As a historical process— the nation's adjustment to the destruction of slavery— Reconstruction continued well after 1877. But as a distinct era of national history, when Republicans controlled much or all of the South, blacks exercised significant political power, and the federal government accepted the responsibility for protecting the fundamental rights of all American citizens, Reconstruction had come to an end.

The former slaves reacted in numerous ways to this turn of events. Emigration movements such as the one organized by Henry Adams in Louisiana were one expression of a wide-

THE MODERN ST. GEORGE.

Republican president Rutherford B. Hayes is portrayed in this cartoon from the satirical weekly Puck *as the "Modern St. George," freeing the South from the "misrule" of Reconstruction.*

spread sense of aborted hopes and constricted opportunities. Local organizations devoted to emigration sprang up throughout the South, like the Liberia Exodus Association of Pinesville, Florida, and the Pilgrem Travelers of Robertson County, Texas. Hundreds of letters from blacks anxious to leave the country poured into the offices of the American Colonization Society. "The colored man has no home in America," declared Harrison N. Bouey, a teacher and Baptist minister who organized an emigration movement in South Carolina in 1877. "We have no chance to rise from beggars. Men own the capital that we work, who believe that they still have a right to either us or our value from the general government." Bouey sailed for Liberia on the *Azor* in 1878, along with two hundred black Carolinians.

Most black southerners who contemplated leaving the region, however, preferred to seek improved conditions elsewhere in the United States. "We are not Africans now, but colored Americans, and are entitled to American citizenship," wrote a correspondent of Senator Blanche K. Bruce of Mississippi. If blacks could not enjoy this status in the South, he added, the government should set aside "one of the States or Territories" for their settlement. And in 1879 and 1880, an estimated twenty thousand to thirty thousand African Americans migrated to Kansas, mostly in groups of families from neighborhoods and small towns scattered throughout the South. The migrants sought political equality, protection against violence, access to education, and economic opportunity—in a word, the substance of freedom so frequently denied them in the South now that Reconstruction had ended. Those promoting the movement, including freedman Henry Adams and former fugitive slave Benjamin "Pap" Singleton, organizer of a real estate company, distributed flyers and lithographs picturing Kansas as an idyllic land of opportunity. Lacking the capital to take up farming, most migrants ended up working as unskilled laborers in Midwestern towns and cities. But few chose to return to the South. In the words of one minister active in the movement, "we had rather suffer and be free."

"We wants to be a people," two leaders of a local emigration movement wrote from Mississippi; "we can't be it here." Whether their destination was Africa or Kansas, emigration movements reflected the sense of collective identity forged in the crucible of slavery, emancipation, and Reconstruction. Being a "people" for these refugees from the South meant living where black families could create communities enjoying economic independence and political and civil equality. Until well into the twentieth century, however, the large majority of African Americans had little alternative but to remain in the southern states. For them, the demise of Reconstruction ushered in a period of shattered hopes and limited opportunities.

The creation of a new system of race relations in politics, labor, and

An 1877 handbill urged African Americans to leave Kentucky and join a new settlement in Kansas.

society at large after Reconstruction did not occur overnight. But the South's "Redeemers"—as the coalition of merchants, planters, and business entrepreneurs who now took control of the region's politics styled themselves—swiftly moved to undo as much as possible of Reconstruction. To begin with, having promised to reduce taxes and state expenditures, they drastically scaled back the scope and responsibilities of government. State budgets were slashed and taxes, especially levies on landed property, diminished. "Spend nothing unless absolutely necessary," Democrat George F. Drew, Florida's new governor, advised his legislature in 1877. Throughout the South, spending on schools, hospitals, and other social services was decimated. In the name of strengthening male authority within the family, Redeemer courts and legislatures also reversed some of the gains in women's rights legislated under Reconstruction. In Mississippi, the courts ruled that Reconstruction laws protecting a woman's right to own property in her own name did not allow a married woman who worked on her husband's land an independent title to the fruits of her labor. The crop belonged to the husband, not the wife, regardless of who had worked in the fields. Property generally owned by white women—land, buildings, cash gifts—continued to be protected against her husband's creditors. But a growing crop was owned by the husband and could be seized to pay his debts.

Hardest hit were the new public school systems, one of the greatest achievements of the Reconstruction era. Black schools suffered the most, but education for whites was affected as well. Louisiana spent so little on education that it became the only state in the Union in which the percentage of whites unable to read and write actually increased between 1880 and 1900. Simultaneously, the gap between expenditures on black and white schools widened steadily. In the final year of Reconstruction, for example, South Carolina's per capita expenditure on education was $1.85 for white and black pupils alike. By 1895, the amount spent on whites had risen to $3.11 per pupil, while for the state's black majority, it had declined to less than $1.00. Twenty years later, the figures for Mississippi stood at $8.20 per white student, and $1.53 per black. The history textbooks used in southern schools taught the lessons of white superiority and black backwardness. Slavery was described as a benign institution that brought a benighted people into the heart of Western civilization, and Reconstruction was a terrible error, never to be repeated. Many whites opposed maintaining schools for blacks at all. "What I want here is Negroes who can make cotton," declared one planter, "and they don't need education to help them make cotton"—an attitude reminiscent of the darkest days of slavery.

Change after the election of 1876 was immediate in labor relations as well. What one black political leader called "the class legislation of the Democrats against the race" included vagrancy laws, restrictions on "enticing" a worker to leave his employment for another job, and criminal penalties for breach of contract. Measures reminiscent of the Black Codes of 1865–66 authorized the arrest of virtually any person without employment. Unlike the laws of Presidential Reconstruction, the new ones ostensibly applied to members of both races, otherwise they would have violated the Civil Rights Act of 1866 and the Fourteenth Amendment. But they were enforced in a blatantly discriminatory manner. "A single instance of punishment of whites under these acts has never occurred," a Tennessee black convention declared.

Meanwhile, southern legislatures greatly increased the penalties for petty crimes, a strategy targeted especially against blacks. Mississippi's famous "pig law" defined the theft of any cattle or swine as grand larceny punishable by five years in prison. "They send [a man] to the penitentiary if he steals a chicken," complained a former slave in North Carolina. As the South's prison population rose, the leasing of convicts became a lucrative business. Railroads, mining companies, and other businesses vied for this new form of involuntary labor, the vast majority of them blacks imprisoned for minor offenses. Conditions in labor camps were often barbaric, with disease rife and the death rate high. "One dies, get another" was the motto of the system's architects, since thanks to discriminatory law enforcement by all-white police forces and the exclusion of blacks from juries, there seemed to be an endless supply of black convicts to replace those who perished.

The Radicals' failure to achieve land reform had ensured that most black southerners would be confined to agricultural labor on white-owned land, or menial jobs in southern cities. Sharecroppers frequently found themselves in debt at the end of a crop year. "We make as much cotton and sugar as we did when we were slaves," noted a Texas sharecropper, "and it does us as little good now as it did then." New laws passed by the Redeemers added to the tenants' problems. During Reconstruction, many states had awarded tenants the first lien on a crop, with preference over merchants or others to whom landowners owed money. Now, courts ruled that the tenant was, legally speaking, nothing more than a wage laborer, with no claim to compensation until the planter's other obligations had been discharged. North Carolina placed the entire crop in the hands of the landlord until rent was fully paid, and allowed no challenge to his decision as to when the tenant's obligations had been fulfilled. Throughout the South, if the planter was heavily in debt to a merchant, the sharecropper might end up with nothing. Finally, with Redemption, the balance of power at the local level shifted in the planters' favor in terms of the use of governmental force. This was clearly demonstrated in November 1887, when field laborers in the Louisiana sugar district organized a strike for higher wages. Planters called in the militia to force the strikers back to work, and the troops stood by as local posses massacred more than fifty workers, effectively ending the walkout.

Under the Redeemers, the rural South sank even further into poverty, a trend that would continue into the twentieth century, so that by the 1930s, President Franklin D. Roosevelt would declare the region the nation's "number one" economic problem. As the most disadvantaged rural southerners, black farmers in the post-Reconstruction decades suffered the most from the region's overall condition.

In southern cities, the situation for the descendants of slaves was more complex. The network of institutions whose foundations had been laid during Reconstruction—schools and colleges, churches, businesses, fraternal orders, women's clubs, and the like—served as the infrastructure for thriving and increasingly diverse black urban communities. These institutions also formed the basis for the rapid growth of the black middle class, mostly professionals such as teachers and physicians, or businessmen serving the needs of a black clientele. Even in cities, however, most blacks were relegated to menial and unskilled employment. Most urban black males worked as manual laborers or as personal servants in white homes. The large majority of employed black women labored as laundresses and domestic workers. A rigidly segmented job market kept blacks excluded from nearly all skilled employment. Black men had little access to supervisory positions in factories and workshops or to the burgeoning white-collar workforce of clerks in offices. Black women could not find employment as secretaries, typists, or department store clerks.

Most labor unions, north and south, barred blacks from membership. The few exceptions, such as the Knights of Labor, which flourished in the 1880s, attracted a large membership of blacks eager to find allies in the struggle for economic empowerment and respect in the workplace. Although most of their local assemblies were segregated, the Knights welcomed blacks as members. Their demise in the 1890s left some local unions of longshoremen and mine workers with significant numbers of both black and white members. But in most occupations, the few unions that existed in the South formed yet another barrier to blacks' economic advancement.

Overall, one historian has written, the New South was "a miserable landscape dotted only by a few rich enclaves that cast little or no light upon the poverty surrounding them." Trapped at the bottom of a stagnant econ-

*African American workers prepare tobacco in Richmond, Virginia, stripping
stems from the leaves.*

omy, excluded from jobs in the textile factories that burgeoned in the
southern piedmont, and denied access to industrial employment in the
North, blacks had few chances to improve their situation in life or to fulfill
the long-standing desire for land of their own. In the Upper South, economic development offered some opportunities—mines, iron furnaces,
and tobacco factories employed black laborers, and because a shift from
tobacco to truck farming encouraged planters to sell off some of their hold-
ings, a good number of blacks managed to acquire land, albeit usually small
plots of marginal fertility. In the Deep South, however, African Americans
owned a smaller percentage of the land in 1900 than they had at the end of
Reconstruction.

Neither black voting nor officeholding came to an abrupt end in 1877.
In many states, blacks continued to cast ballots in large numbers, although
in some states Redeemers solidified their control of state and local affairs
by redrawing district lines and substituting appointive for elective officials
in counties with black majorities. In cities such as Mobile, Alabama, blacks
continued to serve on juries after 1877. Small numbers of blacks continued
to win election to southern legislatures, and a few, representing heavily
black districts, even served in Congress in the 1880s and 1890s. Thanks to

Republican control of the White House for most of the years from 1876 to 1912, many African Americans held patronage posts distributed by federal officials in Washington. Joseph H. Lee, a graduate of Howard University Law School who moved to Florida in 1873 and was elected to seven terms in the state legislature, served as customs collector at Jacksonville from 1880 to 1913. Robert Smalls, the daring slave pilot who brought his vessel over to the Union navy during the Civil War, held a string of offices during and after Reconstruction. He was elected to five terms in the House of Representatives, and represented Beaufort County in the South Carolina Constitutional Convention of 1895, where he spoke out eloquently against the movement to disenfranchise black voters.

Black political leaders operated in a profoundly altered context after the end of Reconstruction. Local officials confronted hostile state governments and national administrations indifferent to their constituents' concerns, and black lawmakers found it difficult to exert influence as a tiny minority in Democratic-dominated legislatures. Most black officials now depended for their power on the goodwill of prominent Democrats or patronage dispensed by the federal government, rather than on the backing of a politically mobilized black community. For men of talent and ambition, avenues other than politics—business, the law, the church—increasingly seemed to offer greater opportunities for personal advancement and community service than did politics. One interesting result was that by the 1890s, black women activists, including antilynching crusader Ida B. Wells and temperance and women's suffrage activist Frances Ellen Watkins Harper, seemed to have taken up the banner of political leadership abandoned by so many black men. The National Association of Colored Women, founded in 1896, brought together local and regional women's clubs to press for both women's rights and racial uplift. Most female activists emerged from the small urban, black middle class and

Antilynching crusader Ida B. Wells and the widow and orphans of a black businessman murdered in Memphis in 1892

preached the necessity of "respectable" behavior and demeanor as essential to the struggle for equal rights. By claiming the mantle of respectability for black women, they implicitly challenged dominant racial ideologies, which consigned all blacks to the status of degraded second-class citizens.

In a few areas, enclaves of genuine black political power survived the end of Reconstruction—including Robert Smalls's bailiwick in the South Carolina low country, the "black second" congressional district of Virginia, and Galveston, Texas, where former slave Norris W. Cuney headed a political machine that made him the state's most powerful black politician. In several states, the victorious Democrats fractured, with Independent movements challenging tax and spending policies that favored urban and rural elites at the expense of small farmers. These divisions created new political opportunities for black voters. In Mobile, for example, black voters helped one Democratic faction with local elections in 1885, and were rewarded with the appointment of more black teachers in segregated schools. In Virginia and North Carolina, blacks took part in interracial coalitions that briefly took control of state government and instituted policies—including expanded education and more equitable law enforcement—reminiscent of Reconstruction. In Virginia, the Readjuster movement (so named because it called for reducing payment of the state debt, which was starving schools and other public responsibilities) brought together Republicans and dissident Democrats and ousted the Redeemers from power in 1879. In North Carolina, a coalition of black Republicans and white Populists took over the state government between 1894 and 1898. In other states as well, the People's Party, or Populists—composed mainly of white farmers who believed the Democrats indifferent to their economic plight—sought to attract black votes. By and large, their challenge to the Redeemers' political order failed. But as long as black suffrage survived, so too did the possibility of significant political change within the South.

For nearly a generation after the end of Reconstruction, despite fraud, violence, and redistricting, most black southerners continued to cast ballots. Beginning in 1890, however, every southern state enacted laws or constitutional provisions designed to eliminate the black vote entirely. Since the Fifteenth Amendment prohibited the use of race as a qualification for suffrage, these new measures were ostensibly color-blind. The most popular devices included poll taxes, without payment of which a voter lost the franchise; literacy tests and requirements that a prospective voter demonstrate an "understanding" of the state constitution; and stringent residency requirements. Some white leaders presented disenfranchisement as a "good government measure"—a means of ending the fraud, violence, and stuffing of ballot boxes used against Republicans since 1877. But whatever the motivation, the aim, as a Charleston, South Carolina, newspaper declared, was to "reduce the colored vote to insignificance in every county in the State," and to make clear that the white South "does not desire or intend ever to include black men among its citizens."

The result was the virtual elimination of black voting in the South. And although sympathetic election officials often allowed whites who did not meet the new qualifications to register, the number of eligible white voters declined as well. Louisiana, for example, reduced the number of black voters from one hundred thirty thousand to one thousand. But eighty thousand white voters also lost the franchise. In 1898, the Supreme Court encouraged the disenfranchisement movement by ruling, in *Williams v. Mississippi*, that the suffrage provisions of the state's 1890 constitution did not violate the Fifteenth Amendment, since they did not "on their face discriminate between the races."

The elimination of almost all black and many white voters not only reversed the long nineteenth-century trend toward universal suffrage, but also transformed much of the South into a series of rotten boroughs, whose representatives in Congress would long wield far greater power on the national scene than their tiny electorates warranted. The Fourteenth Amendment provided that if any state deprived a group of male citizens of the franchise, it would lose part of its representation in Congress. But like much of the federal Constitution, this provision became a dead letter so far as African Americans were concerned.

Along with disenfranchisement, the 1890s saw the widespread imposition of racial segregation in the South. Of course, de facto racial separation had existed in Reconstruction schools and many other institutions, and among the first acts of the Redeemers had been to institutionalize in the law the principle of separate schools for white and black students. But it was not until the 1890s that the Supreme Court, in the landmark decision *Plessy v. Ferguson*, gave its approval to state laws requiring separate facilities for blacks and whites. The case arose in Louisiana, where the legislature had enacted a law requiring railroad companies to maintain a separate car for black passengers. Homer Plessy, a local shoemaker and an official of the New Amis Sincere, an organization formed in 1887 to promote public education in New Orleans, challenged his exclusion from a whites-only first-class car. Several former black Reconstruction officials organized the Citizens' Committee, which filed a court challenge. The issue was not simply comfort while traveling, but the implications for the idea of equal citizenship of "caste legislation" of any sort. To argue the case before the Supreme Court, the committee hired Albion W. Tourgée, a native of Ohio who as a judge during Reconstruction had waged a courageous battle against the Ku Klux Klan. "Citizenship is national and knows no color," Tourgée asserted. The state's requirement that blacks be segregated from whites violated the Fourteenth Amendment's guarantee of equal protection before the law. But in an 8–1 decision, the Court upheld the law, arguing that separate facilities were not discriminatory so long as they were "separate but equal." The lone dissenter, John Marshall Harlan, hurled at the majority the oft-quoted dictum: "Our Constitution is color-blind."

More than simply an interpretation of the equal protection clause, Harlan's dissent was a rumination on the meaning of freedom and citizenship in a racialized democracy. Segregation, he insisted, sprang from whites' conviction that they were the "dominant race" (a phrase employed by the Court's majority), and this violated the principle of equal liberty spawned by the Civil War and institutionalized during Reconstruction.

As Harlan predicted, the *Plessy* decision was quickly followed by state laws mandating racial segregation in every aspect of life, from schools to hospitals, waiting rooms to toilets, drinking fountains to cemeteries. In some states, taxi drivers were forbidden by law to carry members of different races at the same time. But more than simply a form of racial separation, segregation was part of a complex system of white domination, in which each component—disenfranchisement, unequal economic status, inferior education—reinforced the others. The system's major premise, as Dunbar Rowland, a Mississippi historian, explained in 1903, was that

John Marshall Harlan

no black person would ever "be accepted as an equal no matter how great his future advancement." The point was not so much to keep the races apart as to ensure that when they came into contact with each other, whether in politics, labor relations, or social life, whites held the upper hand. Jim Crow, a term that originated as the name of a stock character in nineteenth-century minstrel shows, became a popular shorthand for racial segregation, and more generally for the South's all-encompassing system of racial inequality.

Those blacks who sought to challenge the system, or who refused to accept docilely the insults and demands for demeaning behavior that were a daily feature of life, faced not only overwhelming political and legal power, but also the very real threat of violent reprisal. Between 1880 and 1968, nearly 3,500 persons were lynched in the United States, the vast majority of them black men in the South. Some lynchings occurred secretly at night; others were advertised in advance and attracted huge audiences of onlookers. In 1899, Sam Hose, a plantation laborer who killed his employer in self-defense, was brutally murdered near Newman, Georgia, before two thousand onlookers, some of whom arrived on a special excursion train from Atlanta. The crowd watched as Hose's executioners cut off his ears, fingers, and genitals and burned him alive, and then fought over "souvenirs," such as pieces of his bones. Law enforcement authorities made no effort to prevent the lynching or to bring the assailants to justice. Like many victims of lynchings, Hose was retrospectively accused of raping a white woman, a deed almost universally considered by white southerners as justification for extralegal vengeance.

By the turn of the century, a new system of racial subordination had come into being in the South. In the words of the black historian Rayford Logan, blacks occupied a "separate wing" of the "edifice of national unity," and "on the pediments . . . were carved Exploitation, Disfranchisement, Segregation, Discrimination, Lynching, Contempt." But the white South did not create the new system of white supremacy alone. The effective nullification of the laws and constitutional amendments enacted during Reconstruction could never have occurred without the full acquiescence of the North.

The resurgence of racism was both cause and effect of the nation's abandonment of the Reconstruction ideal of color-blind citizenship. If racism helped to undermine Reconstruction by offering a convenient explanation for southern governments' "failures," the relegation of blacks to the position of an economically dispossessed and politically disempowered caste fit neatly with the general pattern of racial thinking in the late nineteenth century. By 1900, the language of "race"—race conflict, race feeling, race problems—had assumed a central place in American public life, more central, in fact, than during the days of slavery. The supposed inborn capacity of one or another "race"—a term applied not only to blacks but to Italians, Jews, Slavs, and other "new immigrants" then entering the country, as well as to mythical constructs such as "Anglo-Saxons"— was commonly invoked to explain everything from the standard of living of various groups of workers to the worldwide dominance of European powers in the age of imperialism. Just as individual character was thought to explain success or failure in the economic marketplace, "racial" and "national" character—terms used more or less interchangeably—took on an ever larger role in explaining historical outcomes. Nativists claimed that immigration weakened the fiber of American society by allowing "inferior" races to outnumber sturdy Anglo-Saxons. Meanwhile, the boundaries of nationhood and citizenship, expanded so dramatically in the aftermath of the Civil War, contracted. Beginning in 1882, for example, Congress excluded Chinese immigrants from entering the country. In 1898, the triumphant appearance of the United States on the world stage as an imperial power during the Spanish-American War—in which northern and southern whites fought side by side, while blacks continued to be relegated to segregated units—reinforced the identification of democracy and nationhood with notions of racial superiority. Anglo-Saxons would now take up the "white man's burden" of spreading liberty and self-government throughout the world. Whether in the newly acquired territories of Puerto

The racial justification for American and European imperialism is questioned in this 1899 cartoon, "The White (?) Man's Burden."

Rico and the Philippines or in the South, the domination of nonwhite peoples by white Americans was part of the progress of civilization.

Beginning in 1890, prominent white educators and reformers, including ex-president Hayes, who had driven the final nail into the coffin of Reconstruction, met periodically at Lake Mohonk, New York, for conferences on the "Negro Question." The participants concluded that blacks' problem was deficient "personal conduct and character," and that self-help, not national assistance or political agitation, offered the best route to racial progress. No blacks were present at the conferences. The only discordant note was sounded by former Reconstruction judge Albion W. Tourgée, who observed that those participating ought to devote some attention to the "white" problem, since "the hate, the oppression, the injustice, are all on our side." Tourgée's, however, was a lone voice.

Even within the black community, prominent leaders took to emphasizing economic self-help and individual advancement into the middle class as an alternative to popular mobilization and political agitation. Symbolizing the change was the juxtaposition, in 1895, of the death of Frederick Douglass with Booker T. Washington's widely praised speech at the Atlanta Cotton States and International Exposition urging blacks to adjust to segregation and forgo agitation for civil rights and suffrage. Like Douglass, Washington had been born a slave, but as a young man during Reconstruction, rather than becoming involved in politics, he had studied at Hampton Institute, a newly established vocational training center for blacks in Virginia. Washington imbibed the ethos of Hampton's founder, General Samuel Armstrong, which emphasized that obtaining farms or skilled jobs was far more important to African Americans just emerging from slavery than the rights of citizenship.

In his Atlanta speech, Washington explicitly repudiated the abolitionist-Reconstruction tradition embodied by Douglass, which stressed ceaseless agitation for full equality. It was more important, Washington declared, for blacks to "prepare" themselves for the exercise of citizenship rights than to achieve them through "artificial forcing." As to segregation, Washington accepted that as well: "In all the things that are purely social we can be as separate as the fingers, yet one as the hand in all things essential to mutual progress." "The whole future of the Negro," Washington declared in his autobiography, *Up from Slavery*, rested not on the premature exercise of political power, but "upon the question as to whether or not he should make himself, through his skill, intelligence, and character, . . . of undeniable value to the community."

Given economic independence, political rights would soon follow, Washington insisted. But in the meantime, blacks should accept without challenge their second-class status, while seeking the assistance of white employers and philanthropists who, in a land wracked by labor turmoil and unchecked foreign immigration, would value blacks as a docile, dependable labor force. Indeed, Washington's ascendancy depended in large part on his success in channeling aid from white philanthropists—the Carnegies, Rockefellers, and Peabodys of the North—to his center for vocational education, Alabama's Tuskegee Institute, and to black politicians and newspapers that supported his program. But his base in the black community also arose from a sense that frontal assaults on white power were suicidal, and from the desire of the emerging black middle class for recognition as the true leaders of the race.

Years later, black writer Blyden Jackson recalled growing up in early-twentieth-century Louisville, Kentucky, a city in many ways typical of the New South. It was a divided society. There was the world "where white folks lived . . . the Louisville of the downtown hotels, the lower floors of the big movie houses . . . the inner sanctums of offices where I could go only as a humble client or a menial custodian." Then there was the black world, "the homes, the people, the churches, and the schools," where "everything was black." "I knew," Jackson later recalled, "that there were two Louisvilles and . . . two Americas."

Thus, the aspirations embodied in Reconstruction remained largely unfulfilled at the dawn of the twentieth century. "The slave went free;" W. E. B. Du Bois would later write in *Black Reconstruction in America*, "stood a brief moment in the sun; and then moved back again toward slavery." To be sure, the tide of change could never be completely reversed. Despite the North's complicity in segregation and disenfranchisement, the South's racial system remained regional, not national. Segregation was pervasive in the North (although by custom, not law), but northern blacks retained the right to vote, a matter of considerable importance once migration from the South began in significant numbers. Although black schools and colleges remained woefully underfunded, education continued to be available to most African Americans. And the autonomous family and church, pillars of the black community that emerged during Reconstruction, remained vital forces in black life, and the springboard from which future challenges to racial injustice would emerge. Finally, although grievously violated, the laws and constitutional amendments of Reconstruction remained on the books—"sleeping giants," as Charles Sumner had once called them, ready to be reawakened when the struggle for racial justice revived.

When the Reconstruction Act of 1867 was passed, granting southern blacks the right to vote for the first time in American history, Senator Timothy Howe, a Wisconsin Republican, wrote to his niece, "we have cut loose from the whole dead past and have cast our anchor out a hundred years." Howe proved more prescient than he could have imagined in the heady days of 1867. After the end of Reconstruction, it would take nearly a century for the nation to begin to come to terms once again with that era's political and economic agenda, and with the continuing struggle for genuine freedom by the descendants of slavery.

JIM CROW

In the depressing chronicle of racism and Jim Crow, what role could pictures have played?

The answer lies in the language of the notorious 1896 *Plessy v. Ferguson* U.S. Supreme Court decision. The majority opinion, written by Justice Henry Billings Brown, denied that violations of either the Thirteenth or Fourteenth amendments were relevant to the case. African Americans and white Americans had equal political rights, but those rights could not transcend black citizens' inherent inferiority and consequent unequal social status.

> Legislation is powerless to eradicate racial instincts or to abolish distinctions based on physical differences. . . . If the civil and political rights of both races be equal, one cannot be inferior to the other civilly or politically. If one race be inferior to the other socially, the Constitution of the United States cannot put them on the same plane.

As if in service to that judgment, artists, photographers, editors, publishers, and film-makers—a new category—had by 1896 created a visual culture based on racial difference. An avalanche of racist imagery in new mass-circulation publications and on movie screens reached every corner of the country, establishing racial distinctions through apelike, child-like, and criminal stereotypes of African Americans. And in grotesque lines, brushstrokes, and visual performances, this imagery legitimized the Supreme Court's decision. In a travesty of Frederick Douglass's post-emancipation hope for equality of representation in the spheres of politics and art, a Jim Crow visual culture accentuated inequality; helped along by cruel imagery, the nation descended into a deep trough of racial injustice.

The conjunction of social and visual discrimination was readily apparent three years before the Supreme Court justices codified inequality. The World's Columbian Exposition that opened in Chicago in 1893 marked (albeit a year late) the four hundredth anniversary of Columbus's arrival in the Americas and the establishment of the United States as a leading industrial power now expanding its influence across the globe. In the fair's brief six-month existence, an astonishing twenty-seven million visitors flocked to the "White City" built along Lake Michigan. In its neoclassical grandeur, the fair provided a majestic diversion from the turmoil the nation then faced from the worst economic depression it had ever experienced.

The White City's spectacle was complemented by the popular focal point of the fair, the Midway Plaisance, a cluttered mile-long series of exhibits and eateries that cleverly merged sideshowlike entertainment with elucidation of contemporary scientific theory. With the participation of the Smithsonian Institution, the Midway—in particular, its simulated ethnic villages peopled by "genuine" Indians, Asians, and Africans—explained the nation's stunning material growth on the basis of racial hierarchy: a visit to the Midway, in the words of one observer, was "a walk through the past history of the [human] race,

preparing and conducting one to the highest development which it has attained." That ideal was prominently displayed in two statues of a white man and woman, based on students from Harvard and Radcliffe.

Such a show had no room for African Americans. As at the 1876 Centennial Exposition, blacks were excluded from decision-making positions in preparation for the Chicago fair. Fair officials blocked plans by some African American leaders to open an exhibit heralding black achievements; the black leaders instead were invited to submit their ideas to all-white committees running separate state exhibits. In a pamphlet called "The Reason Why the Colored American Is Not in the World's Columbian Exposition," co-edited with antilynching activist Ida B. Wells, an aged Frederick Douglass declared that he hoped that the fair,

> with its splendid display of wealth and power, its triumphs of art and its multitudinous architectural and other attractions, [would be] a fair indication of the elevated and liberal sentiment of the American people, and that to the colored people of America, morally speaking, the World's Fair now in progress, is not a whited sepulcher.

"All this, and more," he concluded, "we would gladly say of American laws, manners, customs and Christianity. But unhappily, nothing of all this can be said, without qualification and without flagrant disregard of the truth."

When the fair's directors designated August 25 as the "Jubilee" or "Colored People's Day," many African Americans feared that the special date would serve only as an opportunity for blacks themselves to become exhibits, to be gawked at and derided by the largely white crowds. These trepidations were confirmed four days before the event, when the "World's Fair" edition of the popular satirical weekly *Puck,* published at the exposition, featured cartoonist Frederick Opper's extravagantly insulting "Darkies' Day at the Fair." And, indeed, the small number of African Americans who attended the fair on August 25 were appalled to discover upon their arrival that stands had been erected throughout the Midway to sell 2,500 watermelons specially shipped in for the day.

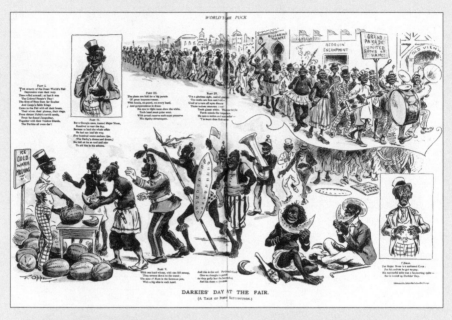

DARKIES' DAY AT THE FAIR.
(A TALE OF POOR EXTINCTION.)

In the end, the day was saved by the seventy-six-year-old Douglass, who, in an impromptu speech, shamed heckling white onlookers into silence with his fiery demand that "the American people have honesty enough, loyalty enough, honor enough, patriotism enough to live up to their own Constitution." But *Puck's* treatment was typical of the pictorial derision, in official pamphlets and magazine reporting, directed at African American visitors to the Chicago exposition.

Three decades after the Civil War, America's Jim Crow visual culture was imbued with the prevailing myth of "The Lost Cause." In this revision of the past, the antebellum South was recalled as a benevolent, orderly society that pitted its noble values against the aggressive greed of northern industrial society. Denying slavery as the root cause of the war, the proponents of The Lost Cause achieved an ideological victory—even as the South was defeated in the war—by shaping the popular memory of the conflict. In the process, this ideological victory helped ensure widespread white American acceptance of the South's justification for the racial status quo.

Hundreds of town squares and urban crossroads throughout today's South still display the physical remnants of The Lost Cause crusade in memorial sculptures and monuments that were erected at the turn of the century and in the early twentieth century to mark the heroism of Rebel soldiers and the sacrifice of southern white women. Many southerners, particularly the United Daughters of the Confederacy and other voluntary groups that campaigned for memorialization, believed that their cause was best served through the opaque symbolism of regal bronze and stone soldiers, or in the gentility of elderly southern veterans gathering for reunions or other commemorative rituals.

But The Lost Cause's most popular manifestation was the romantic resurrection of the Ku Klux Klan that appeared in the fiction, theater, and, eventually, the films of Thomas Dixon, Jr. Born in 1864 in North Carolina, Dixon marched through careers in law, politics, the ministry, and popular lecturing before turning to writing. In 1902, in a blaze of anger provoked by attending a performance of the abolitionist play *Uncle Tom's Cabin,* Dixon wrote a fictional recollection about the defeated South. Under the imprimatur of a major New York publisher, Dixon's *The Leopard's Spots: A Romance of the White Man's Burden, 1865–1900* became an instant best seller, with one out of eight Americans purchasing the book. An equally successful sequel, *The Clansman: An Historical Romance of the Ku Klux Klan,* followed in 1905, and was joined two years later by the last volume in Dixon's Reconstruction trilogy, *The Traitor: A Story of the Rise and Fall of the Invisible Empire.*

"The chaos of blind passion that followed Lincoln's assassination is inconceivable today," Dixon explained to his readers in his introduction to *The Clansman.* "The Revolution it produced in our Government, and the bold attempt of Thaddeus Stevens to Africanise ten great states of the American Union, read now like tales from 'The Arabian Nights.' " Indeed, Dixon's novels were successful because they offered in mesmerizing detail a panoramic historical fantasy about the defeated South—a tale with clear-cut heroes and villains that was steeped in a virulent, unrestrained racism.

At the heart of Dixon's story was the southern black man's innate bestiality and bloodlust, unleashed by emancipation. No longer constrained by benevolent slavery, African American men reverted during Reconstruction to their primitive evolutionary state, subjecting southern whites to an incessant reign of terror, epitomized by the rape of white women. In defense of the purity of southern womanhood, the white-swathed knights of the South finally saw no choice but to rise up to free their civilization from the yoke of black misrule and the white race from the curse of miscegenation.

The novel's graphic descriptions and evocative illustrations—picturing, for example, Anglo-Saxon crusaders standing over a cringing black villain—influenced subsequent popular theatrical versions (which featured onstage lynchings and cross burnings) and, ultimately, D. W. Griffith's cinematic vision, the landmark 1915 film *The Birth of a Nation,* which was co-written with Dixon and based on *The Clansman.*

Dixon's and Griffith's romantic vision of the Klan, and popularity among white readers and moviegoers, revealed the extent of American racism. The Reconstruction trilogy and *The Birth of a Nation* also provided justification for the actual terror that gripped the nation at the time—the epidemic of lynching. Of the three thousand victims of lynchings carried out between 1882 and 1930, 88 percent were African American men, most of whom had been charged, with little or no evidence, with sexual offenses against white women.

The imaginary romance of violence in print and on the screen found its everyday counterpart in a new, sinister addition to the country's visual culture: the commemorative pictorial record of vigilante murders. During Reconstruction, beatings and murders often were carried out under the cloak of darkness. But by the turn of the century the summary execution and mutilation of African Americans had become a public spectacle—or, as W. E. B. Du Bois wrote in 1925, "Negro baiting and even lynching became a form of amusement." Drawing huge crowds of onlookers, lynchings also attracted professional photographers. With the assistance of more flexible cameras, their widely disseminated pictures became a crucial factor in encouraging such gruesome events, serving not just to record but also to circulate news of the lynchings far and wide. Images such as this photo of a crowd burning the corpse of William Brown after his hanging in Omaha, Nebraska, in September 1919, were reproduced and sold as postcards, stereographs, and souvenirs. Photography became essential to lynching, a device for circulating the graphic tenets of white supremacy.

By the turn of the century, Americans awakened every morning to a recurring bombardment of visual images conveyed through new mass-market publications and commercial pastimes. As they read their newspapers and the increasingly popular "funny papers," or gazed at flickering movie screens, one message appeared with stunning regularity: the broad and general acceptance among white Americans of the notion of racial inferiority, inscribed on the popular mind by the incessant messages emanating from mass visual culture.

The rise of mass-circulation newspapers at the end of the nineteenth century was based in large part on their lavish layouts and the variety of features they offered readers every day. Among the most popular of these new features was the comic strip, a new form of popular art that from the start found a special role for African Americans in its graphic stories. Cartoonist Richard Outcault gained fame with his pioneering comic strip *Hogan's Alley*, which celebrated the antics of a gang of raucous juvenile inhabitants of an urban immigrant neighborhood. His next venture was a comic strip in the *New York World* called *Here's the New Bully,* whose protagonist had the distinction of being the first black comic strip character. But it was not an auspicious beginning. The straight razor—wielding leader of a street-corner gang, the New Bully represented the epitome of the stereotype of the dangerous, predatory black. Outcault soon dropped *Here's the New Bully* (perhaps his readers did not find the brutish figure funny) for another comic strip starring an African American character, Pore Lil Mose, a rural black child, before finally settling on his greatest comics success, the mischievous upper-class white character Buster Brown.

But it was another black child in the comics—with a bulbous head and garbled language—who would become for a decade a ubiquitous figure in the nation's funny pages. William Marriner's *Sambo and His Funny Noises* appeared in papers across the country between 1905 and 1914. Its premise was simple and predictable, and seemingly addressed the expectations of its white readers. In each installment, Sambo (later Samuel Johnson) clashed with and lost, usually catastrophically, to a duo of tough white tykes, Mike and Jim Tanks. The "funny noises" in the strip's title referred to Sambo's tortured dialect. And while he occasionally prevailed over his tormentors, Sambo's momentary victory was usually the

result of luck or, more often, of the physical traits that were popularly ascribed to black people—particularly their purported insensitivity to pain, which in Sambo's case was found in his amazingly hard head.

The visual conventions employed in comic strips made an easy transition to the new form of film that emerged in the first decade of the twentieth century: short animated cartoons. In common with comic strips, the original animated cartoons were riddled with racist language and racist visual conventions. A black character first appeared in a 1906 three-minute film called *Humorous Phases of Funny Faces.* Working with chalk and the stop-motion technique that would define the medium, former vaudevillian J. Stuart Blackton magically created a series of cartoons that included a leering black caricature formed out of the verbal epithet "coon."

While animator Pat Sullivan's character Sammy Johnsin (a screen variation of the discontinued Sambo comic strip) was the only black "star" of a cartoon series in the silent era, grotesque renditions of African Americans were typical fare on the popular screen. Rendered in rapidly produced black-and-white ink drawings, displaying popping eyes and bulbous lips, a parade of loose-limbed minstrels, randy cannibals, menacing criminals, massive mammies, and mischievous pickaninnies articulated old racial prejudices in new ways. In their fantastic settings and wild appearances, movie animation, more than live-action film, declared to mass audiences how utterly different black Americans were from white Americans. Animation was a medium that would continue to ridicule African Americans well into the 1950s.

If any medium characterized the new century, it was advertising. With the rise of mass-market magazines, which relied on advertisers instead of subscribers for revenue, advertising came into its own. Lavish illustrated ads, more and more of them in color, filled the pages of periodicals; meanwhile, billboards, posters, and other forms of display advertising crammed thoroughfares and roadways. In the increasingly competitive commercial landscape, businesses sought ways to grab consumers' attention, and symbols and trademarks linked to popular products became enduring parts of the nation's culture. Many of these symbolic representatives were African Americans or, more accurately, fictional black Americans who embodied the subservient stereotypes with which white Americans felt comfortable.

CREAM
of WHEAT

Maybe *Cream of Wheat*
aint got no vitamines.
I dont know what them
things is. If they's bugs
they aint none in *Cream of
Wheat* but she's sho' good
to eat and cheap. Costs 'bout
1¢ fo' a great big dish.
                    Rastus

The most popular product logos were black figures whose history in the visual culture immediately recalled good-natured servitude in the kitchen. "Aunt Jemima," who was first introduced at the 1893 World's Columbian Exposition to sell a brand of instant pancake flour, harked back to the figure of the Mammy in the southern plantation big house glorified by The Lost Cause. "Rastus," the chef who adorned the package of Cream of Wheat farina, also first appeared in the 1890s. Like that of Aunt Jemima, Rastus's perpetually sunny disposition beamed from magazine ads and billboards as the twentieth century progressed. The Cream of Wheat advertisements often featured Rastus's rural relatives, who expressed in garbled dialect their pride in his commercial status. And, on those rare occasions when Rastus "spoke" to the viewer, his ignorance was at the heart of the advertising pitch. Their faces peering from ads and from the boxes and containers of everyday products, these benign black figures domesticated prejudice, using racist stereotypes to sell products found in the kitchen.

It was the familiarity and alarming pervasiveness of these stereotypes that the National Association for the Advancement of Colored People challenged in the pages of its monthly magazine, *The Crisis,* launched in 1910 and edited by W. E. B. Du Bois. *The Crisis* made a point of featuring illustrations and photographs of young and very real African Americans, an archive of actual faces to confront the Moses, Sambos, New Bullies, and the host of other caricatures flooding the nation's visual culture.

By the 1920s, *The Crisis* promoted African American art by publishing the work of and sponsoring contests for visual artists, writers, and composers. Its pages reflected the work of the artists of the Harlem Renaissance, including Aaron Douglas, William Johnson, and Lois Mailou Jones. These talented artists were inspired to confront Jim Crow culture by combining a rich folk heritage, ways of seeing rooted in African art, and contemporary modernism. In all, style merged with substance to declare, in visual terms, racial pride.

In the twenty-first century, the Jim Crow images

This is my CRISIS—

OCTOBER 1916

of the late nineteenth century and the first half of the twentieth century still have the capacity to hurt—and distort—our understanding of the nation's past. Some people advocate covering up these pictures, believing that acknowledging their existence only lends legitimacy to a racist pictorial record. But the remnants and resonances of those images still appear today in myriad and diverse ways. Racist imagery will simply not go away.

Over the last thirty years, a number of African American artists have grappled with Jim Crow visual culture by using its invidious signs and stereotyped conventions to draw attention to the history of American racism. Among the work of a number of important black American artists, including Kara Walker and Emma Amos, Kerry James Marshall's *Heirlooms and Accessories* stands out, turning the visual record back on itself.

In this typically challenging piece, Marshall begins with one of the most infamous lynching photographs, which records an enthusiastic white crowd in Marion, Indiana, in

August 1930, gathered about the corpses of two African American teenagers. *Heirlooms and Accessories,* a large triptych completed in 2002, isolates three white women captured in the original photograph, reinstalling their isolated portraits into bejeweled lockets and mounting each one against a faint reproduction of the full lynching photograph. The work is, as Marshall explained in a recent interview, "a reminder that these people are accessories to a crime in the first place, and that the heirlooms and the things that their offspring inherited from them were inherited from them because they were engaged in this kind of violence." By implicating the white spectators at the lynching and the past purchasers of the souvenir photograph of that abominable crime—turning their gazes back upon themselves—*Heirlooms and Accessories* offers one strategy for contending with a painful visual record of racism that requires both our ongoing recognition and our active condemnation.

EPILOGUE

THE UNFINISHED REVOLUTION

THE EFFORT TO RECOVER what John R. Lynch called the "facts of Reconstruction" has always been part of the unfinished struggle for racial justice in the United States. For nearly a century after the end of Reconstruction, a grossly distorted memory of that critical era overwhelmed the dissenting account that survived in black communities and received eloquent scholarly expression from W. E. B. Du Bois. An inaccurate picture of Reconstruction as a time of rampant misgovernment presided over by unscrupulous carpetbaggers, duplicitous scalawags, and former slaves incapable of exercising responsibly the freedom that had been thrust upon them helped to justify the racial system that dominated the South and profoundly affected the entire nation for the first six decades of the twentieth century. This was a time when the guarantees of equal rights enshrined in the laws and the Constitution after the Civil War became dead letters, and all too many public officials, popular writers, and scholars glorified or failed to condemn the violent terrorists who had used murder and intimidation to roll back the gains achieved by former slaves and their white allies.

Only in the 1950s and 1960s, when the edifice of racism began to crumble in the face of a massive popular challenge, did it become possible to begin to recover the full story of emancipation and Reconstruction and to understand their connections to our own time. That process continues to this day. Sadly, it will take a long time for scholarly writing to overcome the distorted image of Reconstruction that so powerfully penetrated the national consciousness. But for history to have any value, it must be remembered accurately. That is why this book was written.

One of the most celebrated orations in American history was delivered by Martin Luther King, Jr., on an August afternoon in 1963 on the steps of the Lincoln Memorial. The occasion was the March on Washington, the largest public demonstration in American history to that date, which

The August 28, 1963, civil rights demonstration in Washington, D.C.

brought a quarter of a million Americans, black and white, to the nation's capital to demand "jobs and freedom." King began the legendary "I have a dream" speech with a reference to the Emancipation Proclamation: "One hundred years later, the Negro still is not free." He then spoke of the "promissory note" on which the nation had defaulted in the aftermath of emancipation, a note that guaranteed "the unalienable rights of life, liberty, and the pursuit of happiness" to all Americans.

The "dream" King outlined that day—of an America where all persons would enjoy equality, dignity, and opportunity—has become a staple of our historical aspiration. But the era that first promised participation in that dream to African Americans has been too long forgotten. The twentieth-century civil rights revolution, the Second Reconstruction, embraced the ideals and in many ways fulfilled the revolutionary political and social agenda of the era of Reconstruction.

History never really repeats itself. But the parallels between the two Reconstructions are indeed striking. The shock troops of the mass movement in the South in the 1950s and 1960s emerged from black churches and schools—institutions created by African Americans after the Civil War. As during Reconstruction, ministers, such as King himself, played a key role in the movement's political leadership. Central to King's theology was the story of Exodus, a mainstay of black preaching in the days of slavery and Reconstruction, which interpreted the African American experience as a divinely guided progress toward Canaan, the promised land of freedom. And for its legal strategy, the civil rights movement turned to the laws and constitutional amendments enacted during Reconstruction, demanding that the nation live up to the letter of the law and to its professed beliefs.

King always linked the struggle for racial justice to the unfulfilled promises of the Civil War era. He first voiced his demand for equality during World War II, when as a high school student he won a contest with a speech on "The Negro and the Constitution." His talk, delivered in 1944, invoked the spirit of Lincoln and the "new birth of freedom" that came out of the Civil War, as well as the legacy of Reconstruction. The task facing the younger generation, he said, was to translate the constitutional amendments of Reconstruction "from writing on the printed page to an actuality," to reclaim the right to vote and to abolish segregation. While the struggle for racial justice has been a constant theme of African American history, World War II was a time when the struggle for racial justice became a matter of intense interest at home and abroad. Indeed, as King's youthful oration suggests, the modern civil rights movement emerged during World War II.

American wars have not always promoted greater justice. While most black leaders urged African Americans to enlist in the army in World War I, for example, seeing such participation as an opportunity to make real the promise of equality—even though the armed forces were segregated—that conflict was followed by widespread racial violence in the nation's cities and an upsurge in lynchings, including of several returning black veterans still in their uniforms. The combination of increased wartime production and the cutoff of immigration from Europe opened thousands of industrial jobs to black laborers during and after World War I. By 1920, nearly half a million blacks had left the South. But the black migrants found not "social and economic freedom," as Alain Locke explained in the preface to his influential book *The New Negro,* but vast disappointments—severely restricted employment opportunities, exclusion from unions, rigid housing segregation, and machine control of urban politics that limited the impact of the right to vote.

World War II was different. For the first time since Reconstruction, the status of black Americans was placed on the national agenda, challenging the hold of racial thinking and policy on national life. The struggle against Nazi tyranny and its theory of a master race gave new emphasis to a definition of American nationality, pioneered by the abolitionists and written into the Constitution after the Civil War, as equal citizenship regardless of racial or ethnic origins. Public and private pronouncements celebrated a pluralist vision of American society. Racism was the enemy's philosophy; Americanism rested on toleration of diversity and equality for all. The writings of Franz Boas, Ruth Benedict, and other anthropologists critical of the supposed link between race, culture, and intelligence, now for the first time reached a mass audience. Benedict's book *Races and Racism,* published in 1942, described racism as "a travesty of scientific knowledge."

Of course, the internment of tens of thousands of citizens of Japanese descent during the war belied the new spirit of racial accommodation. So, too, did the persistence of segregation, disenfranchisement, and lynching. Until the final months of the war, the one million African Americans in the armed forces served in segregated units, mostly confined to construction, transport, and other noncombat duties. Washington, D.C., remained rigidly segregated. Detroit in June 1943 experienced a race riot that left thirty-four

While police stand by, white crowds terrorize African Americans on Detroit's Woodward Avenue on June 21, 1943.

persons dead and a "hate strike" of twenty thousand white autoworkers protesting the upgrading of black workers in a plant manufacturing aircraft engines.

In 1942, a public-opinion survey reported that a large majority of white Americans did not believe "that there is any such thing as a 'Negro problem.' " But the wide disparities between wartime ideology and the actual condition of black Americans helped to spawn a renewed movement for equality. Angered by the almost complete exclusion of blacks from employment in the rapidly expanding war production industries, labor leader A. Philip Randolph in July 1941 called for a March on Washington to demand defense jobs and an end to segregation in government departments and the armed forces. To persuade Randolph to call off the march, President Franklin D. Roosevelt issued an executive order banning discrimination in defense employment and establishing a Fair Employment Practices Commission to monitor compliance. The first federal agency since Reconstruction to campaign for equal opportunity for black Americans, the FEPC played an important role in obtaining jobs for black workers in wartime industrial plants and shipyards, an enormous step forward for migrants from the rural South. By 1944, more than one million blacks held manufacturing jobs, three hundred thousand of them women. ("My sister always said that Hitler was the one that got us out of the white folks' kitchen," recalled one black woman.) Other egalitarian steps soon followed. In 1944, the Supreme Court took a small step toward reinvigorating the Fifteenth Amendment, outlawing all-white primaries, one of many mechanisms by which blacks had been deprived of the franchise in the South.

The phrase that came to epitomize black attitudes during the war—the "double-V"—was coined in 1942 by a leading black newspaper, the *Pittsburgh Courier*. Victory over Germany and Japan, it insisted, must be accompanied by victory over segregation at home. While most of the white press supported the war as an expression of American ideals, black newspapers persistently pointed to the gap between those ideals and reality. During the war, the NAACP's membership grew from fifty thousand to nearly half a million. "*Our* fight for freedom," said a black veteran returning from Pacific combat, "begins when we get to San Francisco."

The new attention to the question of racial justice spawned by the war spilled over into postwar America. It was especially evident in President Truman's decision to make civil rights a major plank in the Democratic platform of 1948, prompting delegates from several southern states to walk out of the gathering. But as the Cold War deepened, criticism of American society became increasingly suspect. Aside from the integration of the armed forces, ordered by the president in 1948, little came of the Truman administration's civil rights flurry. Indeed, during the postwar suburban boom, federal agencies continued to insure mortgages with racially restrictive provisions, thereby financing housing segregation.

In 1954, in the historic decision *Brown v. Board of Education,* the Supreme Court finally rediscovered the promise of racial justice inherent in the Fourteenth Amendment, overturning the "separate but equal" doctrine of *Plessy v. Ferguson* and declaring school segregation unconstitutional. The black press hailed the decision as "a second Emancipation Proclamation." But the real inauguration of the civil rights revolution as a nonviolent crusade based in the black churches of the South came the following year. On December 1, 1955, Rosa Parks, a veteran of civil rights activities in Montgomery, Alabama, was arrested for refusing to surrender her seat on a city bus to a white rider, as required by municipal law. The incident, reminiscent of Reconstruction movements to integrate public streetcars, sparked a year-long bus boycott, the beginning of the greatest mass movement in modern American history.

Today, with King's birthday a national holiday, and streets, office buildings, and education institutions named after participants in the movement, the civil rights revolution has been assimilated into mainstream historical memory. It is difficult to recall that when the mass movement for racial equality arose during the 1950s, it came as a great surprise and roused bitter opposition. In retrospect, its precipitating causes seem clear: the destabilization of the racial system during World War II; the migration out of the segregated South that made black voters a major part of the northern Democratic Party coalition; and the Cold War and rise of independent states in Africa, both of which made the gap between American rhetoric and the reality of American race relations an international embarrassment.

Yet the movement was hardly inevitable. With blacks' traditional allies on the left decimated by McCarthyism; union leaders, by and large, unwilling to challenge racial inequalities within their own ranks; and the NAACP concentrating almost entirely on court battles, the challenge to segregation and racial inequality desperately needed new constituencies and tactics. The movement found in the black church the organizing power for a militant, nonviolent assault on the edifice of segregation. Then, beginning with the sit-ins of 1960, students from the black colleges established after the Civil War propelled the struggle to a new level of mass activism and civil disobedience. Within a decade, the civil rights revolution would overturn the system of de jure segregation and win the ballot for black citizens in the South. Although today many Americans equate the civil rights struggle with the actions of King, Parks, and a handful of other larger-than-life individuals, as during Reconstruction, the movement rested on the courage of thousands of ordinary men and women—maids and laborers alongside teachers, businessmen, and ministers—who, like their counterparts a century earlier, risked physical and economic retribution to lay claim to freedom.

Civil rights activists also demanded the enforcement of the laws and constitutional amendments enacted after the Civil War and resurrected the Reconstruction vision of federal authority as the custodian of American citizens' rights. Unlike the more recent struggle against apartheid in South Africa, the overthrow of an oppressive system did not require adopting a new national constitution; it simply meant enforcing the one under which the country already lived, yet which had in effect been nullified in many states. Despite the long history of federal complicity in segregation, black Americans' historical experience suggested that they had more hope for justice from national power than from local governments or the voluntary acquiescence of well-meaning whites. The civil rights movement reinforced the tradition, which originated with emancipation, that saw black Americans rely much more strongly on an activist national state than did most white citizens.

In the 1960s, the movement's growing militancy and the violent resistance it encountered created a national crisis that propelled the federal government, for a time, to champion the cause of black freedom. Like the first Reconstruction, the second encountered massive white resistance, in the North as well as in the South. Sometimes, resistance was violent, although nothing occurred on the scale of the depredations of the original Ku Klux Klan. This time, violence against civil rights activists deepened the national commitment rather than precipitated a retreat. Time and again, violence against nonviolent demonstrators flashed across television screens around the world, embarrassed the federal government, aroused the conscience of many white Americans, and forced national authorities to take action. Doing so led some leaders to think in new ways about the first Reconstruction. When the court-ordered integration of the University of Mississippi in 1962 inspired riots that left two persons dead and required the intervention of federal troops to restore order, President John F. Kennedy remarked, "It makes me wonder whether everything I learned about the evils of Reconstruction is really true." (Less than a decade earlier, Kennedy himself had contributed to the enduring mythology about Reconstruction in his book *Profiles in Courage*, which grossly exaggerated corruption in the Reconstruction South and presented as the era's heroes the seven Republicans who voted to acquit Andrew Johnson during his 1868 impeachment trial.)

In June 1963, with demonstrations sweeping the country (in one week, more than fifteen thousand Americans were arrested in 186 cities) and the violence unleashed against black protesters in Birmingham, Alabama, attracting worldwide attention, Kennedy went on television to announce that the nation was confronting a "moral crisis." Two years later, the crisis in Selma—where voting rights marchers were assaulted by the Alabama State Police—led Kennedy's successor, Lyndon B. Johnson, to secure passage of legislation restoring the right to vote to African Americans in the South. Never since the days of the Thirty-ninth Congress a century earlier had the cause of black rights received so sweeping or powerful an endorsement from the federal government. By 1965, with court orders having dismantled legal segregation and new federal laws prohibiting discrimination in public accommodations, employment, and voting, the movement had succeeded in eradicating the legal bases of second-class citizenship. The political agenda of freed slaves and Radical Republicans after the Civil War had once again been written into national law.

Economic injustice, however, remained an intractable problem. Just as the first Reconstruction had failed to address adequately the economic legacy of slavery, the Second Reconstruction found it difficult to attack the economic consequences of a century of segregation and economic and

Demonstrators are pummeled by water cannons in Birmingham, Alabama, in 1963.

political disempowerment. Civil rights activity had not entirely ignored the economic dimensions of the black condition: expanded employment opportunity was one part of the "treaty" that ended the Birmingham crisis of 1963. But the issue had been muted, partly because of the pressing need to challenge the legal and political dimensions of black inequality. Violent outbreaks in black ghettos outside the South—Harlem in 1964, Watts in 1965 (just a few days after Johnson signed the Voting Rights Act), Detroit, Newark, and other cities in ensuing years—drew attention to the inequalities in employment, education, and housing that the dismantling of legal segregation left intact.

In the mid-1960s, with black unemployment two and a half times that of white and the average black family income little more than half the white norm, economic issues moved to the forefront of the civil rights agenda. King in 1964 proposed a "Bill of Rights for the Disadvantaged" to mobilize the nation's resources to combat economic deprivation. He insisted that after "doing something special *against* the Negro for hundreds of years," the United States had an obligation to "do something special *for* him now"—a call reminiscent of Wendell Phillips's insistence in 1870, noted earlier, that the descendants of slavery continued to deserve the nation's "special sympathy." King was one of the most prominent advocates of what soon came to be termed "affirmative action." (Today, his call, in the "I have a dream" speech, for Americans to be judged by "the content of their character" rather than the "color of their skin" is often wrenched out of context by opponents of affirmative action to try to demonstrate that King opposed such policies, which he in fact strongly supported.)

In 1966, King took the struggle for racial justice into the North when he launched the Chicago Freedom Movement, whose demands included upgraded black employment, an end to discrimination by employers and unions, equal treatment in granting mortgages, and the construction of low-income housing scattered throughout the region. As during the first Reconstruction, the white North seemed much more willing to attack the legacy of slavery in the South than to alter its own less overt but no less pervasive structures of racial inequality. By 1967, when he wrote his last book, *Where Do We Go from Here?*, the optimism that had sustained King during the southern phase of the movement had faded. Open housing and equal employment opportunity remained "a distant dream," he wrote, and radical economic reforms—full employment, a guaranteed annual income, "structural changes" in capitalism itself—were necessary to bring blacks fully into the social mainstream.

In the nineteenth century, the waning of Reconstruction had opened the door to the rise of emigrationist and nationalist movements that emphasized the creation of economically and politically self-sufficient black communities. In the early 1960s, the fiery orator Malcolm X had drawn on the nationalist tradition that stretched back to Martin Delany in the Civil War era, to repudiate the integrationist ideal and insist that blacks must control the political and economic resources of their own communities and rely on their own efforts in order to achieve full emancipation. Malcolm X was assassinated in 1965, but his views helped to inspire the rise of Black Power, a slogan that first came to national attention in 1966 when Stokely Carmichael and other young African Americans employed it during a civil rights march in Mississippi. Black Power suggested everything from the election of more black officials to the belief that black Americans were a colonized people, analogous to inhabitants of the third world, whose freedom could be won only through a revolutionary struggle for self-determination. But however the slogan was employed, its prominence marked a significant shift in the goals of the civil rights movement.

The retreat from the Second Reconstruction in many ways paralleled the nation's abandonment of the first. Like the election of 1876, that of 1968 marked the inauguration of a long period of more conservative policies in Washington, during which civil rights issues faded slowly from the national

Malcolm X and trade union leader A. Philip Randolph share a platform during a 1962 rally celebrating a successful hospital workers' strike.

agenda. Republican presidential candidate Richard Nixon pioneered a "southern strategy" that was so successful that today the South is almost entirely Republican. Many issues contributed to this historic shift in the region's political loyalties. But there is no question that divisions and resentments among white voters, inspired by the civil rights revolution, proved to be an electoral gold mine for political conservatives. The conservative litany of law and order, local autonomy, the evils of welfare, and the sanctity of property often had strong racial overtones. The language of Andrew Johnson in his vetoes of the civil rights measures of the Thirty-ninth Congress gained a new lease on life in modern conservative rhetoric—that enhancing the rights of blacks amounted to reverse discrimination against whites, and that civil rights enforcement constituted a dangerous enhancement of federal power. If the first Reconstruction was followed by a long retreat from the principle of equality, the Second Reconstruction was also succeeded by a second Redemption.

Just as the retreat from Reconstruction was a long process that con-

Antibusing demonstrators assault labor lawyer Theodore Landsmark outside of Boston's City Hall on April 5, 1976.

sumed most of the final quarter of the nineteenth century, so the waning of the civil rights impulse took place slowly after the 1960s. As in the nineteenth century, the modern Supreme Court retreated from its commitment to civil rights, interpreting the Reconstruction amendments and modern civil rights laws in the narrowest possible manner. In celebrated cases, the Court limited the right to sue to enforce equal treatment on the job, invalidated government programs that sought to compensate for past discrimination by allotting a percentage of contracts to minority firms, and made it easier for school districts to free themselves from judicial orders mandating desegregation.

Of course, the Second Reconstruction has proved to be far more deeply entrenched than the first. A pluralist vision of nationality and a broad commitment to equality before the law have become deeply ingrained in American culture. It is impossible to imagine that black Americans will again be deprived of the right to vote, as they were a century ago. Nonetheless, as in the late nineteenth century, the issue of how to deal with continuing racial inequality has faded from the nation's political agenda.

At the dawn of the twenty-first century, what is remarkable is both how much America's racial situation has changed, and how much it remains the same. Thanks in large measure to a generation of civil rights activism and affirmative action policies adopted by public and private institutions, not only has the traditional color line been dismantled, but in every realm of American life—from sports and entertainment to universities, corporate boardrooms, and the military—nonwhites are playing roles that would have been inconceivable only a few decades ago. The right to vote has been guaranteed, and blacks cast ballots throughout the country in about the same proportion as whites. Several thousand African Americans now hold public office.

Nonetheless, progress in many areas remains decidedly mixed. Far more blacks live in suburbs than ever before, but predominantly in largely black suburban communities. The black middle class has grown dramatically, but so, too, has a black "underclass" trapped in urban poverty. The gap in income, job categories, and education between white and black families has narrowed significantly since 1960, but the median wealth of black families remains far below that of their white counterparts, and black unemployment remains double that of whites. In life expectancy and health, the gap between the races remains enormous. Despite the nation's growing racial diversity, school segregation—now resulting from housing patterns and the divide between urban and suburban school districts rather than laws requiring racial separation—is again on the rise. In the year 2000, the nation's black and Latino students were more isolated from white pupils than in 1970. In the same year, the percentage of the black population in prison stood eight times higher than that for white Americans. With twenty-nine states denying the right to vote to those on probation and several barring ex-felons from voting for their entire lives, an estimated four million black men (one-seventh of the black male population) could not cast a ballot at the beginning of the twenty-first century. In Florida, which George W. Bush carried by fewer than six hundred votes in the 2000 election, six hundred thousand persons—overwhelmingly black and Latino men—had lost the right to vote for their entire lives after being convicted of a felony. In 2004, more than four and a half million citizens nationwide, one-third of them African Americans, could not vote because of a past felony conviction.

Even more significant, perhaps, than statistical indices of difference in status, are differences in outlook. On issues ranging from the proper role of the federal government to economic policy and the equity of the criminal justice system, public-opinion polls consistently reveal an enormous difference between black and white attitudes. Most striking of all are different perceptions of race itself as a salient feature of modern American society. Most whites tend to think that race has only a minor impact on the daily experiences and future expectations of Americans whatever their background, and that blacks receive the same treatment as whites from individuals and institutions of authority. Most nonwhites feel that race still matters a great deal and that equal treatment remains a distant goal.

The United States has made enormous progress in eradicating historic wrongs. But much remains to be accomplished. Issues central to the Reconstruction era—the relationship between political and economic democracy, for example, and the proper role of the federal government in defining and protecting the rights of all citizens—remain as controversial today as they were after the Civil War. Studying Reconstruction can help us understand the world in which we live. Like the Reconstruction generation, we have witnessed how social movements led by ordinary citizens can transform society. Like them, we know, as Thomas Wentworth Higginson warned during the Civil War era, that "revolutions may go backward," and that the consequences of counterrevolutions can be damaging and long-lasting. Like the Reconstruction generation, we have seen radical movements rise to prominence, then shatter and retreat. Like them, we have experienced political terrorism, and like them we have seen that just because rights are enshrined in the Constitution does not mean that they are necessarily secure.

One reason, perhaps, why Reconstruction was for so long shunted to an obscure backwater of national memory is that Americans, like other people, prefer historical narratives with happy endings. Certainly, Reconstruction was in many ways a failure. In part, the story of Reconstruction history reveals in vivid hues aspects of our national history—especially our long experience with racial violence—that are hardly pleasant to contemplate. Yet properly understood, Reconstruction was also an era of noble dreams, of inspiring efforts by ordinary men and women to create a more just society for themselves and their countrymen. As South Africans demonstrated in the 1990s by establishing a Truth and Reconciliation Commission to uncover and publicize the history of apartheid, the search for historical truth can be simultaneously empowering and healing. In this country as well, "the facts of Reconstruction"—the era's true history—can serve as an inspiration for the unfinished task of forging from the ashes of slavery a society of interracial democracy and social justice.

BIBLIOGRAPHY FOR
FURTHER READING

Bennett, Lerone. *Black Power, U.S.A.: The Human Side of Reconstruction, 1867–1877.* Chicago: Johnson Publishing Company, 1967.

Bercaw, Nancy. *Gendered Freedoms: Race, Rights, and the Politics of the Household in the Delta, 1861–1875.* Gainesville: University Press of Florida, 2003.

Berlin, Ira. *Generations of Captivity: A History of African-American Slaves.* Cambridge, Mass.: Harvard University Press, 2003.

————, ed. *Slaves No More: Three Essays on Emancipation and the Civil War.* New York: Cambridge University Press, 1992.

Blight, David W. *Frederick Douglass' Civil War: Keeping Faith in Jubilee.* Baton Rouge: Louisiana State University Press, 1989.

————. *Race and Reunion: The Civil War in American Memory.* Cambridge, Mass.: Harvard University Press, 2001.

Carter, Dan T. *When the War Was Over: The Failure of Self-Reconstruction in the South, 1865–1867.* Baton Rouge: Louisiana State University Press, 1985.

DuBois, Ellen C. *Feminism and Suffrage: The Emergence of an Independent Women's Movement in America, 1848–1869.* Ithaca, N.Y.: Cornell University Press, 1978.

Du Bois, W. E. B. *Black Reconstruction in America.* New York: Harcourt, Brace, 1935.

Edwards, Laura. *Gendered Strife and Confusion: The Political Culture of Reconstruction.* Urbana: University of Illinois Press, 1997.

Fairclough, Adam. *Better Day Coming: Blacks and Equality, 1890–2000.* New York: Viking, 2001.

Fields, Barbara J. *Slavery and Freedom on the Middle Ground: Maryland During the Nineteenth Century.* New Haven, Conn.: Yale University Press, 1985.

Fitzgerald, Michael W. *Urban Emancipation: Popular Politics in Reconstruction Mobile, 1860–1890.* Baton Rouge: Louisiana State University Press, 2002.

Foner, Eric. *Freedom's Lawmakers: A Directory of Black Officeholders During Reconstruction.* Rev. ed. Baton Rouge: Louisiana State University Press, 1996.

————. *Reconstruction: America's Unfinished Revolution, 1863–1877.* New York: HarperCollins, 1988.

Foner, Eric, and Olivia Mahoney. *America's Reconstruction: People and Politics After the Civil War.* New York: HarperCollins, 1995.

Goodman, Paul. *Of One Blood: Abolitionism and the Origins of Racial Equality.* Berkeley: University of California Press, 1998.

Gutman, Herbert G. *The Black Family in Slavery and Freedom, 1750–1925.* New York: Pantheon, 1976.

Hahn, Steven. *A Nation Under Our Feet: Black Political Struggles in the Rural South from Slavery to the Great Migration.* Cambridge, Mass.: Harvard University Press, 2003.

Harding, Vincent. *There Is a River: The Black Struggle for Freedom in America.* New York: Harcourt Brace Jovanovich, 1981.

Holt, Sharon Ann. *Making Freedom Pay: North Carolina Freedpeople Working for Themselves, 1865–1900.* Athens: University of Georgia Press, 2000.

Hyman, Harold M. *A More Perfect Union: The Impact of the Civil War and Reconstruction on the Constitution.* New York: Alfred A. Knopf, 1973.

Jaynes, Gerald D. *Branches Without Roots: Genesis of the Black Working Class in the American South, 1862–1882.* New York: Oxford University Press, 1986.

Joyner, Charles D. *Down by the Riverside: A South Carolina Slave Community.* Urbana: University of Illinois Press, 1984.

Kerr-Ritchie, Jeffrey. *Freedpeople in the Tobacco South: Virginia, 1860–1900.* Chapel Hill: University of North Carolina Press, 1999.

Lawson, Melinda. *Patriot Fires: Forging a New American Nationalism in the Civil War North.* Lawrence: University of Kansas Press, 2002.

Litwack, Leon F. *Been in the Storm So Long: The Aftermath of Slavery.* New York: Alfred A. Knopf, 1979.

McPherson, James M. *Battle Cry of Freedom: The Civil War Era.* New York: Oxford University Press, 1988.

Penningroth, Dylan C. *The Claims of Kinfolk: African American Property and Community in the Nineteenth-Century South.* Chapel Hill: University of North Carolina Press, 2003.

Quarles, Benjamin. *Lincoln and the Negro.* New York: Oxford University Press, 1962.

Rable, George C. *But There Was No Peace: The Role of Violence in the Politics of Reconstruction.* Athens: University of Georgia Press, 1984.

Ransom, Roger L., and Richard Sutch. *One Kind of Freedom: The Economic Consequences of Emancipation.* New York: Cambridge University Press, 1977.

Regosin, Elizabeth Ann. *Freedom's Promise: Ex-Slave Families and Citizenship in the Age of Emancipation.* Charlottesville: University Press of Virginia, 2002.

Richardson, Heather C. *The Death of Reconstruction: Race, Labor, and Politics in the Post–Civil War North, 1865–1901.* Cambridge, Mass.: Harvard University Press, 2001.

Rodrigue, John C. *Reconstruction in the Cane Fields: From Slavery to Free Labor in Louisiana's Sugar Parishes, 1862–1880.* Baton Rouge: Louisiana State University Press, 2001.

Rose, Willie Lee. *Rehearsal for Reconstruction: The Port Royal Experiment.* Indianapolis: Bobbs-Merrill, 1964.

Saville, Julie. *The Work of Reconstruction: From Slave to Wage Laborer in South Carolina, 1860–1870.* New York: Cambridge University Press, 1994.

Stanley, Amy Dru. *From Bondage to Contract: Wage Labor, Marriage, and the Market in the Age of Slave Emancipation.* New York: Cambridge University Press, 1998.

Stevenson, Brenda E. *Life in Black and White: Family and Community in the Slave South.* New York: Oxford University Press, 1996.

Summers, Mark W. *Railroads, Reconstruction, and the Gospel of Prosperity: Aid Under the Radical Republicans, 1865–1877.* Princeton, N.J.: Princeton University Press, 1984.

Trefousse, Hans L. *The Radical Republicans: Lincoln's Vanguard for Racial Justice.* New York: Alfred A. Knopf, 1969.

Webber, Thomas L. *Deep Like the Rivers: Education in the Slave Quarter Community, 1831–1865.* New York: W. W. Norton, 1978.

BIBLIOGRAPHY FOR
THE VISUAL ESSAYS

Allen, James, et al. *Without Sanctuary: Lynching Photography in America.* Santa Fe, N.M.: Twin Palms, 2000.

Boime, Albert. *The Art of Exclusion: Representing Blacks in the Nineteenth Century.* Washington, D.C.: Smithsonian Institution Press, 1990.

Fahs, Alice. *The Imagined Civil War: Popular Literature of the North and South, 1861–1865.* Chapel Hill: University of North Carolina Press, 2001.

Fried, Gregory. "True Pictures." *Common-place* 2, no. 2 (January 2002), http://www.common-place.org/vol-02/no-02/fried/

Fusco, Coco, and Brian Wallis, eds. *Only Skin Deep: Changing Visions of the American Self.* New York: International Center of Photography/Harry N. Abrams, 2003.

Gordon, Ian. *Comic Strips and Consumer Culture, 1890–1945.* Washington, D.C.: Smithsonian Institution Press, 1998.

Harris, Michael D. *Colored Pictures: Race and Visual Representation.* Chapel Hill: University of North Carolina Press, 2003.

Honour, Hugh. *The Image of the Black in Western Art. Volume IV: From the American Revolution to World War I: 1. Slaves and Liberators.* Cambridge, Mass.: Harvard University Press, 1989.

Jeter, Marvin D. "H. J. Lewis and His Family in Indiana and Beyond, 1889–1990s." In *Indiana's African-American Heritage: Essays from Black History News & Notes,* edited by Wilma L. Gibbs, pp. 161–76. Indianapolis: Indiana Historical Society, 1993.

Kimball, Gregg D. " 'The South as It Was': Social Order, Slavery, and Illustrators in Virginia, 1830–1877." In *Graphic Arts and the South: Proceedings of the 1990 North American Print Conference,* edited by Judy L. Larson, with the assistance of Cynthia Payne, pp. 129–57. Fayetteville: University of Arkansas Press, 1993.

Lapansky, Phillip. "Graphic Discord: Abolitionist and Antiabolitionist Images." In *The Abolitionist Sisterhood: Women's Political Culture in Antebellum America,* edited by Jean Fagan Yellin and John C. Van Horne, pp. 201–30. Ithaca, N.Y.: Cornell University Press, 1994.

LeBeau, Bryan F. *Currier and Ives: America Imagined.* Washington, D.C.: Smithsonian Institution Press, 2001.

Lott, Eric. *Love and Theft: Blackface Minstrelsy and the American Working Class.* New York: Oxford University Press, 1993.

McClinton, Katharine Morrison. *The Chromolithographs of Louis Prang.* New York: Clarkson N. Potter, 1973.

McElroy, Guy C. *Facing History: The Black Image in American Art, 1710–1940.* Washington, D.C.: Corcoran Gallery of Art, 1990.

Peters, Harry T. *Currier and Ives: Printmakers to the American People.* Garden City, N.Y.: Doubleday, Doran, 1929.

Powell, Richard J. "Cinqué: Antislavery Portraiture and Patronage in Jacksonian America," *American Art* 11, no. 3 (Fall 1997): 48–73.

Reilly, Bernard F., Jr. "The Art of the Antislavery Movement." In *Courage and Conscience: Black and White Abolitionists in Boston,* edited by Donald M. Jacobs, pp. 47–73. Bloomington: Indiana University Press, 1993.

Reiss, Benjamin. *The Showman and the Slave: Race, Death, and Memory in Barnum's America.* Cambridge, Mass.: Harvard University Press, 2001.

Rydell, Robert W. *All the World's a Fair: Visions of Empire at American International Expositions, 1876–1916.* Chicago: University of Chicago Press, 1984.

Sampson, Henry T. *That's Enough, Folks: Black Images in Animated Cartoons, 1900–1960.* Lanham, Md.: Scarecrow Press, 1998.

Savage, Kirk. *Standing Soldiers, Kneeling Slaves: Race, War, and Monument in Nineteenth-Century America.* Princeton, N.J.: Princeton University Press, 1997.

Stauffer, John. *The Black Hearts of Men: Radical Abolitionists and the Transformation of Race.* Cambridge, Mass.: Harvard University Press, 2002.

Strömberg, Fredrik. *Black Images in the Comics: A Visual History.* Seattle: Fantagraphics Books, 2003.

Thompson, William Fletcher, Jr. "Pictorial Images of the Negro During the Civil War." *Wisconsin Magazine of History* 48, no. 4 (Summer 1965): 282–94.

Trachtenberg, Alan. *Reading American Photographs: Images as History: Mathew Brady to Walker Evans.* New York: Hill and Wang, 1989.

Turner, Patricia A. *Ceramic Uncles and Celluloid Mammies: Black Images and Their Influence on Culture.* New York: Anchor Books, 1994.

West, Richard Samuel. *Satire on Stone: The Political Cartoons of Joseph Keppler.* Urbana: University of Illinois Press, 1988.

Westerbeck, Colin L. "Frederick Douglass Chooses His Moment." *The Art Institute of Chicago Museum Studies* 24, no. 2 (1999): 9–25.

Willis, Deborah. *Reflections in Black: A History of Black Photographers, 1840 to the Present.* New York: W. W. Norton, 2002.

Wood, Peter H., and Karen C. C. Dalton. *Winslow Homer's Images of Blacks: The Civil War and Reconstruction Years.* Austin: University of Texas Press, 1988.

ILLUSTRATION CREDITS

38 "Mr. T. Rice as the Original Jim Crow," Harvard Theatre Collection, The Houghton Library

38 Edward W. Clay, *Life in Philadelphia Plate 4*, etching with color (Philadelphia: S. Hart, 1829), The Library Company of Philadelphia

39 Edward W. Clay, *Practical Amalgamation*, colored lithograph (New York: John Childs, 1839), The Library Company of Philadelphia

39 J. C. Buttre (engraver), Frederick Douglass, frontispiece engraving, in Frederick Douglass, *My Bondage and My Freedom* (New York: Miller, Orton & Milligan, 1855), Prints and Photographs Division, Library of Congress

40 J. T. Zealy, *Portrait of Renty, African-born slave*, quarter-plate daguerreotype (March 1850), Peabody Museum, Harvard University Photo T1867

41 *Harper's Weekly*, June 14, 1862, American Social History Project

45 James F. Gibson, United States Army Military History Institute

46 Prints and Photographs Division, Library of Congress

49 V. Blada (A. J. Volck), *Sketches from the Civil War in North America, 1861, '62, '63* (1863), American Social History Project

53 The Library Company of Philadelphia

54 F. H. Schell, *Frank Leslie's Illustrated Newspaper*, June 27, 1863, American Social History Project

56 *Illustrated London News*, August 8, 1863, American Social History Project

59 R. A. Holland, ed., *Letters and Diary of Laura M. Towne* (1912), American Social History Project

63 *Frank Leslie's Illustrated Newspaper*, February 25, 1865, Prints and Photographs Division, Library of Congress

66 *Harper's Weekly*, March 18, 1865, American Social History Project

69 Theodore Davis, "Scene in the parlor of Mr. Barnwell's house at Beaufort, South Carolina," *Harper's Weekly*, January 18, 1862, Prints and Photographs Division, Library of Congress

69 Henry Louis Stephens, "Gentleman of Color.—Yah! Yah! Darkey hab de best ob it now. Dat's de white man's draff, and here's de niggah's!" *Vanity Fair*, July 26, 1862, Prints and Photographs Division, Library of Congress

70 "A Rebel Captain forcing Negroes to load cannon under the fire of Berdan's Sharp-Shooters. Seen through a Telescope from our Lines, and Sketched by Mr. Mead," *Harper's Weekly*, May 10, 1862, American Social History Project

70 Frank Vizetelly(?), "The War in America: Negroes at Work on the fortifications at Savannah," *Illustrated London News*, April 18, 1863, American Social History Project

71 Edwin Forbes, " 'Contrabands' coming into the lines," May 29, 1864, Prints and Photographs Division, Library of Congress

72 Frank Bellew, "Dark Artillery; or How to Make the Contrabands Useful," *Frank Leslie's Illustrated Newspaper*, October 26, 1861, Prints and Photographs Division, Library of Congress

72 "Wilson Chinn, a Branded Slave from Louisiana. Also exhibiting Instruments of Torture used to punish Slaves," *Carte de visite*, 1863, Photographed by Kimball, 477 Broadway, N.Y., Prints and Photographs Division, Library of Congress

73 Winslow Homer, *The Bright Side*, 1865, oil on canvas, 12¾ × 17 inches (32.4 ×

43.2 cm), Fine Arts Museums of San Francisco, Gift of Mr. and Mrs. John D. Rockefeller III, 1979.7.56

73 James Walker, "The True Defenders of the Constitution," *Harper's Weekly*, November 11, 1865, Prints and Photographs Division, Library of Congress

74 Tintype of a Black Soldier, 1863–65, Chicago Historical Society

74 Automaton ad, *Harper's Weekly*, December 17, 1864, Prints and Photographs Division, Library of Congress

75 "Contrabands accompanying the line of Sherman's March through Georgia," *Frank Leslie's Illustrated Newspaper*, March 18, 1865, American Social History Project

77 H. P. Moore, New-York Historical Society

78 Thomas Nast, *Harper's Weekly*, April 14, 1866, American Social History Project

83 Drawing by J. Wells Champney [W. L. Sheppard, office artist], Edward King, *The Great South* . . . (1875), American Social History Project

85 R. A. Holland, ed., *Letters and Diary of Laura M. Towne* (1912), American Social History Project

88 Chicago Historical Society

93 *Frank Leslie's Illustrated Newspaper*, October 6, 1866, American Social History Project

95 James E. Taylor, *Frank Leslie's Illustrated Newspaper*, January 19, 1867, American Social History Project

97 A. R. Waud, *Harper's Weekly*, July 25, 1868, American Social History Project

99 Stanley Fox, *Harper's Weekly*, October 14, 1865, American Social History Project

101 Hiram R. Revels, photograph, Prints and Photographs Division, Library of Congress

102 L. Prang and Company (after a painting by Theodore Kaufmann), 1870, chromolithograph, 14 × 11¼ inches, Prints and Photographs Division, Library of Congress

103 Alfred R. Waud, *Marriage of a Colored Soldier at Vicksburg by Chaplain Warren of the Freedmen's Bureau*, c. June 1866, The Historic New Orleans Collection, accession no. 1965.71

103 *Frank Leslie's Illustrated Newspaper*, October 20, 1866, American Social History Project

104 American Tract Society, *The Freedman's Second Reader* (1865), American Social History Project

104 James E. Taylor, "The Misses Cooke's school-room, Freedmen's Bureau, Richmond, Va.," *Frank Leslie's Illustrated Newspaper*, November 17, 1866, American Social History Project

105 Alfred R. Waud, " 'Zion' school for Colored Children, Charleston, South Carolina," *Harper's Weekly*, December 15, 1866, American Social History Project

106 *Harper's Weekly*, July 25, 1868, American Social History Project

108 Thomas Nast, *Harper's Weekly*, October 27, 1866, American Social History Project

110 *Frank Leslie's Illustrated Newspaper*, August 1865, American Social History Project

112 John L. Magee, *Southern Chivalry—Argument versus Club's*, lithograph, 1856, American Social History Project

114 *Harper's Weekly*, December 9, 1865, American Social History Project

116 *Harper's Weekly*, April 28, 1866, American Social History Project

117 *Harper's Weekly*, October 27, 1866, American Social History Project

119 Thomas Nast, *The Massacre at New Orleans*, 1867, oil on canvas, 7 feet 10¾ inches × 11 feet 6½ inches, Prints and Photographs Division, Library of Congress

120 *Harper's Weekly*, September 15, 1866, American Social History Project

121 Thomas Nast, *Harper's Weekly*, March 16, 1867, American Social History Project

126 Joseph Keppler, *Die Vehme*, April 2, 1870, American Social History Project

130 William L. Sheppard, *Frank Leslie's Illustrated Newspaper*, July 24, 1869, American Social History Project

132 Theodore R. Davis, *Harper's Weekly*, February 6, 1869, American Social History Project

133 Prints and Photographs Division, Library of Congress

135 Alabama Department of Archives and History, Montgomery, Ala.

136 Mifflin Gibbs, *Shadow and Light: An Autobiography* (1902), American Social History Project

136 Prints and Photographs Division, Library of Congress

138 Drawing by J. Wells Champney [W. L. Sheppard, office artist], Edward King, *The Great South . . .* (1875), American Social History Project

141 James E. Taylor [Albert Berghaus, office artist], *Frank Leslie's Illustrated Newspaper*, November 30, 1867, American Social History Project

145 General Collections, Library of Congress

151 *Harper's Weekly*, February 24, 1872, American Social History Project

152 "The Louisiana murders—Gathering the dead and wounded," *Harper's Weekly*, May 10, 1873, Prints and Photographs Division, Library of Congress

152 *Harper's Weekly*, October 28, 1876, American Social History Project

153 The Library of Virginia

154 *Every Saturday: An Illustrated Journal of Choice Reading*, December 31, 1870, Prints and Photographs Division, Library of Congress

155 *New York Daily Graphic*, March 11, 1874, American Social History Project

156 Thomas Ball, *Freedmen's Memorial to Abraham Lincoln*, 1876, Lincoln Park, Washington, D.C., Prints and Photographs Division, Library of Congress

157 Sol Eytinge, Jr., "The Centennial—Visit of the 'Small Breed' family," wood engraving based on a sketch by Sol Eytinge, *Harper's Weekly*, November 4, 1876, Prints and Photographs Division, Library of Congress

158 Fernando Miranda, "Philadelphia, Pa.—The Centennial Exposition—The statue of 'The Freed Slave' in Memorial Hall," *Frank Leslie's Illustrated Newspaper*, August 5, 1876, American Social History Project

161 Collection of Greg French

164 *Frank Leslie's Illustrated Newspaper*, June 13, 1874, Prints and Photographs Division, Library of Congress

165 Thomas P. Anshutz, *The Way They Live*, 1879, oil on canvas, 24 × 17 inches, Metropolitan Museum of Art, Morris K. Jesup Fund, 1940, accession no. 40.40

166 Frank Bellew, *New York Daily Graphic*, April 14, 1874, American Social History Project

170 John R. Lynch, *The Facts of Reconstruction* (1913), American Social History Project

172 *Frank Leslie's Illustrated Newspaper*, April 8, 1871, Prints and Photographs Division, Library of Congress

174 William L. Sheppard, *Harper's Weekly*, May 10, 1873, Prints and Photographs Division, Library of Congress

176 *Frank Leslie's Illustrated Newspaper*, October 7, 1871, American Social History Project

179 Thomas Nast, *Harper's Weekly*, August 24, 1872, American Social History Project

181 *The Old Plantation Home*, lithograph (New York: Currier and Ives, 1872), Prints and Photographs Division, Library of Congress

182 Thomas Worth, "De Cake Walk: For Beauty, Grace and Style; de Winner Takes de Cake," lithograph (New York: Currier and Ives, 1884), Harry T. Peters Collection, Museum of the City of New York

183 "Missouri.—Remarkable exit of Negroes from Louisiana and Mississippi—Incidents of the arrival, support and departure of the refuges at St. Louis. 1. Procession of refugees from the steamboat landing to the colored churches," *Frank Leslie's Illustrated Newspaper*, April 19, 1879, American Social History Project

184 "Virginia.—A family of negroes who do not favor the exodus, returning from a purchasing trip to New Market," *Frank Leslie's Illustrated Newspaper*, May 10, 1879, American Social History Project

184 Joseph Keppler, "Now Boss How You Like It You' Self?" *Puck*, April 16, 1879, Prints and Photographs Division, Library of Congress

185 Frederic Remington, "Sign Language," *The Century* 37 (April 1889), Prints and Photographs Division, Library of Congress

186 F. C. Burroughs, "Virginia.—The fatal explosion at the Midlothian coal mine, February 3d—carrying from the shaft-cage a rescue party overcome by gas," *Frank Leslie's Illustrated Newspaper*, February 18, 1882, American Social History Project

187 Joseph Becker, "Virginia.—Tenth annual Convention of the Knights of Labor, held at the First Regiment Armory, Richmond, October 4th–9th. General Master Workman Powderly addressing the Convention," *Frank Leslie's Illustrated Newspaper*, October 16, 1886, American Social History Project

187 Henry Jackson Lewis, self-portrait in the offices of *The Freeman* in Indianapolis, c. 1890, pen and ink drawing, DuSable Museum of African American History, Chicago

188 *The Freeman*, October 19, 1889, Prints and Photographs Division, Library of Congress

191 Frank Bellew, *New York Daily Graphic*, September 29, 1873, American Social History Project

193 *Atlas of the World* (n.d.), American Social History Project

196 James T. Pierson, *Frank Leslie's Illustrated Newspaper*, December 26, 1874, Prints and Photographs Division, Library of Congress

198 Thomas Nast, *Harper's Weekly*, August 12, 1876, American Social History Project

199 Joseph Keppler, *Puck*, May 2, 1877, New-York Historical Society

200 Kansas State Historical Society

204 Valentine Museum, Richmond, Va.

205 W. F. Griffin, Special Collections, University of Chicago Library

208 Prints and Photographs Division, Library of Congress

210 William Walker, "The White (?) Man's Burden," *Life*, March 16, 1899, American Social History Project

215 *Special Catalogue of Exhibits on the Midway Plaisance* (Chicago, 1893), Chicago Historical Society

216 Frederick Opper, "Darkies' Day at the Fair (A Tale of Poetic Retribution)," *World's Fair Puck* 16 (August 21, 1893), Prints and Photographs Division, Library of Congress

217 Arthur I. Keller, " 'The Fiery Cross of old Scotland's hills!' " in Thomas Dixon, Jr., *The Clansman: An Historical Romance of the Ku Klux Klan* (New York: Doubleday, Page & Co., 1905), Prints and Photographs Division, Library of Congress

218 Motion Picture, Broadcasting, and Recorded Sound Division, Library of Congress

219 Courtesy of the Allen / Littlefield Collection

220 Richard Outcault, "Here's the New Bully," *New York World*, February 13, 1898, Prints and Photographs Division, Library of Congress

220 William Marriner, "Sambo's Birthday," *San Francisco Chronicle*, December 7, 1913, Prints and Photographs Division, Library of Congress

221 Motion Picture, Broadcasting, and Recorded Sound Division, Library of Congress

222 Edward V. Brewer, *Needlecraft Magazine*, v. 13 (December 1921), General Research Division, The New York Public Library, Astor, Lenox and Tilden Foundations

222 *The Crisis*, October 1916, Prints and Photographs Division, Library of Congress

223 *The Crisis*, May 1929, Prints and Photographs Division, Library of Congress

223 Bettman / CORBIS

224 Kerry James Marshall, *Heirlooms and Accessories*, 2002, inkjet prints on paper in wooden frames with rhinestones, three parts, each 51 × 46 inches. Courtesy of Jack Shainman Gallery, New York

226 Leonard Freed / Magnum

228 *Detroit News*

232 Charles Moore—ICP / Black Star

234 *1199 News*, Local 1199, Health Care Employees Union, New York City

235 Stanley Forman, Pulitzer Prize 1977

ACKNOWLEDGMENTS

This book evolved through many processes and involved many collaborators. Chief among them are authors Eric Foner and Joshua Brown, *Forever Free* project editor Christine Doudna, and project administrator Audrey Rapoport. All four made critical contributions to the entire *Forever Free* project. Research and planning for our television series led to the development of this book, a process that now returns to the television enterprise and to preparation of a Web site (www.foreverfreeproject.org) for general use.

We came to do this project because of our immersion in the rich historical materials now available on the emancipation and Reconstruction era. A group of historians and popular writers, including Benjamin Quarles, Herbert Aptheker, Philip Foner, John Hope Franklin, George Rawick, John Blassingame, Vincent Harding, Lerone Bennett, Jr., and Dorothy Sterling plumbed unknown and neglected historical archives and government publications that contained vivid firsthand accounts and observations of the events surrounding slavery, emancipation, and Reconstruction. In doing this they were carrying on the work of W. E. B. Du Bois, who, working alone in 1935, published *Black Reconstruction in America*, a volume rich in archival sources and unique in historical perspective. Their work proved invaluable as we shaped our projects.

Our colleague and friend the late historian Herbert Gutman, at The City University of New York, also drew on Du Bois's work. Gutman looked at these historical documents and sources about the African American experience in new ways. How, Gutman wondered, should we explain the articulate and compelling voices of the freedpeople, so recently liberated from bondage? How did such a clear vision of freedom and the detailed understanding of how to achieve it emerge so quickly following the demise of slavery? In a 1983 interview Gutman addressed the historical implications of these important questions:

> The important discovery . . . is not that slaves lived in families that were frequently broken, but that the family could serve the slaves as a way of creating social and class connections. . . . These new connections, occurring so early in time, make the entire Afro-American experience look different. . . . If one

essential part of the picture is changed, then the other parts of the picture also change. It becomes a different picture, a very, very different history.

Gutman sought an explanation for these powerful and previously ignored stories of the black experience by revisiting what black people did during the era of their enslavement. The result was his pathbreaking book, *The Black Family in Slavery and Freedom, 1750–1925* (1976).

An explosion of academic scholarship in the 1970s quickly followed upon Gutman's work, fundamentally rewriting the history of African Americans in the era of emancipation and Reconstruction. Ira Berlin, Leslie Rowland, and their colleagues at the University of Maryland undertook a monumental editing and publication project, beginning in the mid-1970s, of the unpublished records of the Freedmen's Bureau, the federal agency set up in the midst of the Civil War to aid the newly freedpeople. Their Freedmen and Southern Society Project has published four volumes to date of letters, reports, and other primary documents (with a fifth on the way) filled with the beautifully articulate voices of the freedpeople. The *Forever Free* project used this rich source material extensively in our early research on the television programs. In the same vein, another historian, Leon Litwack at the University of California, Berkeley, in his Pulitzer Prize–winning *Been in the Storm So Long* (1979), describes the "many meanings of freedom," illustrating the ways in which recently emancipated slaves in the war's immediate aftermath embraced the personal, political, economic, and educational expressions of their newly won freedom. David Blight, a scholar of uncommon wisdom, illuminated the themes of unsettled history and contested memory.

Much as our textual analysis benefited from such scholarly assistance and support, so too did the visual essays, which were greatly enhanced by the help of scholars. Jeanie Attie, David Jaffee, Ellen Noonan, and Donna Thompson Ray read early drafts of the essays and provided crucial advice about addressing gaps in our knowledge of the nation's visual history. We also must thank the many scholars whose work informed the visual essays, with special thanks to Charles Lawing and Marvin Jeter, who generously shared their ongoing research. We are indebted to these scholars, and other, more recent writers too numerous to name, in helping to shape the basic historical approach that we took in this project.

Charles Burnett joined the struggle to make *Forever Free* a film and television project, and gave us his signature quiet and artful determination. The Corporation for Public Broadcasting and the National Endowment for the Humanities supported several years of research and writing in connection with the television effort. The Koldyke Foundation of Chicago provided much-needed support. The Koldyke family convened a distinguished group of Chicagoans to hear "our story," and the sociologist William Julius Wilson addressed the gathering with a sharp set of remarks demonstrating the connection of Reconstruction to contemporary social-welfare struggles. Jack Willis, now head of LinkTV, gave us his cheerful commitment to getting the story right. Eric Foner, David Blight, James Horton, Leon Litwack, Michael Perman, Ira Berlin, and Jacqueline Jones served as advisors to the TV project and distinguished themselves, as always, with their kind and intelligent support.

Forever Free, Inc., the project, has a loyal board, including Constance Rice, Sarah Pillsbury, and Rudy Langlais. We are grateful for their continued interest and support. The Center for Media and Learning and the American Social History Project at The City University of New York provided a home and an intellectual and political framework for our work. Beacon Pictures provided another base for the idea of television programming and a cinema of commitment.

Along the way people have stepped in just in the nick of time. Katie Kleinsasser, of the Public Media Center, provided facilities and sympathy for our work. Ben Koldyke sat for an entire year in the basement of our California headquarters and so thoroughly absorbed W. E. B. Du Bois's *Black Reconstruction* that this landmark book took on the authority of scripture in our work that it so richly deserves. Jeremy Stein tackled any number of research, planning, and conceptual challenges with energy and intelligence. If there is such a thing as a quiet anchor, Audrey Rapoport provided it, giving us the bridge between television logistics and research and book manuscript preparation.

Jonathan Segal, our editor at Alfred A. Knopf, and Sonny Mehta, Knopf's editor in chief, have supported the book and its approach through thick and thin. We treasure our association with them. Ida Giragossian at Knopf has also proved indispensable in helping us get the book to press.

We feel a great debt to our families, in particular to our parents, who oriented us to the decency and importance of the struggle for rights: to Charles and Evelyn Doudna, who have always kept the faith; to Florence and Harry Brier, whose lives gave friendship and support to committed people and revolutionaries; and to Dorothea and Gabriel Almond, "let [their] own works praise [them] in the gates. . . ."

These individuals and institutions provided inspiration and support in many ways, to this book and to the *Forever Free* project. We alone are responsible for any failings or shortcomings.

INDEX

Page numbers in *italics* refer to illustrations.

A NOTE ABOUT THE AUTHORS

Eric Foner was born in New York City. He is DeWitt Clinton Professor of History, Columbia University, and specializes in the Civil War and Reconstruction, slavery, and nineteenth-century America. He received his B.A. from Columbia in 1963 and his Ph.D. from Columbia in 1969. In 2000, he served as President of the American Historical Association.

Joshua Brown was born in New York City and received his Ph.D. from Columbia University. He is Executive Director of the American Social History Project / Center for Media and Learning at The Graduate Center, City University of New York. He has written extensively on the history of U.S. visual culture and the visualization of the past, and his cartoons and illustrations—including his weekly online *Life During Wartime* commentary—appear in popular and scholarly publications and digital media.

A NOTE ON THE TYPE

Pierre Simon Fournier *le jeune,* who designed the type used in this book, was both an originator and a collector of types. His services to the art of printing were his design of letters, his creation of ornaments and initials, and his standardization of type sizes. His types are old style in character and sharply cut. In 1764 and 1766, he published his *Manuel typographique,* a treatise on the history of French types and printing, on typefounding in all its details, and on what many consider his most important contribution to typography—the measurement of type by the point system.

Composed by North Market Street Graphics, Lancaster, Pennsylvania

Printed and bound by Berryville Graphics, Berryville, Virginia

Designed by Robert C. Olsson

973.8
F6738

112462